Wild Orphan Babies: Mammals and Birds

Wild Orphan
Babies MAMMALS AND BIRDS

Caring for Them + Setting Them Free

WILLIAM J. WEBER, D.V.M.

photographs by the author

Holt Rinehart and Winston
New York

Published simultaneously in Canada by Holt, Rinehart and
Winston of Canada, Limited.

Printed in the United States of America

Designed by Sandra Kandrac

Library of Congress Cataloging in Publication Data

Weber, William J
  Wild orphan babies.

  Bibliography: p. 151
  SUMMARY: A handbook offering instruction on the
housing, feeding, and general care of orphaned wild
animal babies and how to prepare them for life in the
wild.

  1. Wildlife rescue—Juvenile literature. 2. Wildlife diseases—Juvenile literature. [1. Wildlife
rescue. 2. Wild animals as pets] I. Title.
QL83.2.W4   639.9   74–23811
ISBN 0–03–014211–3

10 9 8 7 6 5 4 3

For my family, sons Bill and John, who help feed and care for a great many of the orphaned and injured, and helped develop the techniques we use, and for my wife Barbara, who cares for all the babies, makes formula, feeds orphans, corrected the grammar in my manuscript, and did all the typing. This is really her book.

WJW

Virtually all of us making a career of conservation, display, or control of wildlife began our careers (and our undying love for animals) with a pet squirrel, toad, snake, crow, or praying mantis. I've always felt, as a naturalist and veterinarian, that my responsibility was not to discourage this normal urge, but to direct it toward the love and respect for our natural wilderness and its inhabitants.

Dr. Don Collins
Veterinary Consultant
Topeka, Kansas

Preface

I am a veterinarian in private practice in a small city in central Florida. In 1964 my family and I moved from that city to a three-and-one-half-acre site on the shore of a clear lake. Being an Audubon member of long standing, in due course I persuaded our neighbors to join with us in having the area declared an Audubon sanctuary. Our home now occupies the center of that sanctuary.

Gradually, word of the sanctuary and our interest in wildlife spread throughout the community, and my veterinary hospital became the drop-off point for injured and orphaned wild birds and animals.

My family and I agreed to do our best to raise or heal the sick and orphaned animals and birds that were brought to us with the understanding that we would set them free when they were able to survive on their own.

Before long, the assistance we were called upon to give required more time than we had. In addition, we discovered that what little information has been published on this subject is neither practical nor accurate. These two factors brought us to the realization of the need for this book.

The fear has been expressed that a book which teaches one

how to raise wildlife babies might encourage some people to steal baby animals in order to raise them as pets. In our experience, this fear is groundless. We have had contact with hundreds of people who have adopted and cared for wild babies. Most of them have acquired the babies as the result of legitimate accidents. Their concern is for the welfare of the baby. And they would regard anything less than total freedom, when the time comes, as "cruelty to animals."

The mutual bond of affection which is established between orphan and foster parent remains even after the youngster is given its freedom. The bluejay that has been set free still comes back to visit, landing on your hand for food. The squirrel is equally at home on your shoulder as in the tree. And the raccoon comes around to your house whenever it fishes along the edge of the lake. The experience of raising and freeing an orphan generates an interest in wildlife that seems to last forever. For many young people, the experience has led to a career in wildlife biology, veterinary medicine, or conservation.

WJW

Acknowledgments

I wish to thank:

Mrs. Trudy Farrand, Publishers Services Inc., for her constant encouragement and suggestions.

Dr. Ben Sheffy, Professor of Nutrition and the Assistant Director of the Virus Research Institute at Cornell University, who read an early draft of the manuscript and made excellent suggestions.

Dr. Bill Jackson, a Lakeland, Florida, veterinarian and good friend, who read the text and offered practical comments.

WJW

Contents

Preface   9
Introduction   19

MAMMALS

1. **Basic Care of Orphan Mammals**   27
   What Is an Orphan?; Approaching the Baby; A
   Nest for the Baby; Keeping the Baby Warm;
   Warming a Chilled Baby; Bowel and Urine Con-
   trol; Houses and Cages; The Nest-Box House; The
   Cage; Water

2. **Feeding Orphan Mammals**   40
   When to Start Feeding; The Formula; Formula
   for Babies Which Will Be Small as Adults; For-
   mula for Baby Rabbits; Formula for Babies Which
   Will Grow into Large Adults; Formula for Larger
   Mammals; Sweetener; Ways of Feeding Formula;
   Dropper Feeding; How Much to Feed; Bottle
   Feeding; How Much to Feed; Weaning the Baby;

Stomach-Tube Feeding; Equipment; How Far to Baby's Stomach?; The Feeding Process; How Much to Feed; Gagging; Veterinary Assistance; Washing Up; Foods for the Older Baby; Flying Squirrels, Squirrels, and Mice; Baby Rabbits; Fox Puppies, Skunks, Opossums, Raccoons, Bobcats; Canned Dog Food; Dry Food; Diet Supplements

3. Petting, Handling, and Freedom   **63**
Petting and Handling; If Baby Bites; Setting Your Orphan Free; First Step; Second Step; Freedom

4. Ailing or Injured Mammals   **67**
Intestinal Infection; Antibiotics; Dehydration; Ticks, Fleas, and Lice; Bathing; Injury; Should . Help Be Given?; Abnormal Physical Appearance; Abnormal Behavior; Pain; When Not to Help; How to Administer First Aid; Moving the Animal to Safety; Fluids; Adding Formula

BIRDS

5. Altricial Birds   **79**
What is an Altricial Bird?; What is an Orphan?; Determining Baby's Age; Putting Baby Back in the Nest; For Most Birds; For Owls and Hawks; Warmth and Shelter; The Nest; Temperature Control; The Cage; Feeding Most Baby Birds; The Basic Diet; Liquids; Expanding the Menu; Feeding Hawks and Owls; Several at a Time; Handling and Freedom; Freeing Most Birds; Freeing Owls

6. Precocial Birds   **100**
What is a Precocial Bird?; The Orphan; Approaching the Orphan; Chicks Less Than Three

Days Old; Chicks More Than Three Days Old;
Warmth and Shelter; The Cage; Warmth; Feeding;
What to Feed; Teaching the Chick to Eat; Feeding
Ducklings, Geese, and Water Birds; Special Hous-
ing and Feeding; Precocial Land Birds; Housing;
Feeding; Setting Them Free; Setting the Single
Bird Free; Precocial Water Birds; Diet; Housing;
Setting Them Free

7. **Feeding Injured and Very Weak Birds
   and Dietary Supplements**   **114**
   Toothpick Formula Feeding; Stomach-Tube Feed-
   ing; Force-Feeding Solid Foods; Force-Feeding
   Hawks and Owls; Dietary Supplements and Calcium Deficiencies

8. **First Aid for All Birds**   **125**
   Which Birds Need First Aid?; Approaching an In-
   jured Bird; Basic Care; Chilled Birds; Concussion-
   Type Injuries; Intestinal Infection; Antibiotics;
   Problem Eater; Oil-Contaminated Birds; Frac-
   tures; Lower Leg; For Small Birds; For Larger
   Birds; Upper Leg; Amputation; Fractured Wings;
   Open Wound or Compound Fracture; Fractures
   in Large Birds

Migratory Birds   142

Regional Offices of Fish and Wildlife Service   144

Rare and Endangered Species   146

Composition of Animal Milks by Percentage   149

Suggested for Further Reading   151

Index   153

Wild Orphan Babies: Mammals and Birds

Introduction

WILDLIFE

Just what is wildlife? In fact, it means different things in different places. In Florida, wildlife includes all wild or non-domesticated birds, mammals, reptiles, and amphibians. What legally constitutes wildlife differs from state to state, as do the laws governing the keeping, holding, and sometimes even helping of wildlife. By law, species such as hawks, owls, mockingbirds, or alligators may not be taken, possessed, harmed, or killed. Thus, these species and many others are given full protection by law.

Wildlife classified as game species is afforded a different kind of protection. Animals such as deer and quail may be hunted, but only at certain times of the year. The law restricts the dates of the hunting season, it limits the time of day, it specifies how these animals may be hunted, and it limits the numbers which may be taken. These wildlife species represent a resource which can be harvested, and this hunting helps keep game animal populations in balance with their available habitat.

There are also species which are classified as unprotected. In Florida, for example, English sparrows, crows, and starlings are not considered valuable, and therefore receive no protection by law. These, along with mice, rats, raccoons, opossums, and armadillos, may be shot, captured, or disposed of in any fashion. While the law does not regard these creatures as valuable, we offer them our help whenever we can, for we enjoy them all.

The law states you may not keep or possess protected wildlife. You must have permission from a game warden or wildlife officer to care for any animal or bird on the protected list. If you acquire an orphan that needs help, the first thing to do is consult a local state wildlife officer or warden. He will tell you if the creature you are trying to help is protected.

Every area of every state has a local game warden or wildlife officer. If you cannot find the officer for your area listed in the telephone directory, call your local police department, sheriff's office, or highway patrol. They will refer you to him.

When you contact the wildlife officer, tell him who you are, the circumstances under which you obtained the orphan or injured creature, what you are planning to do for it, and when you plan to release it. These are sincere, dedicated men who are devoting their lives to helping wildlife. Their advice will therefore be based on what is best for the animal involved. When you have their permission to care for the animal involved, contact your family veterinarian for information on health and professional care.

Additional permission may sometimes be required, as in the case of migratory birds. Birds which migrate across state borders are considered a national asset. They are valuable from an aesthetic point of view, and some, such as ducks, geese, and doves, are also sources of food. The federal government, by agreement with the individual states and the countries of Canada and Mexico, makes the regulations governing these birds. For a list of these birds, see the back of the book.

According to a strict interpretation of the law, you must have a federal permit to keep a bird on this list. However, to confine such a bird temporarily to help with a specific problem, permission from your wildlife officer or warden is usually sufficient.

If, however, you become involved in caring for migratory birds on a year-round basis, you must obtain first a state permit and then an annual federal permit from the Regional Director, Bureau of Sport Fisheries and Wildlife. A list of the Regional Directors appears at the back of the book.

If you find a baby or injured creature on the Rare and Endangered Species list, which includes all the fish, birds, mammals, reptiles, and amphibians in danger of becoming extinct in North America, contact your local wildlife officer. In order to ensure its survival, he will probably want to see that it receives a more professional level of care than you may be able to give. There are presently over one hundred creatures on this list. See the list found at the back of the book.

WARNING TO FOSTER PARENTS

Contact with wild animals can carry an element of risk. Most obvious is the danger of being bitten or scratched.

There is little danger of bite wounds from a tiny orphan if it is given lots of attention and love while growing up. When this baby becomes an adult, however, and the instinct to be with its own kind becomes strong, it can become dangerous. This alone is an excellent reason for raising your orphan to go free.

If you find an injured mature mammal or bird, notify the local wildlife officer of its location and type of injury. Do not try to handle the animal yourself. This is a task only for a professional. Coping with any grown wild animal, such as a raccoon, fox, or otter, is very dangerous. It will bite and can inflict severe injury.

Birds of prey also require caution, for, if frightened, they will defend themselves with their sharp beaks and claws.

A less obvious danger is exposure to disease. To minimize any danger to yourself, follow these basic rules of hygiene:

1. Immediately after you work, play with, or clean up after a wild creature, wash your hands thoroughly with soap and water.

2. Wash any bite wound or scratch thoroughly with soap and water and apply an antiseptic.

3. If an animal dies while you are caring for it, notify your physician or local health department. Based on the information you give, they may or may not suggest further examination.

Few diseases are transmitted directly from birds to man. Based on the experiences of many people in the field, we feel there is little danger.

Of the diseases that can be transmitted from mammals to man, rabies concerns us most. The other communicable diseases represent little practical hazard with the very young animals.

One basic rule is to avoid all wild animals which appear tame. This type of altered or abnormal behavior has always been a sign of rabies in wild animals.

In the last ten years most cases of wildlife rabies have occurred among skunks, raccoons, foxes, and bats. These particular species should, therefore, always be regarded with caution.

In a six-year study conducted by Dr. Paul Schnurrenberger, a public-health veterinarian in Illinois, 911 cases of rabies were diagnosed in wild animals. Fourteen of these animals were being kept as pets at the time. No one died, but several people had to undergo a painful series of injections.

In the Western states a unique hazard exists. Some ground squirrels and prairie dogs carry fleas which are capable of transmitting the organism that causes bubonic plague. For this reason, these ground squirrels and prairie dogs should not be handled. Those which appear tame may be sick, and the fleas leaving these animals can spread plague to people.

While contact with wild animals may carry an element of risk, the care, handling, and raising of wild animals is very satisfying.

Although the information presented in the following pages can also be used to raise an orphan puppy or kitten, I have not included these and other common pets because information on caring for them is available from your local veterinarian. Nor have I included frogs, toads, snakes, and other amphibians and reptiles. From the time of hatching they have the ability to care for themselves and do not require assistance.

Mammals

1

Basic Care of Orphan Mammals

WHAT IS AN ORPHAN?

There are two types of orphans: animals which have lost their mothers and are too young to survive on their own; and animals which, though physically old enough to care for themselves, cannot do so because they have been weakened or injured.

It is commonly believed that once a human being has touched a wild baby, its mother will abandon it. In most cases, this is not true. Babies should not be handled, but for a different reason: they may flee from you and get lost or hurt trying to escape.

A fully furred orphan that can walk rather than crawl and whose eyes are open and bright is usually old enough to care for itself, even though it may be tiny. Be kind. Leave this baby in the wild where it belongs. However, a cold, wet baby whose eyes are not yet open needs help. A baby in danger because of the family cat or other predator should also be rescued.

Babies are orphaned in different ways. Most often they are orphaned when their mother is injured or killed in an accident. Sometimes a raccoon mother is killed and the babies she has left high in a tree will grow hungry and begin to cry. Such babies should be rescued. Or an injured raccoon baby may be found on the ground, having fallen or crawled from its tree den. If there is no way to put it back in the den, and the mother is nowhere around, the baby will have to be adopted.

Most squirrels are found in the same way. "Drays," or nests built of twigs and leaves high in a tree, sometimes come apart in a storm, and tiny baby squirrels are found cold and wet under the tree.

Baby rabbits are also frequently found after a storm. The mother rabbit builds her nest in a shallow depression in the grass. When a heavy rain floods the nest, the babies will often crawl to higher ground.

In spring and summer an opossum that has been killed in an accident should be checked to see if she has babies with her. If very tiny, they would be found in the pouch on the mother's abdomen, and if large enough to have their eyes open and to have hair, they would more likely be found clinging to the fur on her back.

APPROACHING THE BABY

A very small baby that has no hair or whose eyes are not yet open may be picked up in your bare hands. Gently slide your fingers under the baby, scoop it up, and cradle it in your palms. Most babies, particularly very small ones, will enjoy the warmth of your hands. Adjust your fingers to fit snugly around the baby, so it can absorb the maximum warmth from your fingers, but not so snugly that it can't shift its posi-

Cupped hands serve as warm substitute nest for gray squirrel.

tion. The tiny, hairless baby will become quiet almost at once and will soon drop off to sleep.

The larger baby should be approached more cautiously. Do not sneak up on it silently, as a predator might. Talk to the baby in a low, soothing voice, and it will have the confidence to let you come close. The baby will be less frightened if you stoop, or in some way come lower to its level, rather than if you tower over it like a giant. When you are close enough, offer your hand for the baby to smell. Do not extend a finger, in case it should attempt to bite. If it doesn't try to bite and seems quite satisfied with the first step you have taken in getting acquainted, slowly change the position of your hand so you can stroke its back, petting it as you would a kitten, only more slowly and more gently.

Be wary until you see how your offer of friendship is received. If the baby tries to bite you when you touch it, start over again. First let it smell your hand, then try to stroke it gently. If it accepts being stroked, then you can try to pick it up.

It is wise to wear gloves or to protect yourself in some other way. If you don't have gloves with you, use your shirt or jacket instead. Open it and place one hand under it. Use the other hand, covered with part of the shirt, to "herd" or push the baby to your outstretched, waiting hand. Move your hands together gently under the baby until one hand is on either side of it, forming a nest in which to carry it. Place a fold of the shirt or jacket over the baby to prevent it from jumping out and injuring itself. As the baby absorbs the warmth of your hands, you have taken the first step in the basic care that will keep it alive.

A NEST FOR THE BABY

To provide warmth and security, the first requirements of care for all very young animals, transfer the baby from your hands to a nest box as soon as possible. Any box the size of a shoe box, lined with cotton, flannel, or a piece of an old sweater, will make a fine nest. The material must be soft and comfortable in order to simulate the mother's nest. The sides of the nest should be high enough so the baby won't accidentally fall out. The baby must have room enough to move around so it can get into a comfortable position. Tiny babies can only turn around by crawling forward.

KEEPING THE BABY WARM

Place the nest box in an area free from drafts. An ordinary 60-watt light bulb will provide adequate heat and warmth for the newborn or very young baby. Hang the light bulb near the

A nest made from an old shoebox, a flannel shirt, and a light bulb is used for young, tiny mammal babies.

nest using an extension cord, like a mechanic's trouble light, or use a flexible gooseneck study lamp. Position the light over one end of the nest, so the temperature will vary from one end to the other. This will enable the baby to move closer to the light when it is cold and farther away when it feels too warm. Place an inexpensive outdoor thermometer in or beside the nest.

By knowing a little about the species of animal you have adopted, you can make a rough estimate of its age. Many mammals, such as squirrels, are born without hair, while some, such as cats, are born already covered with soft, fine hair. All are born with the eyes sealed closed. The hairless babies begin growing hair at once. Within fourteen to twenty-four days after birth, the hairless babies have hair and in almost all mammal babies the eyes have opened.

For the very young hairless baby, adjust the light or the nest until you have a temperature of 95° F.

If the baby has some hair but the eyes are still closed, maintain a temperature of 90° F. until the eyes open. Once the eyes open, drop the temperature of the nest 5° F. each week.

You should have no problem keeping a young baby in the nest. They seem to appreciate the warmth and the security that a comfortable nest affords. A light burning continuously doesn't bother them. They know no darkness, or night as such, and readily accept the light as part of their world.

How long should bulb heat be provided? When you see that the baby no longer sleeps near the bulb or snuggles up close to it after play, you can remove it. The baby no longer needs warmth from this source.

Caution: The temperature-control mechanism of a baby's body functions poorly. It is easy to kill a baby with too much heat. This has happened when heating pads were used to provide heat and the baby couldn't escape from the excessive warmth. Older babies can compensate for a while by panting, but the very young aren't able to eliminate excessive body heat this way. If you must use a heating pad temporarily, leave room for the baby to crawl off it. Use your thermometer to watch the temperature closely.

The temperature-regulating mechanism of the baby's body begins to function more efficiently about the time the eyes begin to open. When this happens, accurate temperature monitoring of the nest is less critical, but still important if the baby is to be kept comfortable.

Warming a Chilled Baby

Never warm a chilled or cold baby too rapidly. A heat lamp, heating pad, or even the light bulb will not warm the baby uniformly. The body surface will warm at once, but the internal structures will remain cool longer. The warm outer tissues demand more nutrients and oxygen. But the baby's heart, which is beating weakly and slowly because of its low tem-

A plastic bottle filled with warm water temporarily keeps a baby raccoon warm.

perature (hypothermia), is unable to supply these. By the time the internal structures are warm and the heart stronger, the outer warm tissues are badly damaged. The accumulation of waste products and the poisons of tissue breakdown entering the system of the weakened baby are enough to cause its death.

The chilled baby should therefore be warmed very gradually with your body heat. Cradle the baby in your hands until it feels warm to your touch. This may take two to three hours, or longer. Of if it is tiny, put the baby in a shirt pocket under your sweater, or just hold it in your lap while you read a book or watch television. When it becomes active and no longer feels cold, place it in its shoe-box nest. We often place a plastic bottle filled with warm water in the nest box. The baby will snuggle up to the warm bottle, drawing both heat and comfort from its presence.

BOWEL AND URINE CONTROL

The nest box rarely has to be cleaned, because you control the elimination of the tiny baby. When it is a little older, it will leave the nest to eliminate.

Controlling bowel and urine eliminations in the very young is not a matter of choice. It is a necessity. The very young baby, hairless and with its eyes closed, will not normally defecate or urinate on its own. It is stimulated to do so by its mother by licking. Since you have taken over the duties of the mother you must stimulate urination. Take a small piece of cotton about the size of a fifty-cent piece. Moisten it with comfortably warm water and squeeze out the excess. Cradle the baby in one hand as it lies on its back, and gently stroke the genital organs with the warm moist cotton. After three to ten quick, gentle strokes, the baby will begin to urinate. Tiny drops of liquid will appear on the genital organs after each stroke. Continue stroking until the flow ceases. The mother stimulates bowel movements, or defecation, in the same fashion, and so must you. Most babies will urinate and defecate each time they are fed. Take care of this chore before each feeding so you aren't "messed upon" during the feeding. Having these two functions under your control helps keep the baby and its nest clean and neat.

When a baby reaches two to four weeks of age, it no longer needs your stimulation to eliminate. However, continue to make it eliminate before you feed or handle it for as long as you can. As it gets older, the baby acquires voluntary control over elimination, and it will take over the function itself.

If you acquire the baby after its eyes are open, you ordinarily cannot stimulate bowel or urine elimination since the older baby already has control over the act. You can try, however. If you are successful, keep control of this function as long as you can. If unsuccessful, you will have a messier baby, but not necessarily a messier nest. If the baby can leave the nest to eliminate, it will usually do so. If it can eliminate but can't get out, it will probably eliminate when you take it from its nest to feed it. After the first couple of "accidents," you will form the habit of placing a tissue or paper towel under the "accident" end during feeding and handling. Once the baby has eliminated, you will be able to play with it safely for several hours.

HOUSES AND CAGES

When the baby begins to crawl out of the nest regularly, it is time for more permanent housing. Needed now are two things: a house and a cage.

The Nest-Box House

This simple wooden structure is intended as a semipermanent home. The orphan will use it while it is growing into a mature animal and even after it has its freedom, so the nest box must be large enough to accommodate an adult animal. Only when the orphan goes back to the wild permanently will it give up this home.

Construct it from any durable wood scraps that can withstand rain and weather when it is moved outdoors. It is better if it is not painted. Many paints contain materials which are toxic.

A mouse or flying squirrel will need a house with dimensions of 4″ × 4″ × 6″ with an entrance hole 1 inch in diameter. A house for a medium-sized animal, such as a gray squirrel, should have inside dimensions of 8″ × 8″ × 8″ with a 2-inch entrance hole. A large orphan, such as a fox, skunk, or raccoon, needs a house with inside dimensions of 12″ × 12″ × 18″ with an entrance hole 6 inches in diameter.

The house should have a hinged or removable top. This will

An albino gray squirrel in its nest-box-house.

make it easy to remove the orphan and also to clean the nest.

Transfer the bedding from the original nest to the new nest-box house. Add to this enough new bedding to line the house adequately. The familiar bedding, even in new surroundings, will make the change easier for the baby. The nest-box house is placed inside the cage.

The Cage

The cage is made from galvanized wire mesh called hardware cloth. Any hardware store sells it. Get a 30-inch-wide piece about 12 feet long and a spool of fine wire. Cut the hardware cloth with a tin snips and bend it with your hands to form the cage sides. Use the fine wire to lace the sides and top together. The door can be fabricated of hardware cloth and wired in place as part of one side of the cage.

A cage can never be too large. The minimum size for a mouse or flying squirrel is 18″ × 24″ × 24″, and for a gray squirrel, 30″ × 36″ × 36″. A fox, skunk, or raccoon requires a

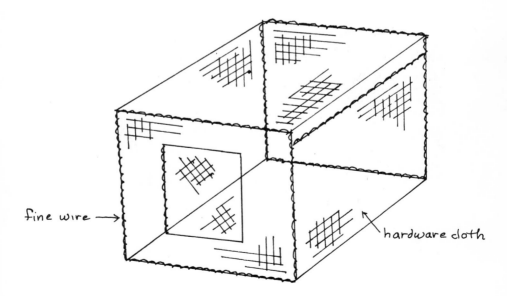

fine wire →

hardware cloth

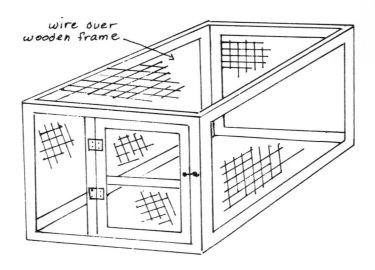

really large house, 48″ × 48″ × 48″. A cage as large as that is best made by tacking hardware cloth over a wooden frame.

The cage must be large enough for the baby to have room to run, climb, romp, and play. Wire a series of limbs, an inch or so in diameter, around the inside of the cage and to each other in order to create a jungle gym for the baby to climb about on. This will ensure a happier and healthier baby with good, sturdy muscles.

When you place the nest home in the cage, you can discontinue using the light bulb for warmth, if you haven't done so before. If there is any doubt about whether to continue it now, place the bulb either in the cage or against the wire outside of it, so warmth is available if the orphan wants it. When the baby no longer seeks the warmth of the bulb and ignores it, remove it.

Line the bottom of the cage with newspapers. At this age the orphan will always leave the nest box to urinate and to eliminate bowel material in the bottom of the cage. Change the paper as needed, which is usually every other day. With smaller babies, such as flying squirrels and baby rabbits, there isn't much "mess" to be cleaned up. Use your own judgment to determine when the cage needs cleaning. It is better to clean it too often than not often enough. Bowel material accidentally swallowed by the baby as it cleans and grooms itself can cause intestinal infection, diarrhea, and even death. Cleanliness is one of the most important factors in raising a healthy, happy baby.

Once the baby becomes active enough to play and romp about in the new cage, give it the freedom of a screened porch and part of the house. At our house, cages are used primarily for sleeping and feeding. We let the babies out in the morning and give them the run of the back screened porch and part of the house during the day. Cages never represent confinement to the babies, but rather a place of rest and security. With the freedom to come and go, they don't resent being placed in them and accept the cage as home.

WATER

Once the nest home is placed in a cage and the baby is actively moving about, supply a source of water. For small creatures such as squirrels, wire a water bottle with a sipper tube (this can be obtained at any pet store) to the side of the cage. For larger animals, place a dish of water in a corner of the cage. Keep the water dish clean and be sure to supply fresh water daily.

Tiny babies in a nest are not given water since, as you shall see, they receive all the fluid they need in their formula.

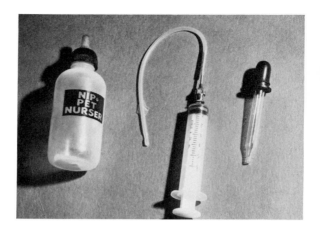

2

Feeding Orphan Mammals

WHEN TO START FEEDING

Now that the baby is comfortable, warm, and no longer frightened, it will be hungry. It is now time to consider feeding.

Do not try to feed the orphan until its body temperature has been brought back to normal. A chilled baby cannot digest food. The chilled baby is cold to the touch and is inactive. The baby with a normal body temperature will move about and feel warm to the touch. You may see it start nuzzling the nest material or begin to crawl and search about the nest. This is the time to start feeding.

THE FORMULA

All young babies are fed a formula as a substitute for its mother's milk. Essentially, the formula consists of homogenized milk and egg yolk.

Prepare 6 to 8 ounces of formula at a time. Mix the formula in a clean bowl with a fork, rotary beater, or in a blender. Transfer it to a clean jar, cover and refrigerate. Remove only enough for one feeding at a time. Pour the formula into a clean glass or measuring cup, and warm it by placing the glass in a bowl of warm water.

Test the temperature by dropping a few drops on your wrist. If it feels barely warm, it is the correct temperature. If it feels warm or hot, it is too hot and should not be used until it cools down.

We use varying combinations of homogenized milk and egg yolk to prepare a formula similar to the mother's milk. Egg yolk is an excellent source of protein. It is easily digested and is rich in vitamins A and D and fatty acids. It adds fat and protein to those present in the milk, making a suitable formula for most mammal babies.* See the back of the book for the composition of milk.

---

* The amounts of food required by an orphan can be figured in calories, which are units of energy. A newborn kitten (this would be close enough for squirrels, raccoons, opossums, and even for fox puppies) requires 250 calories per kilogram of body weight per day. Or, in figures we are more used to considering, this would be 100 calories per pound per day to meet its energy requirements. The basic formula as we mix it contains approximately 28 to 30 calories per ounce. We consider an egg yolk to contain 60 calories and milk, 20.6 calories per ounce. This means a kitten weighing 1 pound (16 ounces) would need about 4 ounces of formula daily.

The requirements of a squirrel or mouse would be higher because of the higher rate of body metabolism. If for the sake of a starting point we say the requirements for the squirrel would be 150 calories per pound or 10 calories per ounce, a 3-ounce squirrel would require 30 calories daily. This is about 1 ounce or 30 cc. of the *concentrated* formula, since each ounce of the more concentrated formula contains 30 to 35 calories. Each dropper delivers ½ cc. per dose which would mean sixty droppers daily or over ten droppers in each of six feedings. We have rarely seen a squirrel that size take that much. This points up the weakness of attempting to make hard and fast feeding rules, and indicates the need for you to use common sense and judgment in your feeding programs.

Warming formula in a bowl of warm water.

Formula for Babies Which Will Be Small As Adults, Such As Mice, Flying Squirrels, Gray Squirrels, and Kittens

These babies require a concentrated formula. Usually, the smaller the animal, the higher its rate of metabolism, and the more calories (energy) it requires. Since it both eats less and has a greater need for energy, formula must be rich for them. Mix one large egg yolk in sufficient milk to make 4 to 6 ounces of formula, or one half to three fourths of a cup.

FORMULA FOR BABY RABBITS.   These babies may be fed exactly as above with the exception that antibiotics may be added to their formula once their eyes are open. For more information on this subject, see the section on antibiotics in the next chapter.

Caution: No other baby mammals should routinely receive antibiotics.

Formula for Babies Which Will Grow into Large Adults, Such As Opossums, Raccoons, and Foxes

Use one large egg yolk or two small egg yolks and add enough homogenized milk to make 8 ounces or one cup of formula. This is the basic formula.

Formula for Larger Mammals, Such As Baby Goats and Deer

Use one egg yolk in sufficient milk to make 8 ounces. When these animals are two weeks of age, make the formula one egg yolk to 12 ounces of milk, and when they are four weeks old, increase it to one egg yolk in 16 ounces (1 pint) of milk. Deer and goats do well on this formula. When they begin to take a pint per feeding, substitute powdered non-fat skim milk for homogenized milk. Use more milk than the directions on the package call for. If package directions say add one and one third cups of powdered milk to enough water to make a quart, use two cups of milk instead. Care of deer, wild goats, wild sheep, or antelope would be very temporary, since all state game commissions have facilities for professional care and insist that these species be turned over to them.

Sweetener

While the simple formula of milk and egg yolk is adequate for all common mammals, a sweetener may sometimes be added for better results.

For any baby that doesn't take to the formula, add a little honey. One level teaspoon to the formula combination does not change the caloric content significantly but does make it a little sweeter. Sometimes a stubborn formula-taker becomes an enthusiastic eater when fed the sweeter formula. Once you start adding honey to the formula, you will have to continue using it, for the baby will not accept the less tasty formula from then on. It is amusing to watch a baby that has had honey being offered the formula without this ingredient. It will begin to suck the formula greedily but will spit it out after the first taste. Its whole attitude is one of disgust, and it resists any further offers of the unsweetened formula.

WAYS OF FEEDING FORMULA

Two different feeding techniques are commonly used, depending upon the age and size of the baby. One is by bottle, the other by medicine dropper.

Dropper Feeding

The most effective way to feed the very young and the very small orphan is with a medicine dropper. A tiny mouse baby, ½ inch long, or a large almost weaned rabbit can be fed

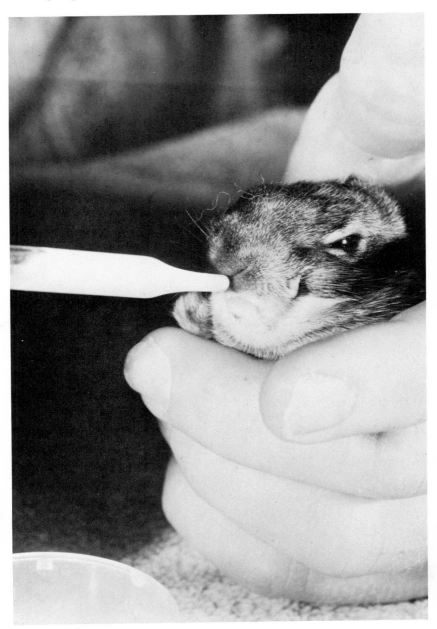

Dropper feeding of a baby rabbit.

equally effectively with a dropper. Some babies do not have the strength to suck on a nipple and bottle. Many babies won't even try. With the dropper, you can force small amounts of the formula into the mouth. Also, with dropper feeding, you can more easily tell if the baby is getting food.

When you are ready to feed the baby, fill your dropper with formula. Hold the baby in the palm of your hand with the head end slightly higher than the rear quarters. The head should be almost horizontal. Do not tilt it up too high. This will stretch the muscles of the throat, and the baby will be unable to swallow.

With the baby in the proper position in one hand and the dropper in the other hand, gently force the dropper just inside the lips. Do not place it deep within the mouth. Pressing the bulb of the dropper gently, release a tiny amount of liquid into the baby's mouth. In all but the very weakest baby this will stimulate a licking motion. A stronger baby will actually grasp the end of the dropper with its lips and start sucking. If it licks and swallows, or begins to suck on the dropper, you can give a silent cheer; the challenge of raising an orphan is half won.

As the baby licks or sucks, you can help it by pressing *very slowly* on the rubber bulb and gradually expelling the contents of the dropper as the baby swallows. If bubbles appear at the baby's nose, or if it opens its mouth very wide (a gagging motion), you are expelling the formula too rapidly. The baby cannot handle the amount you have given it. Remove the dropper and tilt the head down, so the formula can drain out of the mouth, throat, and nose. Wipe the excess formula from the face with a tissue. Give the baby a few moments to recover, then once again start feeding, only this time more slowly.

When the baby has finished eating and the dropper is emptied, use a tissue to wipe the excess formula from the baby's lips and chin. Keeping the baby clean as you feed it keeps the hair around its head and neck from becoming en-crusted with dried formula, which will become sour-smelling.

Refill the dropper and repeat the procedure as long as the baby will accept the formula. As the baby becomes stronger and you become more proficient, you will quickly adapt your ability to give formula to its ability to take it. Each baby varies in the way in which it accepts the feeding procedure, which means you have to learn the best and most effective way for your individual orphan baby.

Some babies, particularly those whose eyes are already open, will often take the formula best if fed drop by drop in the following way: hang one drop of formula at a time on the tip of the dropper and let the baby lick it off; replace it with another drop each time the baby licks it off. This method works particularly well for baby rabbits.

How much food the baby is consuming tells a lot about the condition of your orphan. If at each feeding it takes a little more than the time before, you are making progress.

Once the baby accepts the formula and recognizes it as food, it will usually accept each succeeding dropperful more readily. When it sucks greedily on the end of the dropper, you can change to a bottle.

HOW MUCH TO FEED. The amount to feed depends upon the size and condition of the baby. A baby squirrel with no hair, 1½ inches long, may take only two to ten drops at a feeding. An older squirrel, 3 or 4 inches long, which has hair but whose eyes are closed, will more likely take two to six dropperfuls. A squirrel 4 inches long with its eyes open would take from four to ten dropperfuls at each feeding.

The amount and frequency of feeding will vary but are related. A squirrel 3 inches long, furred, but with its eyes closed, which is strong when you find it, will probably take three to six dropperfuls, sucking vigorously and hungrily. But the same squirrel which was badly chilled and is now warmed but still weak will probably take only one half a dropperful of

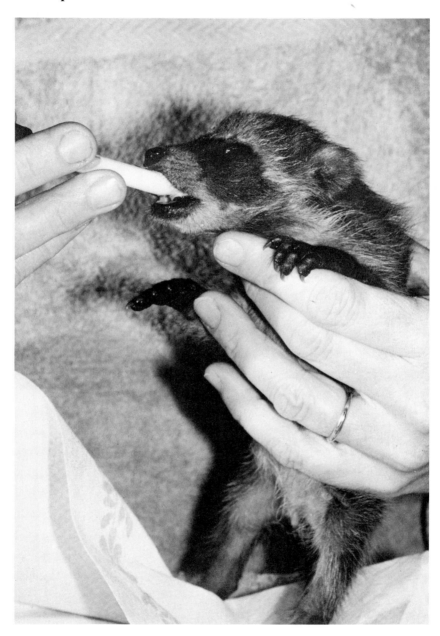

Baby raccoon eats greedily.

formula. The strong squirrel may be satisfied if fed every two or three hours. The weak squirrel should be fed every thirty minutes, in the hope that it will eat a little more each time. When it gets stronger and eats normally, it will eat enough at one time to satisfy its hunger for several hours.

This variation in amounts is true regardless of species. A weak, tiny mouse or flying squirrel will take only one or two drops. A healthy orphan, the same size, might take as much as a quarter dropperful. When a wild baby has had enough, you just can't get it to take any more. After the first few days you will know how often the baby will accept food.

With a little experience, you will often be able to tell whether the baby is ready to eat by watching it for a few moments. The full, contented baby sleeps rather quietly. You may see a little involuntary twitching, which is perfectly normal. The hungry baby is restless. It will raise its head and creep about the nest area every few seconds. The hungry, older baby with its eyes open will be standing in the nest or peering over the edge looking for food. These are your signals that it is time for the next feeding.

Basically, let your orphan tell you how much it wants to eat and when. If it eats less than you expect, you can anticipate that it will be hungry again soon. Most babies want to eat about four times daily and will stop eating when they have had enough.

Therefore, feed only as much as the baby wants. Offer food frequently until you have learned something of your orphan's eating habits and its eating pattern is established.

Bottle Feeding

Larger babies, such as deer and goats, are taught from the start to eat from an infant nursing bottle. Smaller babies are changed over to bottle feeding when they are consuming an ounce or more of formula at each feeding. Because of the stiff

An older baby raccoon is fed with a baby bottle.

nipple, doll bottles are usually not satisfactory for small animals. A baby-animal bottle (Nip·Pet Nurser), which may be obtained from a veterinarian or pet store, works well for small animals. Use a small infant nursing bottle with a "preemie" nipple after the orphan weighs a pound or more. These are purchased at a drugstore.

Since the egg yolk formula is thicker than most prepared milk formulas, the openings in the end of any new nipple must be enlarged for nursing an orphan baby. Pass a heated needle through the existing hole, or enlarge the hole to small slits with a sharp knife. If the nipple has a tendency to plug up, filter the formula through several layers of gauze. This will remove any lumps of yolk material that might stop up the nipple.

How MUCH TO FEED.   Most babies will be bottle-fed three to four times daily. Fill the bottle with the amount of formula the baby will consume at one feeding. You will soon learn how much formula it takes to satisfy your baby at each feeding.

Start with 4 to 6 ounces of formula two to three times daily for a young tiny fawn, and increase the amount as it grows.

After bottle feeding, the baby should be "burped." Hold it in an almost upright position in your hand. Pat its back gently to "coax" out any swallowed air. A larger baby can be placed on your shoulder as a human infant would be and patted in the same way. With hoofed animals, such as deer and goats, this is not necessary.

Weaning the Baby

Most babies wean themselves. They give up the dropper or bottle of formula when they begin eating other foods well. However, some just don't like to give it up. They seem not only to enjoy the formula as food, but also the companionship and attention they receive at feeding time. Even some adult animals enjoy a bottle of formula. We don't force weaning but feed the formula as long as the orphan desires it.

Deer being fed formula from bottle.

Stomach-Tube Feeding

This is for the problem baby. The weak baby that refuses to eat from the dropper, or does not have the strength to suck or the will to swallow, must be fed by stomach tube. Chances are you will not have to do this. Such a baby is not often found. But if you should find and adopt one, it is well to be prepared. This procedure is safe, easy, and effective. You can easily accomplish it on your own. If you have any questions, though, consult your veterinarian.

EQUIPMENT. The necessary equipment will have to be obtained from your veterinarian. You will need a small plastic syringe and a piece of plastic tubing. For most babies, such as squirrels, raccoons, and foxes, tubing ⅛ inch in diameter and 6 or 8 inches long will work best. Your veterinarian will help you select the size syringe and tubing most appropriate for your baby and demonstrate how to use them. Attach the syringe to the tubing. Fill the syringe with formula.

HOW FAR TO BABY'S STOMACH? Before you can place the contents of the syringe directly into the stomach, which sounds more difficult than it is, first measure the distance from baby's mouth to the stomach. Hold the tube alongside the baby, putting the tip of the tube just past the baby's last rib. With a Magic Marker or pen, mark the tube at the nose point. This is the distance to the baby's stomach. When you insert the tube and the mark reaches the baby's lips, you will know the end is in the stomach.

THE FEEDING PROCESS. When you are ready to feed, place the baby on its stomach on a table or counter. Place your left hand around its body, your thumb near the mouth and forefinger on the other side of the head. Gently insert the tips of your thumb and forefinger into the baby's mouth, forcing it slightly open. Moisten the tube with a little formula for lubrication, and insert the tube over the tongue, aiming for the deepest part of the throat. Gently slide the tube down into the

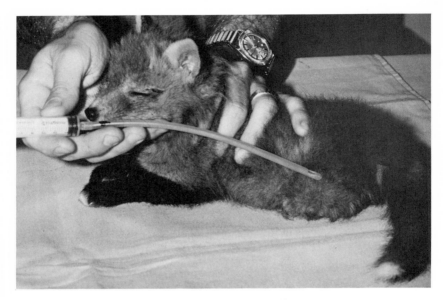

Baby fox being measured for stomach-tube feeding.

stomach. When the "nosemark" is even with the lips, you are there.

All your movements should be gentle. If the tube appears to stop, or doesn't go in readily, withdraw it slightly and then continue. The trachea or windpipe presents no problem. Do not try to avoid it. The tube will go down the right place. If the tube doesn't go to the "nosemark," or if for one reason or another you aren't sure, remove the tube, moisten it with formula again, and start over.

How MUCH TO FEED.   Once the tube is in place, press the syringe very gently and slowly release a small amount of formula into the baby's stomach. If this goes well, press again and give about one fourth the total amount. Pause for five or six seconds to be sure the baby is handling it, then give one half of the remainder. Pause again, and give the balance. When the formula is gone, remove the tube.

Stomach-tube feeding four times a day is sufficient, since more is given at each feeding than with the medicine dropper.

Still, watch for "hungry" signals and feed as your orphan needs it. Since the medicine-dropper method is safer, and since the baby helps and participates in it rather than just being a passive "blob" that you are manipulating, switch to the dropper as soon as possible.

GAGGING. The gagging reflex is not well developed in very young babies. Therefore, it will not interfere with the feeding process. Nor will the baby attempt to get rid of the tube. Since the tube may interfere slightly with breathing, however, don't leave it in any longer than necessary. The gagging reflex develops after the baby's eyes open, and at this age tube feeding is not necessary, except in sick or very weak babies.

If you squirt the formula into the stomach too rapidly, the baby will not be able to handle it, and vomiting will occur. This rarely happens, but if it does, withdraw the tube immediately, hold the baby in a head-down position, and gently pat it over the back and chest area, just as a mother would a human infant. This helps clear the chest of any liquid which might have been sucked into the trachea.

VETERINARY ASSISTANCE. If your veterinarian demonstrates stomach-tube feeding for you, he may use a clear liquid that contains a little sugar and essential salts. This sugar solution is used for the first one or two feedings when the baby is dehydrated (a lack of water in the tissues and circulatory system). The solution is also used when the baby is too weak to accept regular formula. Ordinarily you should not have to use it. Tell your veterinarian that you intend to use the basic egg yolk and milk formula. If he suggests changing it for a few days to combat a specific problem, follow his advice.

If there is no veterinarian in your community, study the illustrations of the feeding utensils and make your own adaptations as best you can. You may find it easier than you expect, and you may save a baby that would otherwise have been lost. Veterinary medicine, and all medicine, has one basic rule: *DO NO HARM*. If it appears that what you are attempting to do might do damage to the baby—don't do it.

Washing Up

Cleanliness is essential for a healthy baby.

Any bacteria present in the warmed formula will grow rapidly and could make the orphan baby sick. Therefore, discard all uneaten formula.

After feeding, clean all utensils thoroughly. Wash them first in cold water, to loosen milk particles, then in very hot water. Place them on a clean paper napkin or paper towel and allow them to air-dry. They will then be clean and ready for the next use.

Detergents should not be necessary. If, however, you did not have an opportunity to clean your utensils after feeding and the milk has dried and hardened, wash them in detergent. Be sure to rinse them thoroughly, for any detergent left on the utensil will make the baby sick. They may be sanitized and disinfected by adding a small amount of Clorox to the final rinse water.

Intestinal upsets caused by detergents or by infection from dirty utensils probably cause more deaths when raising orphan babies than any other factor. The baby's intestinal tract is very sensitive, and in the baby under ten days of age the intestines allow bacteria and poisons to enter its system.

FOODS FOR THE OLDER BABY

As your orphan baby gets older, it will leave the nest to play and explore. This is the time to add other foods to its diet.

Baby cereal, such as Gerber's oatmeal or Hi-Protein cereal, and baby food may be added to its formula to make it more nutritious and satisfying. Just remember that the openings in the nipple must be made even larger to accommodate this thicker formula.

Gray squirrel eats first solid food, dry breakfast cereal.

Flying Squirrels, Squirrels, and Mice

Offer these babies dry breakfast cereals and nuts as their first new foods. Most babies will accept unsweetened oat and wheat cereals. The baby squirrel will usually grasp a piece of cereal in both hands and bite little pieces out of it. Of all the nuts, shelled pecans are the favorite. As soon as the baby is eating nuts well, discontinue the cereal. Continue to feed the formula along with the nuts. Add fruits and other new foods daily. Grapes, orange sections, pieces of apple, lettuce leaves, bits of brown bread, carrots, and any other fruits should be offered if they are available.

If acorns and other seeds that squirrels would normally eat in the wild are available, offer these as well. The sooner these wild creatures begin eating the food they will eat when they are free, the easier will be their transition back to the wild.

Do not try to supply all the foods that an animal would find in the wild. Some animals eat foods such as grasshoppers and

A variety of foods for baby flying squirrel.

other large bugs which are too difficult to obtain. Others are predators who eat smaller creatures such as mice, rats, and rabbits. We feel it is not right for us to kill one animal to sustain another.

Baby Rabbits

Start with dry breakfast food and any green leafy vegetables. Rabbits normally start eating green plant foods at a very early age. When the babies are old enough to start hopping around the cage, offer bits of lettuce, celery leaves, cabbage, apples, and any green plants they will find outdoors.

There are so many foods available to rabbits when they are given their freedom that their dietary transition is not at all difficult. As they eat more of the items you offer, they will take less and less of the formula. When they don't want the formula any more and you have to coax them to take it, it is time to give them their freedom.

Fox Puppies, Skunks, Opossums, Raccoons, and Bobcats

When they are old enough to become playful, usually about four or five weeks of age, offer a little bowl of a complete canned dog food mixed with an equal amount of formula.

CANNED DOG FOOD. A complete canned dog food is a high-quality, balanced food that has met the nutritional requirements of the National Research Council, Washington, D.C. This would be indicated on the label. The label should further state that the contents constitute a complete and balanced diet for a dog. This food, a mixture of meat and cereal grains, should have a meaty consistency and odor. One that is oily, greasy, or has a musty, unpleasant odor should not be used. All-meat dog foods should not be used, because they often cause diarrhea in the young orphan.

Mix the dog food with enough formula to make it the consistency of thick soup or oatmeal, and offer it on your finger. If the baby licks your finger, offer it the entire bowl. As the baby begins to eat more of the dog food-formula combination, it will become less interested in eating formula from the bottle or dropper. Once it is eating well, gradually discontinue feeding the formula and offer only the dog food-formula mixture four to six times daily. Discard what the baby hasn't eaten after five or ten minutes, as a great deal of bacterial growth can take place within a few hours in moist food standing at room temperature. Over the next ten days gradually reduce the amount of formula in the mixture until you are feeding just canned dog food.

DRY FOOD. When the baby is eating canned food well, introduce it to dry cat or dog food. As long as the label states that the dry food is a complete, balanced food, either cat or

Armadillo eating canned dog food.

dog food is satisfactory. Skunks, opossums, armadillos, and cats are usually fed dry cat food. The other species are given dry dog food. Leave a bowl of dry food in the cage at all times for the orphan to snack on. When it begins eating it well, gradually reduce the amount and frequency of the canned dog food feedings.

It is important to change an orphan from the canned to the dry food. Since dry food does not spoil readily, it is easier to keep this food available when the baby is free.

While the dry food will be its basic diet, continue to offer the orphan a variety of foods. Individual babies often show decided food preferences, and it is most interesting to see what a new orphan will like and accept.

Any creature normally has a varied diet in the wild. It is abnormal for an orphan to eat one particular food to the exclusion of all others. If it does, in time it will develop a deficiency. The easiest way to handle this problem is to withdraw the preferred food and offer alternative foods until the baby is eating these other foods well. You may then return the withdrawn food to the diet, but only in small amounts.

DIET SUPPLEMENTS

Dietary supplements are usually added to a diet to make up for a deficiency. The most common dietary supplements are vitamin-mineral preparations. It is not necessary to add a vitamin supplement to the basic milk and egg yolk formula, as this food contains high-quality protein and adequate vitamins and minerals. Nor is it necessary to add supplements to a good canned dog food or dry chow. They have already been supplied with vitamins and minerals.

Cod-liver oil is a widely recommended dietary supplement in animal and bird publications. However, to add it to the diet is to risk permanent damage to your orphan. Cod-liver oil primarily supplies vitamins A and D and affects calcium utilization. In high dosages these vitamins are toxic.

Since vitamin D is the more toxic, it concerns us most. In large amounts, vitamin D increases the level of calcium in the blood. However, unless additional calcium and phosphorus are provided in proper balance in the diet, the vitamin D maintains this higher blood level by drawing calcium from the animal's bones. Prolonged use of cod-liver oil leads to what is called "demineralization" of the skeleton, which simply means the bones lose their density and strength as they lose their calcium. Multiple fractures, bending, and twisting of the bones become commonplace. High calcium levels in the blood also cause damage to blood vessels and kidneys.

The percentage of carbohydrates, fats, and proteins required in the diets of most wild animals is known, but specific information on essential amino acids and vitamin and mineral requirements has not been established. We do know, however, that all these creatures require vitamins and minerals, just as humans do. Our basic formula provides them in adequate amounts.

A neat, healthy appearance in an active orphan is the best evidence that it is being adequately supplied with the vitamins and minerals it requires. As long as an orphan is eating well and eating a variety of foods, extra vitamins and minerals are not necessary.

3

Petting, Handling, and Freedom

PETTING AND HANDLING

Contrary to what you might expect, an orphan should receive a great deal of petting, handling, and attention. After feeding, hold the baby for a little while in your cupped hands. It will burrow around for a few moments, then fall asleep. After it is asleep, place it back in the nest.

The baby will begin to stay awake for longer periods of time once the eyes are open. When this happens, it will be more fascinating to play with and to observe. As with any baby, it will require frequent naps and rest periods. But it will also require large doses of attention and love.

A baby that receives gentle and affectionate handling will respond by becoming very tame. It will rarely bite or become frightened and is a real pleasure to have around. Let the baby sit with you while you are reading or watching television. It over you, exploring and examining everything. will select a warm, snug place in your lap or the chair and curl up and go to sleep. Enjoying baby in this way will cause no difficulty when the time comes to let it go free.

If Baby Bites

As a rule, babies do not bite. If your baby makes an attempt to do so, however, chances are you are doing something wrong. A wild animal cannot stand physical restraint. Petting is one thing, but to clutch a squirrel is to invite a bite. If you try forcibly to subdue a raccoon, bobcat, or fox, you risk not only being bitten or scratched but also losing a friend.

Recognize what is natural and normal for your wild creature. Do not try to impose on your baby what you consider to be socially acceptable behavior. Most animals are guided by strong instincts. To attempt to discourage a bobcat from chasing birds or a raccoon from chasing mice and bugs is to thwart those instinctive urges upon which their survival depends.

As these instinctive urges to chase and pursue become stronger, you can be sure that the time to offer freedom is drawing near.

SETTING YOUR ORPHAN FREE

Offering freedom does not mean that you simply turn your orphan loose. The baby must have time to get used to a new life. It must learn to adapt to the world outside. When your orphan can run, romp, climb, and play, it is time to start the gradual process that will lead to full freedom. Do not make the mistake of waiting for the baby to be an adult. This would be a mistake. Start while the baby is young and flexible in its habits and can still learn about the wide world outside.

First Step

Freedom is given gradually, not all at once. To begin with, take your baby outside for an hour each morning and afternoon. Stay with it for the first few times. Initially, the animal may be afraid of the outdoors, which is a new and strange place. The baby may cling to you and be unwilling to move away. Be patient, for on the second or third try, the baby begins to gain confidence and will begin to do a little exploring close by you. It may go off on its own for a short distance, then come running back to you as if afraid you are going to leave.

As the baby grows accustomed to the outdoors, you will notice that when it is inside it will spend more and more time looking outside or pacing restlessly. It is time to start letting the baby go out on its own.

Second Step

Arrange for the door to be propped open at all times. This will allow the baby to come and go as it pleases, and, most importantly, give it ready access to its cage and nest box. Without a haven to escape to, the baby may be threatened and chased by animals that feel they own the territory around your house. The baby must find its place among the other animals in the area. But until it learns how to "fit in" and make its way among them, it must have the security of its own cage.

Before you know it, your baby will be out most of the time, coming in only for food once or twice a day, and at night to sleep in its nest home. When this happens, move the cage and nest home outside, placing it near the entrance the baby is accustomed to using, so your orphan can find it easily.

The half-grown baby, as it comes and goes, will still be glad to see you. It will like to be picked up and petted by members of the family. While it enjoys its freedom, it has not yet cut the ties with its human friends.

Then, one night, you will notice that the baby is missing, that it hasn't come back to the cage to sleep. You will worry and wonder if it is safe. Just remind yourself that the baby has learned to adapt to the outdoors and that this is another stage in your orphan's development. It is becoming a wild creature again.

Freedom

The cage will be used less and less often over the next weeks. Food will go uneaten. Several months later, the cage and house will be almost totally unused. Food is untouched. You may now and then see a familiar shape around your yard, but you will not be able to touch or handle it any longer. Your orphan has taken its place in nature, where it belongs.

To attempt to hold an orphan captive when it reaches maturity is cruel. It can also be dangerous. Deprived of its instinctive need to be with other animals of its kind, your former baby often becomes cantankerous. Even the handling of routine care can lead to a serious bite or scratch. There is no enjoyment in keeping an unhappy captive that cannot be handled. Nor can you even allow it to be set free. It will be too old to learn how to live successfully in the wild. The great satisfaction is in raising your orphan, in seeing it prepare itself to return to the wild, and in setting it free.

4

Ailing or Injured Mammals

INTESTINAL INFECTION

The most common infection in an orphan animal is an intestinal infection. This usually results from improper cleaning and care of the feeding utensils. The first sign of intestinal infection is a change in the baby's bowel material.

Normally, the bowel material will be slightly darker in color than egg yolk and about the consistency of toothpaste. If an infection is starting, the bowel material will appear at first slightly softer than usual and have little foamy bubbles. In the next stage, it will be more foamy and will look like thin formula, both in consistency and color. When this happens, you should start administering antibiotics.

Antibiotics

Antibiotics prevent or stop infection by killing or preventing the growth of disease-producing bacteria. Except in the case

67

of baby rabbits, antibiotics are used only when an infection is present. Baby rabbits seem to be extremely sensitive to intestinal infection; therefore, as stated earlier, you may add antibiotics to their formula daily once their eyes are open as a preventative measure.

When you notice that the bowel material has become watery or loose, start administering antibiotics right away. Antibiotics are prescription items, so you will have to obtain these from your veterinarian. If you cannot see him personally, perhaps you can do it all by phone. Call him and explain your problem. Ask him if he can call in a prescription to your local drugstore.

One effective antibiotic in most intestinal infections is tetracycline. The usual daily therapeutic dose (the amount of antibiotic that must be given to kill or inhibit growth of disease-producing bacteria) is 50 milligrams (mg.) of tetracycline for each pound your patient weighs. Since most orphans are quite small, you will be dealing with ounces, not with pounds. Weigh the baby on a postal scale or kitchen scale. Use a daily dosage of 3 mg. of antibiotic for each ounce the baby weighs.

For example, a 2-ounce baby should receive 6 mg. of antibiotic, a 3-ounce baby should receive 9 mg., and a 4-ounce baby should get 12 mg. of this antibiotic each day.

To prepare the medication, dissolve one 250-mg. tetracycline capsule in 8 ounces of formula. Eight ounces is 240 milliliters, since each ounce is equal to 30 ml. Each milliliter of this formula thus contains 1 mg. of the antibiotic. If you feed this formula to your baby as you normally would feed plain formula, your baby should receive a satisfactory dosage.

The usual medicine dropper delivers ½ ml. to the baby each time. The average 2-ounce baby will take 12 dropperfuls of formula per day. The total amount of formula consumed is 6 ml. of formula and thus 6 mg. of antibiotic, the correct dosage.

However, your baby may take more or less than the average baby. Therefore, you must make sure it is getting the correct dosage. Calculate how much antibiotic the baby is actually receiving by counting how many dropperfuls it eats daily, divide by two to find out how many milliliters of formula it is taking and thus how many milligrams of antibiotic it is receiving. If the amount is not reasonably close, make an adjustment in the amount of antibiotic you are adding to the formula.

If the baby is not getting enough antibiotic in the formula consumed, add part of the contents of another capsule to the formula. It it is getting too much antibiotic, discard that formula, and mix up a new batch using only a portion of the capsule in your formula.

For smaller babies, add one capsule to their more concentrated 6-ounce formula. There will be slightly more antibiotic per milliliter or formula (1.4 mg. per milliliter), but since these babies consume less formula for their weight, the dosage works out right for them also.

Give the antibiotic until bowel eliminations return to normal and then for two additional days to be sure the infection is cleared up.

One point must be made very clear. Because in time of need a little antibiotic in the formula is good, that doesn't mean a lot is better. Too much antibiotic will reduce the baby's appetite so that it won't eat properly. So follow the guidelines and do not exceed recommended dosages.

DEHYDRATION

Sometimes intestinal infection can lead to dehydration. The formula may move through the intestinal tract so rapidly that the baby doesn't have a chance to digest and absorb the needed nutrients. The intestine becomes irritated. It loses water instead of absorbing it, and the baby becomes dehydrated (drying out from lack of water). Its skin feels dry instead of soft and pliable. Dehydration can progress so rapidly that after twelve hours, a fold of skin picked up between your thumb and fingers and then released may remain standing in a ridge. At this stage your baby will no longer eat. Death will follow shortly. The injection of fluids may save the orphan, but this can properly be done only by a veterinarian.

Sometimes, in spite of all you do, you will not be able to save your orphan. Knowing this can happen does not make it any easier to accept a death when it does occur. But if you do your best, you will have the satisfaction of knowing what you tried, and this is what is all-important.

TICKS, FLEAS, AND LICE

Most new babies you find will be neat and clean, but occasionally one may have fleas, ticks, or lice. In a very young baby with little or no hair, any parasite can be easily seen on the pink skin and removed.

Ticks are tiny, brownish, oval creatures which resemble spiders. They cling tightly to the skin by their mouth parts. You can pull them off with your fingers. Twist or rotate the tick in a clockwise direction as you pull gently, until it comes off.

Wrap the tick in a piece of toilet tissue and flush it down the toilet. Then wash your hands thoroughly with soap and water. Do not kill ticks by crushing them, since some contain disease-producing organisms.

Fleas and lice may not be as easy to spot. Fleas can be seen crawling rapidly through the hair if you check the baby's skin carefully. They are hard, shiny, slender, dark brown in color, and about the same size as the period at the end of this sentence.

Lice was usually slightly larger, soft, and a dull gray in color. They move slowly, if at all.

Treat fleas and lice in the same way. Use a flea spray which states on the label that it is safe for cats. Pyrethrins are generally the active ingredient.

Do not spray the baby directly. Spray into the palms of your hands, rub your hands together to disperse the fluid somewhat, and then rub it into the hair coat of your orphan baby. In this way the "hissing noise" of the spray can doesn't frighten the baby, and the insecticide will be evenly distributed over the entire body.

This spray is mild, so you may repeat the treatment the following day if necessary. If the baby looks grubby from flea dirt, bathe it.

BATHING

A baby may be bathed once, when you first adopt it, or occasionally if it has somehow soiled itself. But bathing should not be a regular weekly event. Most babies learn to clean and groom themselves.

You can bathe even the tiniest baby if you are careful. Adjust the water from the tap until it feels comfortably warm on your arm. Hold the baby gently in the palm of one hand, elevate the head end, so water won't get in its nose or mouth, and place the tail end under the gently flowing warm water.

With your other hand, massage water into the skin, rinsing the dirt away. Work toward the head end, cleaning as you go. Never put the head under the water. Clean the face with the tips of your moistened fingers.

If this rinsing isn't sufficient to clean the baby, use a mild soap, Johnson's Baby Shampoo, or even a mild dishwashing detergent. Lather the baby and rinse thoroughly.

The only real danger in this procedure is allowing the baby to become chilled. After the last rinse, wrap the baby in a towel and rub it gently until dry. Then hold it for a while so it can absorb the warmth of your hands, or place it back in its warm nest and cover it lightly with a piece of towel or some other soft material.

The baby will snuggle into your hands or into its nest and will be content to stay quiet until it is thoroughly dry and warm. Then it will usually become hungry.

Do not bathe the baby when it gets older. You might earn a bite or severe scratches from your usually docile orphan. No wild creature will tolerate being physically restrained, particularly if it becomes frightened.

INJURY

Should Help Be Given?

The first thing to determine is whether a creature really needs first aid. An abnormal physical appearance, abnormal behavior, and evidence of pain are signs that an animal, whether baby or adult, is in need of help.

ABNORMAL PHYSICAL APPEARANCE. An animal walking on three legs, or one with multiple wounds or with some part of its body swollen or enlarged, is one with an abnormal physical appearance.

ABNORMAL BEHAVIOR. A squirrel crawling slowly about in the middle of a busy highway is one example of abnormal behavior. Other examples are a skunk that wanders into your yard in the daytime. Or an adult fox or raccoon that appears friendly and allows you to come close. Abnormal behavior may be a sign of rabies. Avoid these animals completely. Report them at once to the local wildlife officer, health department, or police.

PAIN. The presence of pain is often hard to detect. Even a veterinarian cannot always tell if an animal feels pain. An animal in pain is uneasy and restless. It usually has an anxious expression, but it seldom whines or cries. Often it will lick at the area where the pain is most intense.

When Not to Help

The care and treatment of the smaller animal with concussion is probably the only animal first aid you will be able to handle yourself. When a larger full-grown animal such as a raccoon, opossum, deer, or bobcat is injured or sick, it will usually seek a secluded spot. Such an animal is dangerous and must not be approached without professional assistance. It will bite, scratch, or strike out with its feet if it feels threatened. More important, an injured animal trying to flee will probably do even more damage to itself. You can help most by calling the office of the nearest wildlife officer or game warden and describing the condition and exact location of the animal. He can usually determine if it can be moved.

After an animal with large wounds, fractures, or similar injuries has received the professional care it needs, you may offer to give the animal the necessary nursing care.

How to Administer First Aid

Let's go back to the squirrel on the highway. Let us say that it was able to lift its head and move a bit, but that it would not stand. This animal has undoubtedly been hit by a car. Internal injuries are common when a small animal collides with something as massive as an automobile. Unfortunately most of them will die. Sometimes, however, the animal is merely stunned or has a concussion. If the brain damage is not severe, many of those animals will recover with good nursing care.

MOVING THE ANIMAL TO SAFETY. Without endangering yourself, remove the animal from the highway as quickly as possible. The easiest way to do this is to use a jacket or sweater to protect yourself. Place the jacket over the squirrel and gently slide your hands underneath it, keeping the jacket between your hands and the animal's body.

Once you have the animal cradled in your hands and covered with the jacket, carry it to a place where you can care for it. Place it in a comfortable cage, or even a cardboard box, and allow it to rest. Provide the animal with a dish of fresh water. Maintain the temperature in the box or cage at about 80° F. by using a 60-watt bulb for extra heat, if necessary. Warmth is very important in the treatment of shock.

Lightly stunned animals may recover in one hour or less and can be released as soon as they seem to be walking and moving normally.

If the animal moves feebly but can't walk, it is suffering from a more severe concussion. It may be a month or more before it can move well enough to be set free. Allow it complete rest for the first twenty-four hours.

FLUIDS. If the animal is not drinking water or is semi-conscious, start dropper-feeding it water. While any animal can go without food for several days, without fluids dehydration occurs and death follows.

Place the animal on its side. Do not tip the head up, or the water will run down into the back part of the throat, causing the animal to cough or choke. Fill the dropper with water. Place the tip of the dropper between the animal's lips and allow a few drops of fluid to trickle onto and across the tongue. In many cases the fluid will stimulate your patient to start licking and swallowing. Keep up a steady, gentle, slow trickle as long as your patient keeps licking and swallowing. Then allow it to rest.

ADDING FORMULA. An hour later, try again, using the proper milk and egg yolk formula.

Continue to give water and formula alternately every few hours during the day until your patient is able to drink on its own. This often takes several days. When it can lift its head and is more aware of what is going on, offer formula in a small shallow dish or jar lid. Place the dish under its chin and encourage it to try to lap the formula.

An animal that can take formula or water will almost always recover. However, one that does not respond to your efforts and will not swallow may have severe brain damage. Ask the opinion of your veterinarian on its chances for survival.

If it appears to your veterinarian that the animal will never recover completely, euthanasia may be better than prolonging the animal's suffering.

Birds

5

Altricial Birds

WHAT IS AN ALTRICIAL BIRD?

Altricial birds are born helpless. They are hatched in a weak condition and are, therefore, confined to the nest. Their eyes are usually still closed, and they have few or no feathers. They are completely dependent upon their parents for warmth and nourishment. All songbirds are altricial birds. So are woodpeckers, hawks, owls, crows, and many of the water birds, such as herons, egrets, and pelicans.

Because a baby altricial bird lives in the nest for several days to several months after hatching, it is called a nestling. From the time they leave the nest until they are independent of their parents, they are called fledglings.

WHAT IS AN ORPHAN?

An orphan is a baby bird without a nest or without parents. Many of the birds which need help are birds that leave the

Nestling redwing blackbird, a helpless, blind, naked altricial bird.

nest prematurely. They either tried to fly before they were able, or they have fallen out. If you find a naked, helpless baby on the ground, try to locate its nest. It should be close by. If the baby bird seems warm and active, put it back in the nest at once. If it is trembling and appears cold, gently cup your hands around it until it feels warm, then place it back in the nest. If the nest has been destroyed or if you cannot find it, and if neither parent is anywhere nearby, the baby is an orphan. Adopt it.

Do not worry that because you have touched the baby its parents will abandon both it and the nest. There is truth to the belief that parent birds may desert the nest they are build-ing if they are bothered. They may even do so during the first part of the incubation period. But they are not likely to do so once the eggs have hatched.

If you see the parents watching nearby, it is usually safe to leave the baby on a branch near the nest. They will feed and care for it as if it were in the nest. But if the baby persists in flying to the ground, where it faces constant danger, and you cannot see its parents, the baby is an orphan. Adopt it.

Determining Baby's Age

Since the way these orphans react to you and the care you must give them depend on their age, it is well to have an idea of the baby's age. This can be determined by several factors, but feathering and the presence of an egg tooth are the most important. The egg tooth is a small whitish projection near the tip of the upper beak, which the nestling uses to crack through the shell of the egg when hatching. The tooth usually disappears about three days after birth. Therefore, a naked baby with the whitish egg tooth projecting from the tip of the upper beak is less than three days old.

The nestling one week old or younger will be almost naked,

The egg tooth is the tiny, white projection near the tip of the beak of the baby screech owl on the left. The second one, one or two days older, has already lost the egg tooth.

but will show some dark projections protruding from the skin. These projections, called pinfeathers, will emerge as feathers over the next two weeks. Feathers will first appear along the back and head, then on the wings, and finally on the abdomen and breast area. By two weeks of age, songbird babies have feathers covering most of their skin. By three weeks of age, most songbirds are well covered with feathers and are fluttering about, but not really flying. At four to six weeks of age, they can fly quite well.

Putting Baby Back in the Nest

FOR MOST BIRDS. The tiny altricial bird with only a few or no feathers can be easily picked up. Gently cup the baby in the palms of your hands. It will seldom flutter or struggle and will snuggle down to absorb the warmth of your hands. Usually an alert beady eye will watch you intently, as if to judge whether you are friend or foe.

Baby mockingbird is content being carried in hand-nest.

If the baby you have found is at the stage when it is almost ready to leave the nest, as evidenced by the fact that it has feathers all over, it will be extremely difficult to return this baby to its nest. It is so afraid of you that each time you release it at the nest, it will usually flutter away trying to escape.

A young nestling that has enough feathers to flutter away on short flights is more difficult to catch. Follow it slowly, herding it into the corner of a fence or a building, or into tall grass. Talk gently as you quietly approach. Usually, you will be able to trap the young bird in your hands. Once captured, it will usually sit quietly. However, a sudden movement or noise may frighten it, and it will flutter away again. So confine the baby gently but firmly enough in your hands to keep it from flying away, but don't squeeze it. Then return it to the nest.

FOR OWLS AND HAWKS.   The baby owl or hawk doesn't usually use its sharp beak and claws for defense. If the baby is tiny and downy, pick it up in your hands and return it to its nest. If it is old enough to have some feathers, use a short stick or your fingers as a perch. Gently press the stick or finger against its abdomen. It will usually step on the perch rather than allow itself to be pushed backward. You may have to make as many as ten attempts. But once the bird is securely on the perch, you can carry it to the nest tree. If you can't find the nest, carry it on your finger or the twig perch to your home, where you can properly care for it.

WARMTH AND SHELTER

The Nest

The altricial orphan bird you have adopted must be provided with warmth and a nest. Use a box about 6 inches square as a nest. A quart berry basket will do nicely. Mold a

Mockingbird in nest made from berry box, lined with tissues.

soft piece of cloth, part of an old towel or flannel shirt, into a nest shape and place it inside the box. Then cover the whole nest with fifteen or twenty Kleenex-type tissues. Pat them down to assume a nest shape. The tissues will be used as disposable nest liners. Whenever the baby soils the nest, lift the soiled top tissue out, leaving a fresh one in position. When all the tissues are gone, put in a new stack.

Not all birds require a lot of clean-up care. You may even find a baby orphan that is partially toilet-trained. We raised a tiny bluejay only a few days old whose nest area never needed changing. Each time it felt the need to evacuate, it climbed to the edge of the nest, turned around, backed up close to the edge, and then with several ludicrous wiggles of its sparsely pinfeathered tail, evacuated its droppings well out of the nest area. While this is normal behavior in older nestlings, it is unusual in one so young.

Temperature Control

Provide warmth in the same way as for mammal orphans. Place the nest area away from cold drafts, and use a 60- to 100-watt bulb to provide heat. Place an inexpensive thermometer in the nest and move the light bulb closer and farther away from the nest until a nest temperature of 95° F. is consistently maintained. This temperature is correct for the very young bird with few or no feathers. Allow the bulb to burn night and day to provide constant warmth.

The normal body temperature of most altricial birds is about 102° F. or higher. Although our nest temperature is lower, the bird will receive enough radiant warmth to protect it. Too much heat can cause more harm than too little. A bird begins to acquire the ability to control its body temperature at about the time its feathers start to emerge from the protective sheaths or to change from pinfeathers. This is about midpoint in its nest life.

When the bird is fairly well covered with feathers, begin dropping the nest temperature by moving the bulb farther away from the nest. Decrease the temperature 5° F. each week until it reaches 70° F. Keep the light available as long as the bird sits near it and uses its warmth. Remove the light when the orphan is well feathered and sleeps in another part of the cage.

A baby bird less than a week or two of age will stay in its nest. When it perches on the edge of the nest and becomes more active, it is time to transfer the nest and light to a cage.

The Cage

Build the cage of hardware cloth, as discussed in Chapter 1. The size of the cage will vary a great deal depending on the size the nestling will be when full-grown. All cages should be at least 30″ × 30″ × 36″. This minimum size is adequate if the nestling when full-grown will be the size of a bluejay,

Great horned owl baby in cage with light bulb, nest area, and a perch.

mockingbird, or robin. Wire the nest, in its berry box, in one corner of the cage, about halfway up the side walls. Wire the thermometer in place at the edge of the nest box and the light bulb and socket against the outside of the cage at the same distance from the nest box as it was previously.

Having the bulb outside the cage makes for greater safety for an active, growing nestling, and allows the nest temperature to remain constant. When the orphan hops and flutters about the cage, there is no chance that it will land on the bulb and burn its feet.

Place perches of various sizes in the cage. Dead limbs trimmed from a tree and cut to the correct length are more suitable than smooth, polished perches, since rough bark gives the fledgling a better foothold. Vary the diameter of the limbs to keep the nestling's feet from becoming sore. In a cage 30″ × 30″ × 36″, wire five or six perches at various heights throughout the cage. Design it as you would a playground, with some jumping distance and others flying distance apart. Jumping and flying from perch to perch will help improve the fledgling's coordination.

Cover the bottom of the cage with several layers of newspaper to absorb moisture and help keep the cage clean. Change them about every other day.

We usually leave the cage door open during the day and allow the fledglings the freedom of a screened porch. They flutter and fly around the porch exploring, strengthening flight muscles, and improving coordination. They regularly return to the cage for food, rest, and warmth. When two or three birds are on a porch at once, there can be some confusion. Many birds are very antagonistic toward others on "their" porch. Often, but not always, a larger bird will pick on a smaller one. A tiny titmouse we had adopted would fly into the nest area of three young screech owls and take on all three at once. They had to be rescued from its fierce bites. From then on, we opened the two cages at separate times for the flying exercise periods. For the fledgling or nestling, cages represent security as well as confinement.

FEEDING MOST BABY BIRDS

Eating is one of the first activities a newly hatched altricial bird can perform. When first hatched, any noise or vibration which arouses it will cause the baby instinctively to raise its head and open its mouth wide to receive food. This is called "gaping."

To feed the very young bird, whose eyes are closed and whose egg tooth is still present, tap the side of the nest box gently as you prepare to offer it food. If the baby is healthy, it will gape—lift its head and open its mouth wide. When its beak is open wide, place food in the back part of its mouth.

Young mockingbird gapes for food.

If it is so weak that it does not gape, then forced feeding will be necessary. This will be discussed later in the book, in the chapter on special feeding.

As the nestling learns to eat, it also learns to respond to visual stimulation. At three to four days of age it will open its mouth and gape when it sees your hand approaching the nest. At this time it is no longer necessary to tap or gently shake the nest box before offering each bite of food.

After the nestling is a week old, it will recognize you as an individual. When it is hungry and sees you approaching, it will stand up in the nest, flutter its wings rapidly, and cheep repeatedly as if to say "hurry, hurry, hurry!" This is called "begging posturing" and such behavior is a sign your orphan is maturing. Now it begins to develop "personality" and is the most fun to take care of.

If the bird you have found and adopted is already a week old, it will be shy. It will take patience and gentleness to get it to start eating. However, three or four days after it starts eating, it will accept you as a friend and show this welcoming behavior.

Once the nestling starts begging, lift it out of the nest at each feeding, place it on a perch at about the same distance from the bulb that the nest was, and feed it. Then return it to its warm nest.

The Basic Diet

Basically, the diet for altricial birds, regardless of age, consists of a complete canned dog food and the concentrated formula of one egg yolk in enough homogenized milk to make 6 ounces. Prepare the formula the same way as explained in Chapter 2.

Caution: Be extra careful in your selection of canned dog food. Under no circumstances use one that appears oily or greasy. A high-fat diet binds the calcium in the food so that it

Baby screech owl takes pellet of dog food dipped in formula.

cannot be absorbed by a young bird's intestinal tract. Calcium is necessary for proper growth. Fatty, greasy foods also cause digestive upsets and diarrhea in nestlings.

Once the can has been opened, keep it in the refrigerator. You do not have to warm the food before feeding.

Roll the canned dog food into bite-sized pellets about the size of a pea, or slightly larger. Hold the pellet in your fingers and dip it into the formula. The addition of the formula serves three purposes: it lubricates the pellet so that it can be swallowed more easily, it supplies additional high-quality nutrients, and, since the formula is about 90 per cent water, adds water to the bird's diet.

Once you have moistened the pellet, be sure to feed it to the baby at once, for it becomes wet and crumbly. Even very small birds can usually swallow a pea-sized piece that has been softened and made slippery with the formula. All the altricial species we raise thrive on this diet and grow rapidly and well.

When the baby gapes, stuff the pellet into the back part of its throat. If you have ever watched a mother bird feed her young you know she is not gentle in the feeding process, but just pokes the food down the nestling's throat. But you should be gentle. If necessary, use your little finger to push the pellet partway down the throat—gently. If you don't place the food well back in the throat, the baby will spit it out.

Properly placed, the pellet will be swallowed at once. The small day-old bird may want to accept only one pellet. You can tap the nest box and move your hand toward its mouth to see if it might want more, but the smaller bird will not want any more food for thirty minutes to an hour, or even longer. A bird the size of a week-old blue jay will probably take four to six pellets, but it won't want to eat again for an hour or two.

Overfeeding is not usually a problem, since the babies stop eating when they have had enough. After a few days you will be able to anticipate when your bird will be ready to eat again.

As the baby bird gets older it will eat a little more at each feeding, and the interval between feedings will stretch to two or three hours.

Liquids

Enough formula will cling to the pellet and your fingers to satisfy most babies. However, if the baby swallows the pellet and then immediately tries to grasp your finger and pull any remaining liquid off your fingers, offer additional water by dipping one finger into water or formula and offering the finger to the nestling. Usually one large drop will hang from the end of your finger. The baby will grasp the end of your finger and capture the drop in its mouth.

Offer formula or water in this fashion only after the baby has satisfied its hunger. Offering water when the nestling is hungry may make you mistake its apparent interest in your finger and water for thirst, when all it really wants is to eat.

When the nestling is older, place a water dish close beside the nest. However, continue to dip the pellets in formula.

Expanding the Menu

As the nestling gets older and begins hopping from perch to perch, offer it a variety of foods. Place some on the cage floor, others in small feeders wired to the perches, and still others fastened to the sides of the cage.

Read about your specific bird in a good bird book. For example, the National Geographic Society book *Song and Garden Birds of North America* is an excellent source of this information. It gives a picture of each bird, a brief description of its habits, and information on the bird's usual food. Try to offer some of the foods your bird would eat if it were free. Offer as great a variety as possible and allow the bird to choose what it wants.

Wild bird grain or a seed mixture is essential for seed eaters and will be eaten by many other birds. It is available in grocery stores, pet shops and feedstores. Also provide breakfast cereals, brown bread crumbs, fruits such as grapes, sections of oranges, and apples, and vegetables such as bits of celery, carrots, and lettuce for your birds to try. Bits of eggshell or oystershell should also be offered. They are an excellent source of calcium, and oystershell will help the bird digest its food. Oystershell may be obtained at any livestock feedstore in a rural area or a pet shop in the city.

Since birds have no teeth, most of the food is ground up in the gizzard after it has been swallowed. This heavily muscled organ squeezes food and seeds together rhythmically, breaking them into very small pieces, which then pass into the intestine. Hard materials such as oystershell, called grit, stay in the gizzard and function as a grinding agent to break up the seeds and bits of food. Eventually grit is worn down and the bird eats more to replace it. Your orphan may not eat much oystershell with the diet you are feeding. It is not an absolute necessity, since the dog food contains extra calcium and is easily digested.

As your bird eats more and more of the foods you supply, you will begin to notice which food it likes best. Continue to feed the dog food "baby-style" as long as the bird wants it, but less and less frequently. Soon the fledgling will eat adequately on its own. However, many birds seem to enjoy being fed, so continue hand-feeding your fledgling two or three times a day as long as it wishes.

Many of our birds that are adult in appearance still fly to us and expect to be hand-fed for several months after they are capable of finding food on their own. Other birds are more independent and wean themselves almost at once.

FEEDING HAWKS AND OWLS

Hawks and owls are also altricial birds, but because they are predators they require special care. They normally live by capturing small animals such as mice and rabbits. Although basically meat eaters, along with the muscle or meat of their victim the hawks and owls also eat the skin, stomach contents, internal glands, and sometimes even fur and feathers. Thus, in the wild, they actually eat a variety of substances, not just meat. The digested portion of the prey provides a balanced diet. The undigested material such as bones, hair, fur, or feathers is usually regurgitated (spit up) as a round ball or "pellet" some twelve hours after eating.

When very young, hawks and owls also gape, just as other birds do. Feed the very young baby canned dog food pellets dipped in formula just as you would songbirds. Give them as much as they want to eat four to six times daily. When they have eaten enough, they will refuse to accept more. Each bird seems to establish its own eating pattern.

Baby screech owl eats a piece of beef heart.

When hawk and owl babies are two weeks old, feed them four times daily. While owls normally eat at night, with the light bulb burning all the time there will be no night or day, and they will eat whenever you offer food.

When you see feathers showing through the down, it is time to offer them strips of beef heart at every other feeding. Alternate the canned dog food-formula feeding and beef heart until the baby is eating the beef heart well. You can obtain beef heart at most supermarkets or butcher shops. Cut it into pieces about 2 by 4 by 4 inches in size, wrap each piece individually, and store it in the freezer. Thaw one piece at a time as needed.

Cut the piece into strips about ¼ inch thick. At first, offer tiny bite-sized bits to the nestling. Once it eats a piece or two, it will like both the flavor and consistency. As it gets a little older and eats more readily, offer larger pieces so it will learn to tear and play with the meat. At this time add supplements to the beef heart to make it a balanced food.

Dip the meat strips in egg yolk, which will increase the fat content and add additional vitamins, then powder it lightly with a calcium-vitamin-mineral supplement. Since most birds only have from forty to one hundred taste buds in the back part of their mouths (as compared to nine thousand in man), you will have little difficulty getting your bird to accept the meat coated with the rather bland calcium supplement.

Make the powdered supplement by combining equal parts of calcium carbonate powder and a vitamin-mineral supplement called Unipet Powder (Upjohn Company). Any drugstore has or can get the calcium carbonate powder for you, and your veterinarian will supply you with the Unipet Powder or its equivalent. This is the only time we use a vitamin-mineral supplement in our feeding program.

When your hawk or owl baby reaches the age where it is beginning to fly, discontinue the canned dog food altogether and use only the basic beef heart supplement diet.

Offer the beef in larger slices, about 3 inches long and ½ inch thick, so the fledgling will learn to grasp it in its talons and use its sharp beak to tear it into bite-size portions. It must learn to do this with food if it is to survive in the wild.

Offer fresh road-killed birds and small animals for the same reason. It is a necessary part of their training for them to eat creatures they might prey upon in the wild. We do not, however, offer them live animals as food.

Provide fresh water at all times for all hawks and owls, regardless of their age.

Several at a Time

If you are caring for several birds of prey at one time, it is easier to buy a prepared diet. Zu-Preem Bird of Prey Diet, prepared by Riviana Foods, Inc. (Hills Division, Topeka, Kansas 66601), is an excellent food used by many zoos. It costs about fifty cents a pound. However, 32 pounds is the smallest package size available, and most distributors will not deliver orders of less than 200 pounds. Unless you live in a city with a distribution center that will allow you to pick up one case at a time, or unless you can pool your order with other people, it will not be practical to use this product.

Most birds will accept the Zu-Preem diet well, but they seem to prefer the beef heart supplement diet. For those caring for only one or two birds at a time, the beef heart supplement diet has the advantage of always being available, although it is certainly not any less expensive. We have maintained hawks and owls that could not be freed because of permanent injuries on the beef heart supplement diet for several years. They were healthy, active, and bright, with no sign of dietary deficiency.

Many publications state that it is necessary to feed fur, feathers, and bones to hawks and owls, so that they can properly digest their food. This is not so. We have maintained owls and kestrels for years without ever feeding them a single bone, feather, or bit of fur.

HANDLING AND FREEDOM

You cannot hold, handle, and caress a wild bird as you would a mammal baby. When tiny, birds seem to enjoy being held in a nest of your cupped palms. But they do not enjoy being petted or cuddled.

However, they do enjoy being talked to, and while keeping you company, they will snuggle down to enjoy the warmth that radiates from your body. When the nestling becomes a fledgling, it will enjoy sitting on your finger, riding around on your shoulder, even sleeping on your shoulder. The more time you spend with it, the more tame it will be and the more it will seem to enjoy your company. It flies to you for companionship and food.

If you obtain a bird when it is very small, it will be "imprinted" on you and your family. This means you are its parents and its world. When it is fully feathered and can fly well, you cannot just turn it loose one morning and expect it to survive. It will want to be with you and will fly to you for attention and companionship. This transition to freedom is a gradual process, regardless of species.

Freeing Most Birds

When you notice the fledgling no longer uses the nest or seeks the warmth of the light, it is time to start planning for its eventual release and freedom. Remove the light and place the cage on a screened porch or in some similar place, where the fledgling can see and hear other birds outside. Leave the cage door open whenever possible, so it can practice flying. You will notice it listens attentively to other birds and begins chirping and "singing" when it reaches three to four weeks of age.

At this stage, take the fledgling outdoors for "flying lessons." At first it will appear to be afraid. It may fly to a nearby tree for a moment and then fly back to you. It will hop about the grass exploring, but, unless frightened away, will stay close to you. Start with flying lessons for twenty- to thirty-minute periods twice daily. After three or four days, your orphan will spend more time away from you. It may enjoy being left alone for short periods while you return to the house. But when you go outdoors again, after it has been alone, it will fly to you the minute it sees you. As you start into the house, if it is not ready to go in, it will fly back into a tree. If it has had enough exercise and is hungry, the fledgling will sit on your hand or shoulder for the ride inside to its cage.

If it doesn't come to you, leave it and return in a half hour to try again. We have never had a bird get lost or leave us until it has had many outdoor sessions and has adapted to freedom.

The periods outside will become longer and longer by the fledgling's own choice, but it will still want the security of its cage at night. If you have a screened porch, place its cage where it is safe from cats, and prop the porch door partially open so it can come and go as it pleases. If you have no porch, hang the cage under the eaves where it will have some protection from wind and rain, beside the door you usually use. Keep food and water in the cage, and the bird will use it regularly.

One night you will notice that your bird did not come to the cage. This is a sign your fledgling is growing up. You can place a piece of red or yellow plastic tape loosely on one leg just above the foot to distinguish your orphan from the neighborhood birds. This will wear off in time, but when you see the tape you will know your fledgling is in the yard and that it is all right.

Young hawks are offered freedom in the same fashion as the other altricial birds. They will instinctively try to catch small moving objects. Food is offered and kept available until they learn to capture their own. They gradually adapt to the world and spend less time near their cage.

Freeing Owls

Young owls are more active at dusk and early evening, so they must be given their freedom differently. When owl babies can fly well, move their cage outdoors where it has some protection from wind and rain. Allow them a few days to get acclimated, then start leaving the cage door open in the evening. During the night they will leave the cage and fly about, but usually they will be in their cage in the morning. Even those that prefer to "roost" in a nearby tree will come back each evening for food.

They must have food available while they teach themselves to catch prey. Some, after being freed, will return to be fed each evening for several months. Others strike out on their own sooner.

Usually orphans raised with much love and attention stay tame for the first year, but after they migrate or go through a nesting season they become wild creatures again.

We know very well that helping a single bird isn't going to affect the overall ecosystem of the area, but in our family the joy of helping an orphan is satisfaction in itself. The enjoyment of raising it, of seeing this bit of life mature and return, flying, to its own environment, and of recognizing its individual flash of color in the yard is reward in full for a small amount of effort.

6

![A precocial bird (bobwhite quail) standing near a container of feed.](image)

Precocial Birds

WHAT IS A PRECOCIAL BIRD?

Unlike altricial birds, precocial birds are much more independent when they are hatched. Their eyes are open when they hatch and within minutes they can stand and walk. They are covered with down, and their first feathers begin to appear within five to six days. Precocial birds usually remain in the nest for only a few hours, a day at the most. They may be partially dependent on their parents for food or may have to be taught to eat, but most of them begin immediately searching for food. The downy young of the precocial birds, which are usually called chicks, include killdeer, quail, pheasant, and turkey. But many water birds, including coots, ducks, and geese, are also precocial birds.

With such great differences between altricial birds and precocial birds, the care required varies considerably.

THE ORPHAN

Since precocial baby birds have been taught to eat and find their own food by the time they are two or three days old, they seldom need help. But things might go wrong in very cold or wet weather. The body temperature control mechanism of a chick does not function well until it is about four weeks old. The young chick huddles under its mother for warmth at night, or if it gets chilled. If the chick gets wet, chilling is a distinct possibility if it gets separated from the mother bird, for the down loses its insulating value. A wet, cold chick requires help only until it is warm and dry. Simply placing it in a cardboard box and suspending a 60-watt bulb close to it to provide warmth for a few hours may be all the help it needs. When it is warm and dry, it should be released where you found it. If the mother bird is close by, the chick will call and she will come back as soon as you leave. You can watch from a vantage point to see if the mother returns. If she has not found the chick within three or four hours, it would be best to assume the mother bird's responsibility yourself. If you know the mother has been killed, the chick should be treated as an orphan and offered whatever care is needed until it is old enough to survive by itself.

APPROACHING THE ORPHAN

Chicks Less Than Three Days Old

All tiny birds, whether they are quail-type land birds or baby ducklings, should be approached quietly, while you talk gently to them. The baby three days of age or under will usually sit quietly and allow itself to be picked up in your hands without moving or struggling.

The problem with birds less than three days of age is not in capturing them, but in finding them. For example, a group of birds at the roadside whose mother has just been killed by a car will scatter into the roadside grass. They huddle into tiny, well-camouflaged balls of fluff, and it takes time and diligent searching through the grass to locate the chicks. As you find them, gently pick them up. If you have to carry several, place them in a box or covered basket, or loosen your shirt a little, making a pouch of the material that droops over your belt. This pouch offers warmth, security, and confinement without danger of crushing.

Chicks More Than Three Days Old

If the chicks are more than three to four days old, they will flee from you as you approach. You will have to herd them into a spot where they can't run, and then pick them up. If you find them along the roadside, herding them into the tall matted grass will often slow them down enough to allow you to capture them.

If they are quick and flutter about trying to flee, leave them be. You probably won't be able to capture them, and they stand a better chance of survival in a group than dispersed singly over the whole area. If they can run well and fly a little, they can also find their own food.

WARMTH AND SHELTER

As for altricial birds, two of the primary requirements are warmth and shelter.

Baby precocial birds should be placed in a cage. While birds less than three days old are docile and are not fearful, they can run. They will often try to escape if a noise or sudden movement frightens them and may injure themselves.

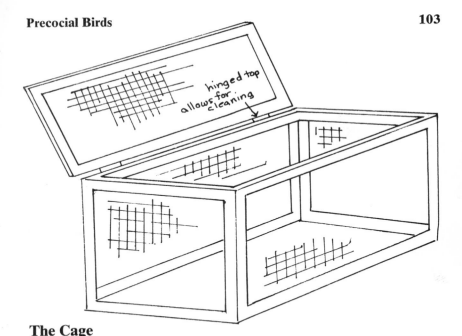

hinged top
allows for
cleaning

The Cage

A baby quail, pheasant, turkey, duck, or goose needs a cage 18″ × 24″ in size, with wire screen sides 12″ to 14″ high. This size would be suitable for several small baby chicks.

The cage sides should be made of hardware cloth or screen material to allow fresh air and light to enter.

It should have a removable top, to make it easy for you to clean, feed, and water your orphans. The cage may be constructed simply by tacking hardware cloth to a simple wood frame.

Place several layers of newspaper in the bottom of the completed cage to absorb water and droppings. Place a small pile of dried grass or shredded paper in one corner to serve as a nest area.

Provide water in a small shallow dish in another corner of the cage.

Put the cage in a draft-free area and place the baby or babies in it. Immediately provide the next essential item of care—warmth.

Warmth

For all precocial chicks use a brooding temperature of 95° F. Suspend a 60- or 100-watt bulb inside the cage in the corner near the nest. Place a thermometer on the floor of the cage under the bulb. As need be, raise or lower the light bulb about every ten minutes until the 95° F. is maintained on the thermometer. Leave the bulb in this position as long as the birds are in the cage. Be sure the bulb does not touch any of the paper or other materials which might burn.

Provide a sheltered corner near the light bulb. Cut a piece of cardboard the height of the sides and about 24 inches long. Fold it in half and tape it to the two adjoining walls. The cardboard will also serve to absorb heat from the bulb and radiate it on the baby when it seeks this spot for warmth and comfort.

The babies will move in and out of the warmth of the light bulb as they become warmer or cooler. Since they select the temperature they desire, you never have to change the position of the bulb. These birds also do not mind the brightness of the light and do not need periods of darkness for sleeping.

FEEDING

What to Feed

As food, offer a quail, pheasant, turkey, or other tiny, downy, seed-eating chick parakeet seed temporarily until a better food is purchased or prepared. Soaking the seed in water for five to ten minutes will make it more palatable.

If you live in a rural area that has a livestock feedstore, they will have a food called "chick starter" which is a finely ground combination of feed grains and vitamin and mineral supplements. If chick starter is not available in your area, make your own. Mix one third cup of dried bread crumbs with one hard-boiled egg yolk, and add sufficient milk to make a mass that will stick to itself but is dry enough to be rather crumbly. Feed it in bits about ⅛ inch in diameter. Chick starter or the homemade starter is suitable for ducks and other water birds, also.

When the birds are two to three weeks old and have more feathers, give them additional foods, such as lettuce, celery tops, or other green, leafy vegetables.

Check in the book already mentioned, *Song and Garden Birds of North America,* or the National Geographic Society companion volume *Water, Prey, and Game Birds of North America* for suggestions on the specific food your orphan would normally eat in the wild. If possible, offer whatever foods you can find that would be the same or similar to what the bird will feed on when it is free.

Teaching the Chick to Eat

Cover part of the floor near the bulb, or even the entire cage floor, with plain brown paper to provide the baby with a feeding area. Scatter the chick starter over the brown paper. It is important to make it as easy as possible for the chick to find its food. Newspaper does not work as well. Bits of food scattered on newspaper tend to confuse the chick. It often cannot distinguish between food and the letters and patterns on the newspaper. On clean brown paper, seeds and bits of food show up distinctly.

Place more food in a shallow dish or jar lid. You can use a chick feeder, a trough-type feeder which can be purchased at a livestock feedstore. This can be used by all precocial birds, including ducks and geese.

In the wild, a chick is taught to eat by the mother bird. Softly chirping or making the specific "food call," the mother bird will pick up a seed or other bit of food and drop it in front of the chick to attract its attention. The chick will usually pick

Bits of food scattered over a plain surface show up distinctly.

it up and swallow it. In this way, it learns to peck at bits and spots it sees on the ground.

The healthy chick will be interested in food as soon as it becomes warm and dry. If it doesn't pick at the food you offer, you must try the mother bird's feeding technique. Repeatedly drop bits of food in front of the chick to draw its attention to it. This must be done without frightening the chick, or it will flee to the far corner of the cage and will not be interested in food until it quiets down. When it appears to be moving about the cage exploring again, you know it is no longer frightened, and by talking quietly and gently to it, you can try feeding it once more, being "mother" again.

Feeding Ducklings, Geese, and Water Birds

Use a similar technique to get baby ducklings and other waterfowl to eat. Ducklings are used as the example, because they will be the most common water bird orphan found. Place bits of food in a shallow feeding dish or bird feeder. Scatter a few more bits around the floor of the cage. If they don't eat, here is a feeding method most ducks can't resist. Place a few bits of food in water in a dish with sides about 1 inch high. Straight-sided dishes are best, so the duckling can walk right up to the water and reach into it and feed without entering the water. It may anyway, but if it stays out, the water and food will stay cleaner. A baby duckling will drink the water, duck its head under the water, and playfully shake water everywhere. In playing, it will pick up and eat any little bits of food it sees in the water, or floating by. In general, if there is water it will make a mess, but that is part of being a duck— and as long as they start to eat, we don't mind.

SPECIAL HOUSING AND FEEDING

All precocial birds whether land birds or water birds are offered the same type of cages and foods until they are two to three weeks old. At this age they should be eating well, have some feathers, and be active and playful.

Because land and water birds are so different, the housing, care, and feeding procedures must be different from this point on.

Precocial Land Birds

Quail are the most common precocial birds which are raised as orphans. We will use them as our example, but the same housing, care, and feeding can apply to all land-type precocial birds whether they are pheasants, turkeys, grouse, chukars, or any other. The following applies to caring for several birds at one time.

HOUSING.   Precocial land birds must have more space than a small cage for exercise and more natural conditions if they are to adapt well to freedom. All land bird chicks should be transferred to a larger movable pen out of doors as soon as they begin to be well feathered. Construct a pen with a wooden frame about 4 feet square and 2 feet high, with sides of fine wire mesh or hardware cloth, but with no bottom. This will allow a natural outdoor environment of grass and weeds in the cage wherever it is set up. The pen must have a top to protect the chicks from predators. Wire one or two low perches in place at one end of the cage.

Place the outdoor pen in a grassy spot close to the house. Connect an extension cord to the same light you used in the smaller cage and place it in one corner of the new pen. Construct a three-sided shelter with a top, large enough to protect the light bulb from rain and to shelter your chicks from the cold, and place it in one corner of the cage. A shelter about 18

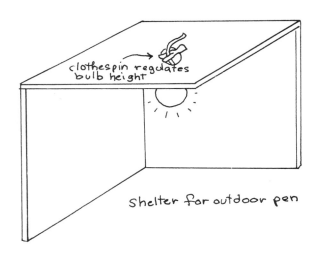

Shelter for outdoor pen

inches square would be right for a group of smaller precocial birds, such as quail, or for one or two pheasant-size birds.

FEEDING. Use the same feeders and waterers as in the smaller cage. Offer the same food for the first few days to keep to a minimum changes which might upset the chicks. When the chicks are no longer frightened and are eating well, begin offering them wild bird grain mix, which consists of cracked corn, wheat, millet, sorghum grain seeds, and often sunflower seeds. It is sold in grocery stores or feedstores.

Offer both this feed and the chick starter in separate feeders and also scatter some in the grass, so the chicks will learn to "scratch" for food. They will instinctively use their feet to stir up the area between the grass roots as they carefully search about for edible bits of food and seeds. Move the pen as often as necessary to keep it clean and to offer a new variety of green plants.

Keep the chicks under these conditions until they are ready to be returned to the wild.

SETTING THEM FREE. Two factors will determine when the birds should be freed: weather and the amount of feathers. As has been said, a precocial chick's body temperature regulating mechanism is not completely functional until about four weeks of age. Since down and feathers act as insulation, the milder the temperature or the more feathers the chick has, the better the chick can survive without supplemental heat and the sooner it can be turned loose.

When you see that your chick no longer sleeps in the lamp-warmed area of the pen, but sleeps on one of the low perches you have provided at the other end of the cage or nestles in the grass elsewhere in the cage, unless colder weather has been forecast for the next few days, you can safely turn your chicks loose. Normally, chicks do not need to be kept past four weeks of age.

If adequate cover, such as heavy grass and bushy thickets, for their protection exists in the area around your home, release them there. Early in the morning open one corner of the cage slightly and allow the chicks to find the opening and to drift out.

Food is fairly abundant in late spring and early summer, and the chicks should have no trouble finding all they need. You may scatter food near the cage, or leave the cage open for several days, but these birds, when raised in a group, rarely return.

SETTING THE SINGLE BIRD FREE. The single bird that has been found and raised by itself will be very attached to you and must be allowed more time to adapt to freedom. Offer it its freedom as you would an altricial bird. Gradually allow it to spend more time outside. In time it will begin to prefer freedom to your companionship. Sooner or later it will find other wild birds and will drift away.

Precocial Water Birds

Ducklings are the most common precocial orphans you will have the occasion to raise. There is seldom a need to raise or rescue other precocial water birds, such as coots, gallinules, limpkins, rails, avocets, or the many others. The parents of these species are very shy and normally would not have their young where they would even be seen by humans. However, if any of these other species are found, housing and care would be the same as for orphan ducklings.

DIET. There would be slight changes in the diet of the different species. Comprehensive information on the subject can be obtained from reading *Water, Prey, and Game Birds of North America,* mentioned earlier. In the wild the various ducks feed on wild celery, a variety of grasses, shellfish and mollusks, pond weeds such as duckweed, aquatic insects, acorns, and the seeds of pond weeds and sedges. You may try to offer some of the foods, such as seeds, green succulent vegetation, grasses, and insects. However, the basic duckling diet which consists of chick starter, wild bird grain, lettuce, celery tops, and other green, leafy vegetables will provide the majority of water birds with the nutrients they need. Chick feeders or other feeding dishes should be provided for the chick starter and wild bird grain mixture. Those for which insects are an important part of their diet may be offered mealworms and earthworms in addition to this basic diet. Mealworms can be obtained at a pet shop and earthworms at a bait-fishing shop.

HOUSING. As soon as baby ducks are eating well, place them in a 4′ × 4′ pen identical to the one used for land bird chicks. In addition to providing warmth and shelter, you must now also provide water for the babies to swim and play in.

Ducklings should have water to swim in as early as possible. If they are raised in a pen without water to swim in, they will be frightened of the water when you free them. If you force ducks that are afraid of the water into the water, they will come out as soon as you allow them to. In time they will adapt to the water, but this can take weeks, and all the time they stay on shore they are vulnerable to predators.

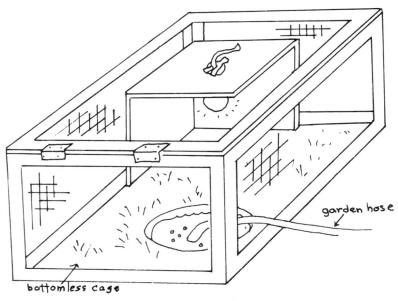

garden hose

bottomless cage

At our home it is easy for us to supply swimming water. We live on the edge of a lake in Florida where during the spring, which is the "duckling" season, the temperature is quite warm. We place our pen half in and half out of the water, in the sunshine. The ducklings can enter and leave the water as they desire. Fresh water is constantly provided in the cage area, and bits of natural food are constantly floating by. Our ducklings can swim, play, and learn to eat without difficulty.

Since we can't provide a light bulb at the lake shore we have to bring the ducklings back to the original, smaller cage at the house every night. On cold days they remain in the smaller cage, where their bulb is available for warmth, but most days they are outside at the lake shore.

If you don't have a lake, pond, or stream you can provide them with a swimming-playing area by digging a shallow hole to fit a large plastic dishpan. Place the dishpan in the ground so that its rim is at ground level. Build a ramp of stones or sand in one side so the ducks can walk in and out of their pool easily. Keep the pan full of water and maintain a constant supply and exchange of clean water by allowing a garden hose to trickle very slowly into the dishpan all day.

Place some of the wild bird mixture you are feeding the chicks in the swimming pool as well. The ducklings will quickly learn to dive and feed off the bottom of the pool, which is the natural way for most ducks to feed.

If you live in a climate that is still cold in duckling season, you must provide your orphans with warmth in their pen. Suspend a 100-watt light bulb in the corner of the pen farthest from the swimming pond and protect it from splashing water. Make a wooden three-sided shelter in that corner to provide a warm, draft-free, protected corner for the ducklings and to protect the bulb further.

SETTING THEM FREE. When it is time to set your ducklings free, do so where they can gradually become acclimated to being on their own. Most ducklings adapt to freedom easily and learn to find their own food readily, but some will need help and encouragement. By providing food grains, you can usually be sure the adaptation will be easy. Choose a place to free them where it will be convenient for you to feed them once a day. Scatter wild bird grain mixture in the shallow water and on the shore at the water's edge. This daily feeding gives you a chance to see how your youngsters are doing. Unless frightened away, young ducklings usually stay in the immediate area where you release them.

Two or more ducklings tend to keep one another company and adapt to freedom much more quickly. Since ducklings are capable of finding their own food at hatching, and are not extremely sensitive to cold temperatures, they can be offered freedom much earlier than most birds.

7

Feeding Injured
and Very Weak Birds
and
Dietary Supplements

TOOTHPICK FORMULA FEEDING

It can happen for one reason or another that a bird is too weak to eat. An altricial baby may be so weak it cannot gape, a precocial chick too exhausted to try to eat, and an injured bird may have no desire for food. These birds require special feeding techniques.

The weak altricial baby and the exhausted precocial chicks are fed in exactly the same way—by "toothpick formula feeding." However, be sure to warm the baby thoroughly before offering it food. Follow the same warming procedures as described earlier. Take the concentrated formula as discussed in Chapter 2 of one egg yolk in a half cup of homogenized milk, and pour a small amount into a small glass or vial.

Cradle the baby in the fingers and palm of one hand in an upright position. With your other hand, dip a flat, thin toothpick into the formula. Hold the toothpick straight up and down as you would a pen or pencil with the wide, flat end downward. A small drop of formula will collect on the end of the toothpick.

Touch this drop to the baby's beak near the tip. The upper and lower beak meet here, and the liquid will flow into the crack where the beaks meet. When most baby birds feel liquid in their mouths, they will swallow.

If your bird is so weak that it doesn't swallow at once, tip the baby forward slightly. This will keep the formula from trickling down the throat by gravity, and will allow it to remain in the tip of the beak until it is swallowed.

Any gentle movement to make the baby aware of its surroundings, such as touching its beak with the toothpick or gently moving your left hand to make the baby shift position, will also help stimulate swallowing.

Even the tiniest quail baby will swallow drop after drop as it is offered on the toothpick. When the baby no longer wants more, it will refuse to swallow and instead will sling its head, throwing the liquid from its beak.

That is the time to put the baby back in its nest, near the light bulb, and allow it to rest. Try to feed it again thirty minutes later. The baby will usually accept and swallow the drops more readily at the second feeding. It may take twenty or more drops this time.

When the baby has taken as much as its wants or as much as it can handle, put the baby back in its nest and try again in an hour. On this third feeding, the bird should open its beak, reach out, grasp the end of the toothpick, and swallow the

Too weak to eat, baby quail accepts formula from end of toothpick.

drop of formula. Feeding has now become an active process, with the orphan helping.

Each time you feed it, the general attitude and appearance of the bird will improve. If the weak, lethargic altricial bird will now gape, you may offer it bits of dog food between each toothpick formula feeding. As the young precocial bird becomes stronger, it will be more interested in food, and will begin moving about pecking at bits in the feeding area.

You may have to use toothpick feeding only once or twice, or you may have to continue for several days. Stop when the orphan is eating other food well.

Most bird books insist that attempting to feed liquids to a bird will kill it. This is not so. The only thing to watch out for is that the bird is swallowing. If the bird is swallowing you have nothing to worry about. Swallowing is an active, voluntary process. The opening to the windpipe closes during this process. If the bird is not swallowing, the fluid may trickle down the throat by gravity and get into the windpipe and lungs. But there is no danger if you use common sense and good judgment when offering liquids.

Use an adaptation of the toothpick-feeding technique for sick or injured adult birds which have lost the desire to eat. You can feed them the same formula, but use a medicine dropper for larger birds instead of a toothpick.

Hold the bird upright. Keep the head tipped slightly downward, and trickle the fluid one drop at a time into the bird's beak until it will not longer swallow it.

STOMACH-TUBE FEEDING

If your bird is so weak that it can't be aroused, there isn't much hope for it. However, as a last resort, you can still try tube force-feeding. For the majority of birds, this will not be necessary.

The same equipment is used for birds as for orphan mammals (see p. 53), but the technique is simpler. Two people are needed for this procedure. Attach a small plastic syringe containing 1 to 5 ml. of formula to a piece of plastic tubing. Hold the tube up beside the bird, the tube end even with the middle of the chest. Make a mark on the tube even with the beak. The mark will act as a guide.

Hold the syringe in your right hand. The bird's body must be steadied by an assistant while you cup the bird's head in your left hand. Force the beak open slightly with the tips of your fingers, tip the head and beak slightly upward, and insert the tube. Direct the tube toward the back of the mouth, down the throat, and into the stomach area. Slowly squeeze the material in the syringe into the bird's stomach, and then gently withdraw the tube.

It is easier to pass the tube in birds than in mammals. Even adult long-necked birds such as herons are not difficult to feed; they merely require longer tubes.

While stomach-tube feeding is effective nutritionally, it should be used only as a temporary measure, when nothing else works, and only until one of the other forms of feeding can be substituted. If a bird is to get well and be self-sufficient, it must learn to feed itself.

FORCE-FEEDING SOLID FOODS

Young birds that don't yet know how to eat and injured adult birds that refuse to eat must be force-fed until they can eat on their own. We force-feed solid food more frequently than we use stomach-tube feeding, but this too is only a temporary measure.

For young birds, mold canned dog food into small pellets about the size of a large green pea. Dip them in formula for lubrication. Grasp the head of the bird gently with your left

Author force-feeding canned dog food to cattle egret.

hand. Pry the beak open with the fingers of your right hand. Hold the mouth open with one finger of the right hand as you place the pellet of food in the back part of the throat. Use a finger to push the pellet well down into the throat, so the bird doesn't spit it out.

Try to be firm, quick, and gentle in force-feeding so that your patient doesn't exhaust itself further by resisting your efforts.

For long-necked birds, such as herons and egrets, the pellet may be the size and shape of a pecan or walnut. After you have placed the pellet in the back part of the throat and poked it well down into the neck with your finger, you must go one step further. Hold the beak or head in your left hand, so you don't get pecked. Then with your right hand gently feel the bird's neck till you locate the pellet of food. Push it downward along the esophagus, and on down into the chest, where it will be only a short distance from the stomach. Unless this is done, the bird will regurgitate the pellet.

Caution: When working with sharp-beaked birds such as herons and egrets, be careful. They can stab quickly with their sharp beaks. Be sure to protect your eyes. Wear protective glasses, or gently hold onto the beak to restrain the bird.

Bites or stabs elsewhere may sting but won't do you any real damage.

Force-Feeding Hawks and Owls

In force-feeding hawks and owls you must also exercise care. You will have to change your technique a little to avoid their sharp claws and beaks. If any bird of prey grasps your hand or wrist with its talons, you must resist the temptation to shake it off. The tendon arrangement in the feet and legs of these birds only makes the sharp, curved claws penetrate more deeply if you struggle. Have a friend grasp the toes of the bird and loosen the claws, or do so yourself with your free hand.

Beef heart held with forceps is offered to an injured adult barred owl.

Until you know the bird, take care to avoid its claws and beak.

Feed smaller birds of prey by offering pieces of beef heart in a blunt forceps. That way your fingers don't get close to the beak. Forceps can be purchased at any drugstore.

A bird the size of a small screech owl or kestrel should be offered two or three pieces of beef heart at a feeding, each about the size of a small lima bean. Hold a piece of meat in the forceps, and touch it to the beak or to the sensitive guard hairs that owls have around their beaks. Many birds will respond by biting at whatever is touching them. When they grasp and bite at the piece of meat, release the forceps and let them have it. Most birds will hold it in their beak for fifteen to thirty seconds and then drop it.

Some hold it for a few seconds, realize it is food, and swallow it. Regardless of whether it is dropped or eaten, repeat the procedure several times until they do finally swallow.

Adult birds are taught to eat this way when they have been brought in for treatment or repair of fractures.

You will have to force-feed those that refuse to eat, by using a modification of the same technique. Place a small piece of meat in the forceps and place the forceps under the tip of the upper beak. Lift upward, and the beak will open. Without losing the upward leverage on the beak, insert the forceps into the back part of the throat and release the meat. Most birds will swallow immediately. If the bird pulls its head away from you, place your free hand behind its head, close but not touching, and try again. If it tries to move its head away from the forceps, your hand will keep it from pulling away. The activity with the forceps is distracting enough so that even adult birds seem to ignore the hand behind them.

After force-feeding several pieces of meat to a hawk or owl, allow the bird to rest for thirty minutes to an hour, then offer more. After each feeding place additional strips or pieces of meat near the bird's perch. When it starts eating on its own, start dusting the beef heart with the calcium-vitamin-mineral supplement as described previously and discontinue force-feeding.

Hawks may eat several times during the day, but fledgling or adult owls eat primarily in the evening or at night. Put four or five strips of the prepared beef heart on the perch next to an owl at dusk, and usually by morning it will have eaten them. After three or four nights you will know how much it will eat.

Some older fledglings may not eat for two or three nights. If they don't eat by the third night, force-feed them small pieces of heart with a forceps. Once an owl or hawk starts eating, it will usually eat readily from then on.

DIETARY SUPPLEMENTS
AND CALCIUM DEFICIENCIES

It is not necessary to feed your bird cod-liver oil or any other vitamin supplement. The only time any supplement is used in any of our diets is when beef heart is being fed. This meat is not adequately balanced.

All raw meat contains insufficient calcium in relation to its phosphorus content. Beef heart, for example, has a ratio of one part calcium to forty parts phosphorus. A calcium-containing powder must be added to the meat to obtain a reasonable balance, since all birds require calcium and phosphorus for building strong, healthy bones and bodies. These minerals must be given in the ratio of 1.2 parts calcium to 1 part phosphorus.

Calcium can be obtained in many forms. Most drugstores sell crushed oystershell or calcium carbonate powder, which is an excellent source of calcium. Mix the crushed tablets or calcium carbonate powder with an equal amount of the vitamin-mineral supplement (Unipet Powder). Dusted on the heart meat, it will increase the calcium level of the diet considerably and balance the diet for feeding a hawk or owl. Use about a teaspoonful of the supplement per ounce of meat.

If calcium carbonate powder or powdered oystershell is not available, use finely crushed eggshells. Spread or dust them over the strip of meat just as you would the vitamin-mineral supplement.

Recently, deaths of seed-eating zoo birds have been traced to a calcium deficiency that resulted from eating an exclusive diet of sunflower seeds. If you are feeding your bird or animal sunflower seeds, and it refuses to eat other foods, take away the sunflower seeds until it is eating other foods. Do this with any food it wants to eat exclusively. Feed fresh, leafy green vegetables such as celery and lettuce, carrots, and fruits such as peaches, grapes, oranges, bananas, and apples. Try to offer a diet as close to what the orphan will find in the wild as is practical. If birds and animals are fed a variety of foods, they are more likely to get the vitamins and minerals they need.

The general appearance and activity of any bird or animal

is the best guide to whether your diet is adequate. If it eats well, has sleek, shiny feathers, flies well, and is strong and vigorous, you are feeding an adequate diet. If the feathers are poor and the bird is weak, consult your veterinarian for help.

8

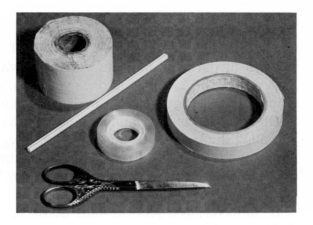

First Aid for All Birds

WHICH BIRDS NEED FIRST AID?

A bird with a leg dangling loose and limp as it hops across the lawn, or with a wing dropping awkwardly at its side, or a bird with an open wound obviously needs help. A bird sitting at the edge of the road in the face of passing traffic, a bird huddled on the sidewalk in the rain rather than taking refuge in a tree, a bird falling each time it tries to hop or fly; all of these birds are in need of help. Not quite so apparent, however, and just as much in need of help is the bird with eyes closed sitting on the ground, resting its head on its shoulders, its feathers all fluffed up. The condition of this bird would be more obvious if other birds of the same species were flying around it, sleek, bright, and chipper, while it sat with the "droops."

Before you attempt to approach or pick up such a bird, study its behavior. Watch it for a while. Try to determine what is abnormal about the bird. Is its leg hurt? Its wing? If so,

125

which one? Can it fly at all? Does it fall if it tries to run? A study of the bird will indicate where and what the problem is. This will not be so apparent once you get it home. For once it is confined to a cage, chances are it won't move.

Do not take the bird home if you don't feel you can help. If you don't think you'll be able to splint a leg or wing or clean up a wound, leave the bird where it is. If the bird can eat and can hop about even awkwardly, it will probably be all right and should be left alone.

If, however, you feel the bird needs help, and if you can find or provide the help that is needed, approach slowly and use the minimum amount of force necessary to capture the bird.

You should keep in mind, if you decide to start treating a weak, injured, or sick bird, that you may not be able to save it. It is sometimes better for an injured creature to die without pain than to spend the rest of its life deformed and caged. At such times, euthanasia, which is a painless death to prevent suffering, may be the best and most humane solution for certain injured animals or birds. To have tried to help a less fortunate creature is what is important. Those that you do save make up for the personal hurt that occurs when a creature must be euthanized.

APPROACHING AN INJURED BIRD

Never chase a bird. Sick birds and injured birds will often die from the extra stress of rough handling or chasing, so patience and gentleness are important.

Very young birds seem to respond quite well when you approach slowly, talk quietly, and handle them gently. However, older birds do not like to be handled. It is better to herd them gently into a corner or even a cardboard box. Approach quietly and cover them gently with your jacket or shirt, which can be tucked around them and used to carry them when nothing else is available. When they are covered and cannot see you, they are much less fearful.

You can most effectively capture injured hawks and owls by herding them into a cardboard box lying on its side. The box seems to represent security to these birds, and many will enter the box with very little herding. Fold in the flaps to confine it and transport the bird to where the necessary aid can be given.

BASIC CARE

Basic nursing care is the same for all birds in need of first aid. It consists of providing warmth, security, water, and food.

Warmth is very important. An adult bird does not need extra warmth under normal circumstances. But it is very much in need of extra warmth if it is sick or has been injured. Warmth is as important as food or medication if your patient is to survive. Provide warmth from a 100-watt light bulb. For an adult bird, suspend the bulb nearby as it rests on a perch or on the floor of the cage.

Select a cage according to the size of the bird. Generally, it should be at least 30″ × 30″ × 36″. Use a smaller cage when you wish to restrict the movement of a severely injured bird.

Often warmth and temporary security are all a bird needs to recover. Do not handle it any more than is absolutely necessary. If it begins to move about normally, without falling or losing its balance, release it.

If a bird is to be kept for additional care or treatment, offer it fresh water and a variety of foods. Some birds are seed eaters; other eat insects or fruits. You must know something about your patient to provide the proper choice of foods. Read about your patient in one of the good bird books. Then offer those foods that it is most likely to be familiar with. When in doubt, offer a wide variety of foods to see what it will eat.

CHILLED BIRDS

Birds may be found wet and chilled after several days of continuous cold rain. Birds that migrate north before much food is available are particularly susceptible. You may find them sitting wet and bedraggled on the ground or on a low limb. Weak from lack of food, they become much more susceptible to chilling.

Once a bird's feathers get wet, they lose their insulation value. The bird becomes chilled rapidly. Such a bird will not resist being picked up. You can easily capture it and carry it inside.

Suspend a 100-watt bulb near a perch in a cage to provide heat to dry the feathers. After the bird is warm and its feathers are thoroughly dry and fluffy, offer it food, and then release it. Since it is wild and may hurt itself by flying into the sides of the cage in an attempt to escape, keep it no longer than necessary.

CONCUSSION-TYPE INJURIES

Sometimes a bird becomes confused and flies into a solid object, hitting its head. This results in concussion. You may find such a bird lying unconscious beside a building. As long as it is still alive, it has a chance. Pick up the bird, bring it indoors, and provide it with warmth and shelter. Surprisingly, after a few hours of rest many of these birds will be completely recovered and can be released. Others, however, recover more slowly and may need several days of rest before they can be released.

A bird suffering from a concussion may remain unconscious for a day or longer. Place this bird in a nest box prepared as for a baby altricial bird, supporting it in a normal, comfortably, semiupright position. Position a thermometer close to the resting bird, and position a light bulb to provide a constant temperature of 85° F.

On the second day, if the bird is not moving about, offer a tiny bird food by the toothpick formula technique, discussed in the previous chapter, and offer a larger bird formula with a medicine dropper.

If a bird is severely injured, it may take a week or longer for your patient to recover. Provide clean, fresh water and food for it and handle it only when absolutely necessary. When it begins to hop about normally, without falling or losing its balance, it is ready to be released. Release the bird in a place where you can recapture it easily in case it cannot fly well.

INTESTINAL INFECTION

The most common bacterial disease is intestinal infection. Normal bird droppings consist of thick black material from the intestinal tract combined with a white paste-like kidney excretion. When the black material becomes soft and light in color, this usually signals the start of an intestinal upset or infection. If allowed to progress, the droppings become watery, light-colored, and foamy in appearance. If this situation develops with an orphan you are raising, or if the droppings are loose in an adult, start administering antibiotic at once.

Antibiotics

Tetracycline, the same antibiotic recommended for mammals, is used for birds as well. You can obtain it from a veterinarian or the pharmacist by prescription.

The amount of antibiotic to use depends on the size of the bird. A bird the size of a screech owl or a blue jay would normally receive a total daily dose of 15 to 20 mg. One 250-mg. capsule contains enough antibiotic to treat a bird this size for about two weeks.

If you wish to be exact, weigh the bird on a postal scale and calculate the correct dosage. Use a figure of 4 mg. of antibiotic per ounce of the bird's weight per day, divided into three to four doses.

A less exacting way would be to place the tiniest pinch of antibiotic in the first piece of canned dog food at each feeding, four times a day. If you remember the amount in the capsule is enough for at least fifty doses for a bird the size of the average blue jay or screech owl, you will realize what is meant by a tiny pinch. Resist the temptation to give more than the smallest amount. If necessary, actually divide the capsules into fifteen separate piles on a piece of wax paper. Each little pile then represents one day's total dosage.

PROBLEM EATER

Your bird patient may not want to eat. If it is running a fever, badly frightened, very weak, or just not familiar with the food offered, the bird usually won't want to eat.

If you are giving medication such as antibiotics, the bird must be force-fed frequently enough during the day to get the required medication into it. The canned dog food dipped in the milk and egg yolk formula is usually used for force-feeding. The antibiotic is mixed into a pea-sized pellet of the dog food and force-fed.

Offer a variety of foods, fruits, and seeds in the hope you can find something to tempt the bird's appetite. In addition, provide good nursing care of warmth, a secure cage, and fresh water.

OIL-CONTAMINATED BIRDS

Oil spills don't occur only on ocean beaches. A bird may become coated with oil from contact with waste oil and with contaminated inland water as well. The oil does damage to the birds in several ways. It mats the feathers together so that they lose their insulation value. The bird then chills, becomes lethargic, and, if the outside temperature is cold, dies of exposure. Or else the bird preens itself and, as it does so, ingests the oil. Among other things this causes damage to its intestinal lining. The intestine can no longer absorb water properly, and the bird often dies of dehydration.

Although the oil spill problem is not a new one, public concern over its effects on wildlife is fairly recent. Techniques in caring for oil-contaminated birds are changing from day to day, and there are no pat answers.

The actual procedure for cleaning a group of oiled birds is a complex one, requiring expensive equipment and materials which may be inflammable. The solvents used are very difficult for the general public to obtain. Therefore, the best action you can take if you find an oil spill involving a large number of birds is to evaluate the situation and seek professional help. Try to determine how many birds are involved. Is the oil a heavy, thick, tarry substance or a thin, volatile oil similar to gasoline? How large an area does the spill cover? When you have as much information as you can gather, report the spill to the nearest Coast Guard station or Environmental Protection Agency office. Also contact the local Audubon Society for volunteers to pick up the birds. Most states have an oil spill plan involving the Coast Guard, game and fish departments, veterinary associations, and wildlife groups. If the spill is serious and involves much wildlife, a professional cleaning team will be sent to the area as well as specialized equipment to clean up the spill itself.

You may collect the contaminated birds and place them in cardboard boxes while waiting for help to arrive. For holding all but the largest of birds, cardboard file boxes 10″ × 12″ × 14″ are satisfactory. Partially fill the boxes with shredded newspaper or other soft bedding. Normally, no more than one bird should be placed in the box. If the birds are quite small, however, two or more of the same species may be placed in the same box. The boxes should have lids in order to create darkness. This will keep the birds quiet and keep them from preening. The birds should be shielded in cool weather to prevent their chilling and in warm weather to prevent heat prostration.

There will be many opportunities for you to assist when the cleaning team moves in to treat the contaminated wildlife.

You may clean them yourself if only one or two birds are found and help is not available. Two people are needed for this procedure.

The safest thing for you to use to clean the birds is mineral oil, which may be obtained at any drugstore. It should be warmed to 100° F. Pour about 2 inches of warm mineral oil into a plastic dishpan. Gently place the contaminated bird in the oil. One person should gently restrain the bird as it stands in a normal upright position while the other does the actual cleaning.

If the bird has been contaminated with a thin oil, such as gasoline, diesel fuel, or waste motor oil, scoop up the mineral oil in your cupped hand and trickle it over the bird wherever the contaminating oil exists. Gently separate the feathers with your hand so the oil penetrates and dilutes the contaminating oil.

If the contaminating oil is a heavy, tarry oil, the warm mineral oil is trickled over the contaminating masses, softening them and dissolving them away. Gently massaging the tarry blobs with your free hand will speed up the softening process.

Discard the mineral oil in the dishpan when it becomes dirty in either cleaning procedure. Place the same amount of clean, warm mineral oil in the dishpan and repeat the cleaning procedure until the oil in the dishpan no longer becomes dirty. A moderately contaminated bird may require two gallons or more of mineral oil to get it clean.

With soft rags, blot the excess mineral oil from the feathers after the bird is clean. When you have finished, the bird will preen itself, removing the balance of the mineral oil over the next several days. The mineral oil is inert and not harmful if it is swallowed by the bird.

The bird must be kept warm for the next several days, since the oily feathers are not good insulators against the cold. Provide the basic nursing care of shelter, warmth, and food, until the plumage is completely back to normal. Then the bird should be freed.

Remember that migratory water birds are protected by federal law. You must have permission to keep one, even for treatment. Notify the local wildlife officer of the number and type of birds you have, and how long you estimate they will be in your care. They will tell you how to obtain whatever additional permission you may need to hold the birds for treatment.

FRACTURES

In any fracture, if you aren't sure how to proceed, take the bird to a veterinarian. If there is no veterinarian available to help you, try gently and carefully to help the bird.

A broken leg is a common injury. It is usually not critical to a bird's survival but, of course, should be repaired if possible. Most of these procedures require two people.

Lower Leg

If the lower part of the fractured leg is still warm, indicating good circulation, healing will probably occur if the leg is properly immobilized. To do this, make a splint and tape it in place.

FOR SMALL BIRDS. For small birds, such as a sparrow, mockingbird, blue jay, or robin, use a large plastic soda straw.

Flattened plastic straw, cut to length, and bent into V shape along its length, is applied to lower leg fracture and taped in place.

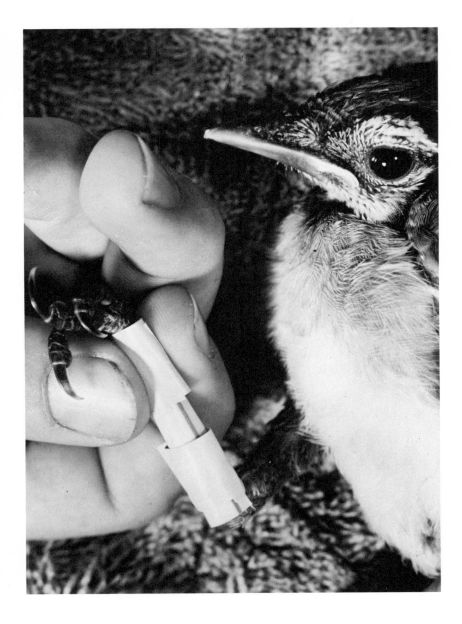

Cut a piece of straw about the same length as the broken bone. Flatten it, then fold it double along its length and bend it into a V shape. Place the injured leg in the V trough of the straw and tape it gently in place with Scotch or Dermalite (Johnson & Johnson). Let the splint remain in place until it wears off or the bird removes it. By that time the leg should be well healed. If the splint comes partially loose and is dangling, remove the rest.

FOR LARGER BIRDS. For larger birds, such as pheasants, owls, hawks, ducks, or egrets, plastic splint material, such as strips cut from a gallon plastic milk jug, is especially good, because it is light, strong, and does not absorb water. The splint material must be as long as the bone to be repaired and rigid enough to support the bone while it heals. Place a thin piece of plastic or rubber foam padding between the splint and the leg. Tape the splint snugly, but not tightly, along the full length of the fractured bone. If the fracture is close to a joint, extend your splint and tape across the joint for additional support. Applied properly, a splint allows the leg almost normal movement.

Upper Leg

This requires two people. Have someone hold the bird while you tape the leg. Use Dermalite tape if you can. Dermalite tape does not damage the feathers as much as Scotch tape or adhesive tapes. Also, it is waterproof, lightweight, easily cut and applied, and sticks well.

In a fracture of the upper leg, tape the leg against the body in a normal position and allow it to remain taped for three weeks, if possible. Three weeks is ideal, but many birds manage to rip the tape off within two weeks. However, if you allow them two more weeks of rest in the cage before permitting them to fly, they will usually be healed.

Be sure the tape is not so tight around the chest that it

Tape wrapped around body and leg immobilizes bone ends in upper leg fractures.

restricts breathing. Be sure, also, not to obstruct the vent, the opening from which fecal material is evacuated.

AMPUTATION.   If the fractured portion of the leg is cold and clammy, it indicates that circulation has been severely damaged. When the break area is badly mutilated and dirty, the fractured bones often will not heal. These must be amputated. Your veterinarian will help you or will do it for you. The nerves have probably also been damaged, so pain is not severe. Amputated legs generally heal well, and birds can manage well with one leg.

Fractured Wings

These, too, are common injuries in birds. Repairing fractured wings usually takes two people. Restrain the bird gently, to avoid further damage to circulation in the fractured wing. If the fractured part is as warm as the other parts of the

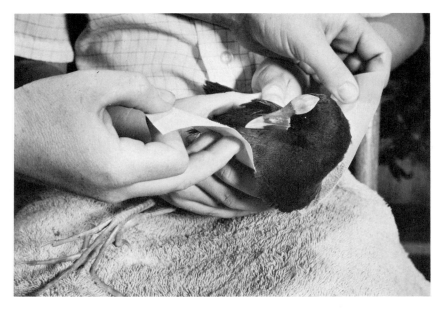

Tape applied to hold injured wing in place. The other wing must be kept free so that the bird can maintain its balance.

bird's body, then circulation is still satisfactory and the wing will usually heal.

For small birds use your fingertips to place the bone ends in position while an assistant holds the bird for you. With Dermalite tape, tape the bird's wing folded against its body in its normal resting position. Tape only the fractured wing. Allowing the other wing to be free will help the bird to balance itself. Allow the wing to remain taped for three weeks.

Open Wound or Compound Fracture

Give an antibiotic for seven to ten days in order to prevent infection to a bird with an open wound or a compound fracture. Administer the antibiotic in the bird's food, as described in the section on intestinal infection.

If the flesh is torn and bone ends are exposed, the treatment is more complicated and proper veterinary care is more essential. Where such help is not available, clean the wound and bone ends with a mild antiseptic such as Zephiran, which can be obtained at a drugstore. After cleaning, place the bones in their normal position with the fractured ends touching and apply an antibiotic powder to the open wound. Then tape the wing folded against the body in the normal resting position.

Here, too, apply the tape just tightly enough to hold the bones in position but not so tightly that it will interfere with breathing.

Fractures in Large Birds

Larger birds, such as herons, egrets, hawks, and owls, usually require professional veterinary care if the birds are to fly again when they recover from a fractured wing. Allow your veterinarian to examine the bird and suggest proper treatment. If he can repair the broken wing, you will still have to provide nursing care if the bird is to survive.

If the wing is not repairable or circulation has been severely damaged, a part of the wing may have to be amputated. If even a portion of a wing has been amputated, the bird will never fly again. Unless you are prepared to take care of the bird for the rest of its life or know of a wildlife sanctuary, zoo, or other place where the bird can receive permanent care, it is probably more humane to let your veterinarian euthanize it than to keep it in a cage for the rest of its life.

Most adult birds accept minimal handling without resentment. Mature, grown birds never become friendly, but they will accept being carried on your hand, being stroked on the head and chest, and will learn not to try to escape when you approach.

When its injury has healed and the bird is able to fly, release it in the area where it was found. If you are doubtful about its ability to fly, and you have space around your home, you may release it there. In this way you can recapture it if necessary, or feed it conveniently until it is completely rehabilitated.

Your patient will usually stay where you release it for several hours or longer. If the bone breaks when it attempts to fly, you must start all over again.

If the bird takes off and flies successfully, you have the deep satisfaction of knowing you have given it another chance at life.

Afterword

Many of the techniques used in this book have been adapted from established techniques in the field of veterinary medicine. Information from colleagues, clients, and veterinary journals, such as the journal of the American Association of Zoo Veterinarians, contributed part of the framework to build upon. Additional information was gleaned from the trials and errors of our personal experiences in raising wild babies.

This book is not meant to be the final work on the raising of wild orphans. Rather it is the first step in the organization and accumulation of knowledge in handling native wild babies.

I have purposely not spoken of seabirds. We live inland in Florida and our experiences with these species have been limited to the care of a few injured gulls.

I would welcome suggestions and comments from people who read this book and use it, and from those engaged in similar endeavors.

W. J. WEBER D.V.M.

Migratory Birds

Game Migratory Birds

Anatidae—Wild ducks, geese, brant, and swans
Charadriidae—Plovers, turnstones, killdeer, and surfbirds
Columbidae—Wild doves and pigeons
Gruidae—Little brown, sandhill, and whooping cranes
Haematopodidae—Oyster catchers
Phalaropodidae—Phalaropes
Rallidae—Rails, soras, coots, and gallinules
Recurvirostridae—Avocets and stilts
Scolopacidae—Sandpipers, curlews, yellowlegs, knots, dowitchers, godwits, willets, woodcock, snipe, and sanderlings

Non-Game Migratory Birds

Alaudidae—Horned larks
Alcidae—Auks, auklets, murres, murrelets, puffins, guillemots, and dovekies
Apodidae—Micropodidae, and swifts
Ardeidae—Herons, bitterns, and egrets

Bombycillidae—Waxwings

Caprimulgidae—Whippoorwills, poorwills, nighthawks, chuck-will's-widows, and pauraques

Certhiidae—Brown creepers

Cuculidae—Cuckoos, anis, and roadrunners

Fringillidae—Cardinals, grosbeaks, buntings, finches, sparrows, towhees, juncos, crossbills, dickcissels, and longspurs

Gaviidae—Loons

Hirundinidae—Swallows and martins

Hydrobatidae—Petrels

Icteridae—Bobolinks, meadowlarks, orioles, grackles, blackbirds, and cowbirds

Laniidae—Shrikes

Laridae—Gulls, terns, and kittiwakes

Mimidae—Mockingbirds, catbirds, and thrashers

Motacillidae—Pipits and wagtails

Paridae—Titmice, chickadees, bushtits, and verdins

Parulidae—Warblers, ovenbirds, water thrushes, chats, and redstarts

Picidae—Woodpeckers, flickers, and sapsuckers

Podicipedidae—Grebes

Procellariidae—Shearwaters and fulmars

Ptilogonatidae—Phainopeplas

Sittidae—Nuthatches

Stercorariidae—Skuas and jaegers

Sulidae—Gannets and boobies

Sylviidae—Kinglets and gnatcatchers

Thraupidae—Tanagers

Trochilidae—Hummingbirds

Troglodytidae—Wrens

Turdidae—Robins, thrushes, bluebirds, solitaires, and wheatears

Tyrannidae—Tyrant flycatchers, kingbirds, peewees, and phoebes

Vireonidae—Vireos

Regional Offices of Fish and Wildlife Service

Mailing Address: Regional Director
                   Bureau of Sport Fisheries and Wildlife
                   (Refer to the lists below for the balance
                   of address that serves your state)

Region 1:   P.O. Box 3737, Portland, Oregon   97208
            234-4050 (Area Code) 503

Region 2:   P.O. Box 1306, Albuquerque, New Mexico   87103
            766-2321 (Area Code) 505

Region 3:   Federal Building, Fort Snelling, Twin Cities,
            Minnesota   55111   725-3500 (Area Code) 612

Region 4:   17 Executive Park Drive, N.E., Atlanta, Georgia   30329
            526-4675 (Area Code) 404

Region 5:   U.S. Post Office and Courthouse, Boston,
            Massachusetts   02109   223-2961 (Area Code) 607

Region 6:   P.O. Box 25486, Denver Federal Center, Denver, Colorado   80225   234-2209 (Area Code) 303

Alaska Area: 813 D Street, Anchorage, Alaska   99501
8-206-583-0150 (Seattle)
Ask for: 907-165-4864

Rare and
Endangered Species

Since 1844, when the great auk disappeared from North America, followed by the Carolina parakeet, the passenger pigeon, the heath hen, and the Labrador duck, some seventy-eight species and forty-nine subspecies have become extinct over the world. The fact that a North American and a World Endangered Species list has been prepared and will be kept up to date demonstrates that governments are becoming concerned over this rapid loss of animal populations. The fact that a species appears on this list does nothing to ensure its survival. For unfortunately, that is all it is—a list. It is up to individual states that have an endangered species within their borders to initiate the measures which will enable these creatures to survive.

Following is the list prepared by the United States Department of the Interior.

Rare and Endangered Mammals

Indiana Bat (E)

Spotted Bat (R)

Utah Prairie Dog (E)

Kaibab Squirrel (R)

Delmarva Peninsula Fox Squirrel
   (E)

Block Island Meadow Vole (R)
Beach Meadow Vole (R)
Whales:
  Gray Whale (R)
  Blue Whale (E)
  Humpback Whale (E)
  Atlantic Right Whale (E)
  Pacific Right Whale (E)
  Bowhead Whale (R)
Eastern Timber Wolf (E)
Texas Red Wolf (E)
San Joaquin Kit Fox (E)
Glacier Bear (R)
Grizzly Bear (R)
Black-Footed Ferret (E)
Southern Sea Otter (R)
Florida Panther (E)
Ribbon Seal (R)
Caribbean Monk Seal (E)
Hawaiian Monk Seal (R)
Guadalupe Fur Seal (E)
Florida Manatee or Florida Sea
  Cow (E)
Tule Elk or Dwarf Elk (R)
Key Deer (E)
Columbian White-tailed Deer (E)
Sonoran Pronghorn (E)
California Bighorn (R)
Peninsular Bighorn (R)

Rare and Endangered Birds

Newell's Manx Shearwater (R)
Hawaiian Dark-rumped Petrel (E)
California Least Tern (E)
Florida Great White Heron (R)
Nene (Hawaiian Goose) (E)
Aleutian Canada Goose (E)
Tule White-fronted Goose (E)
Laysan Duck (E)
Hawaiian Duck (Koloa) (E)

Mexican Duck (E)
California Condor (E)
Florida Everglade Kite (Florida
  Snail Kite) (E)
Hawaiian Hawk (Io) (E)
Short-tailed Hawk (R)
Southern Bald Eagle (E)
Prairie Falcon (R)
American Peregrine Falcon (E)
Northern Greater Prairie Chicken
  (R)
Attwater's Greater Prairie
  Chicken (E)
Lesser Prairie Chicken (R)
Masked Bobwhite (E)
Whooping Crane (E)
Greater Sandhill Crane (R)
Florida Sandhill Crane (R)
Yuma Clapper Rail (E)
California Clapper Rail (R)
Light-footed Clapper Rail (E)
California Black Rail (R)
Hawaiian Gallinule (E)
Hawaiian Coot (E)
Eskimo Curlew (E)
Hawaiian Stilt (E)
Puerto Rican Plain Pigeon (E)
Puerto Rican Parrot (E)
Puerto Rican Whip-Poor-Will (R)
American Ivory-billed Wood-
  pecker (E)
Northern Red-cockaded Wood-
  pecker (E)
Southern Red-cockaded Wood-
  pecker (E)
Hawaiian Crow (Alala) (E)
Puaiohi (Small Kauai Thrush)
  (E)
Large Kauai Thrush (R)
Nihoa Millerbird (E)
Kauai Oo (Oo Aa) (E)

Crested Honeycreeper
(Akohekohe) (E)
Molokai Creeper (Kakawahie)
(E)
Akiapolaau (E)
Kauai Akialoa (E)
Kauai Nukupuu (E)
Maui Nukupuu (E)
Laysan Finch (E)
Nihoa Finch (E)
Ou (E)
Palila (E)
Maui Parrotbill (E)
Bachman's Warbler (E)
Golden-cheeked Warbler (R)
Kirtland's Warbler (E)
Ipswich Sparrow (R)
Dusky Seaside Sparrow (E)
Cape Sable Sparrow (E)

Rare and Endangered Reptiles

Bog Turtle (R)
American Alligator (E)
Blunt-nosed Leopard Lizard (E)
San Francisco Garter Snake (E)
Puerto Rican Boa (E)

**Rare and Endangered
Amphibians**

Santa Cruz Long-toed Sala-
mander (E)
Texas Blind Salamander (E)
Limestone Salamander (R)
Black Toad, Inyo County Toad
(R)
Houston Toad (E)
Pine Barrens Tree Frog (R)
Vegas Valley Leopard Frog (R)

Composition of Animal Milks by Percentage

	Solids	Fat	Protein	Carbo-hydrates
Cow (*Bovidae*)	11.9	3.5	3.0	4.6
Dog (*Canidae*)	24.0	10.5	7.9	3.8
Cat (*Felidae*)	20.0	6.5	9.0	6.8
Rabbit (*Leporidae*)	30.5	10.4	15.5	1.9
Mouse (*Muridae*)	25.8	12.1	9.0	3.2
Pig (*Suidae*)	20.0	7.3	6.6	5.0
Sheep (*Bovidae*)	20.5	8.6	5.7	5.4
Goat (*Bovidae*)	12.8	4.1	3.7	4.2
Opossum (*Didelphidae*)	14.0	4.7	4.0	4.5
Gray Squirrel (*Sciuridae*)	26.6	12.6	9.2	3.4
Beaver (*Castoridae*)	33.0	19.8	9.0	2.2
Coyote (*Canidae*)	24.5	10.7	9.9	2.3
Fox (*Canidae*)	18.1	6.3	6.2	4.6
Raccoon (*Procyonidae*)	13.4	3.9	4.0	4.7
Otter (*Mustelidae*)	35.9	23.9	11.0	.1

149

Deer (*Cervidae*)	23.1	8.0	10.6	2.8
Pronghorn Antelope (*Antilocapridae*)	25.2	13.0	6.9	4.0

This information courtesy of Borden, Inc.

Suggested for Further Reading

1. Cahalane, Victor. *Mammals of North America*. New York, The Macmillan Company, 1961.
   An excellent book on mammals, the best I have read.

2. *Wild Animals of North America*. Washington, D.C., National Geographic Society, 1960.
   A good book with general information on animals.

3. Allen, Arthur A. *Stalking Birds with Color Camera*. Washington, D.C., National Geographic Society, 1963.
   This is more than a photography book. Dr. Allen gives a great deal of background to help the reader understand and work with birds.

4. Pettengill, Olin, Jr. *Ornithology in Laboratory and Field*. Minneapolis, Burgess, 1970.
   A study text on birds for post-high school students.

5. Robbins, C. S., Brunn, B., and Zim, H. S. *Birds of North America*. New York, Golden Press, 1966.
   The easiest to use of the identification guides.

151

6. Wetmore, Alex. *Song and Garden Birds of North America.* Washington, D.C., National Geographic Society, 1964.
Identification and interesting facts about the songbirds.

7. Wetmore, Alex. *Water, Prey, and Game Birds of North America.* Washington, D.C., National Geographic Society, 1965.
General background for understanding this group of birds.

Index

Adult animals, danger from, 22
Age determination
 of animals, 31
 of birds, 81–82
Alligators, 19
Altricial birds, 79–99
 age determination, 81–82
 cage, 85–88
 feeding, 88–96
 handling and freedom, 97–99
 nest, 82–84
 warmth and shelter, 83–88
Amputation of leg (bird), 137
Animal milk composition, 149–50
Animals (mammals), 27–75
 approaching, 28–30

bathing, 71–72
bowel and urine control, 34–35, 38
cage, 37–39
dehydration, 69–70
feeding, 40–62
freedom, 64–66
injury, 72–75
intestinal infection, 67–69
nest, 30
nest-box house, 35–37
petting and handling, 63–64
ticks, fleas and lice, 70–71
warmth, 30–33
 See also under individual species
Antelope, 44, 150

153

Antibiotics
for animals, 67–69
for birds, 129–30, 138
Armadillos, 20, *60,* 61
Avocets, 110, 142

Baby food, 56
Bathing animals, 71–72
Bats, 22, 146
Begging posturing, 89
Birds
altricial, 79–99
feeding, 114–124
first aid, 125–140
migratory, 142–43
of prey, 22
precocial, 100–113
rare and endangered, 146–148
See also under individual species
Bites, Animal, 21–22, 29–30, 64, 66, 73
Bites, Bird, 120
Blue jays, 133
Bobcats, 59, 61, 73
Bottle-feeding animals, 49–52
burping baby, 51
Box-houses for animals, 35–37, 74
Bubonic plague, 23

Cages
for animals, 37–39
for birds (altricial), 85–88, 98
for birds (injured), 127
for birds (precocial), 103, 112
Cat food, 59, 61
Cats, 31, 149
feeding, 41, 43, 61
Chilled birds, care of, 128
Chukars, 107
Cleanliness, 38, 56, 84, 87
Cod-liver oil, 61–62
Compound fractures (birds), 138–140
Concussion-injured birds, 128–129
Coots, 100, 110, 142, 147
Crows, 20, 79, 147

Deer, 73, 150
formula and feeding, 43–44, 49, *52*
Dehydration, 69–70
Dermalite tape, 136, 138
Diet
of altricial birds, 89–93
of precocial water birds, 110–111
See also Feeding animals; Feeding birds
Diet supplements
for animals, 61–62
for birds, 122–24
Diseases from animals to man, 22–23
Dog food
for animals, 59, 61
for birds, 89–90, 93, 95, 118–120
Dogs (puppies), 59, 61, 149

Doves, 20, 142
Drays (nests), 28
Dropper feeding animals, 44–49, 74–75
Dry food, 59, 61
Ducks, 20, 100, 101, 103, 105, 133, 142, 147
  housing and feeding, 107, 110–113

Egg tooth (birds), 81–82, 88
Egrets, 79, *119,* 120, 133, 142
Eliminations, bowel and urine, 34–35, 38, 84, 87
  stimulated, 34–35
Endangered species list, 146–148
Euthanasia, 126

Feeding animals, 40–62
  bottle, 49–52
  diet supplements, 61–62
  dropper, 44–49, 74–75
  foods for older baby, 56–61
  formula, 40–44
  stomach-tube, 53–55
  techniques of, 44–52
  washing up, 56
  weaning, 51
Feeding birds (altricial), 88–96
  basic diet, 89–91
  expanding menu, 92–93
  hawks and owls, 93–96
  liquids, 91–92
Feeding birds (injured and very weak), 114–124, 127
  dietary supplements, 122–124

force-feeding, 118–122
  stomach-tube, 117–118
  toothpick formula, 114–117
Feeding birds (precocial), 101, 104–113
  special housing and feeding, 107–113
  teaching chick to eat, 105–106
  what to feed, 104–105
First aid for animals, 72–75
First aid for birds, 125–140
  amputation of limb, 137
  approaching injured bird, 126–127
  basic care, 127
  chilled birds, 128
  concussion-type injuries, 128–129
  fractures, 133–140
  intestinal infection, 129–130
  oil-contaminated birds, 130–133
  problem eater, 130
Fleas, 23, 70–71
Flying squirrels, 35, 37, 38
  formula and feeding, 43, 49, 57–58
Force-feeding solid foods to birds, 118–122
Formula feeding for animals, 40–44, 74–75
  bottle feeding, 49–52
  dropper feeding, 44–49
  sweetener, 44
Formula feeding for birds, 89–91

toothpick formula, 114–117
Foster parents, warning to, 21–23
Foxes, 22, 35, 37, *54,* 72, 147, 149
  formula and feeding, 41, 43
Fractures (birds), 133–140
  compound, 138–139
  legs, 133–137
  wings, 137–139
Freedom
  for animals, 21, 64–66
  for birds, 87, 97–99, 109–110, 112–113
Frogs, 23

Gagging, 55
Gallinules, 110, 142, 147
Game migratory birds, 142
Game species, 19
Game warden or wildlife officer, 20, 21
Geese, 20, 100, 103, 105, 142, 147
  feeding, 107
Goats, 149
  formula and feeding, 43–44, 49
Gray squirrels, 35, *36,* 37, 149
  formula, 43, *57*
Ground squirrels, 23
Grouse, 107

Hairless babies, 31
Handling birds, 97
Hawks, 19, 79, 147
  capturing injured, 127

feeding, 93–96
force-feeding, 120–22
freeing, 98
nest, 83
Heat (warmth)
  for animals, 28, 30–33, 38, 40
  for birds (altricial), 82–85, 97
  for birds (precocial), 101, 102, 104
Herons, 79, 120, 142
Houses
  for precocial birds, 107–109, 111–112
  nest-box houses for animals, 35–37, 74
Hunting, 19

Intestinal infections in animals, 38, 56, 66
  antibiotics, 66–69
  dehydration, 69–70
Intestinal infections in birds, 129–130
Injury from animals, 21–23
  attempted biting by animals, 29–30
Injury to animals, 72–75
Injury to birds, 125–140
  See also First aid for birds

Kestrel, 121
Kildeer, 100, 142

Land birds, Precocial, 107–110
  feeding, 109
  freedom, 109–110

housing, 108–109
Leg fractures (birds), 133–137
Lice, 70–71
Limpkins, 110
Liquids for birds, 117

Mammals
    ailing or injured, 67–75
    basic care, 27–39
    feeding, 40–62
    petting, handling and freedom,
        63–66
    rare and endangered species,
        146–147
    See also under individual spe-
        cies
Mice, 20, 35
    formula and feeding, 41, 43,
        44, 49, 57–58
Migratory birds, 20–21, 142–
    143
Milk formula, 40–44
Milk of animals, composition of,
    149–150
Mockingbirds, 19, *82, 84,* 86,
    88, 133, 143

Nest-boxes for animals, 30, *31,*
    34–37
    in cage, 37–39
    light for warmth, 30–33
Nest-boxes for birds, 131–132
Nest of altricial birds, 79–80,
    82–84

Oil-contaminated birds, 130–
    133

Orphan birds; *See* Birds
Orphan mammals; *See* Animals;
    Mammals
Opossums, 20, 28, 73, 149
    formula and feeding, 41, 43,
        59, 61
Otter, 22, 147, 149
Outdoor pen for precocial birds,
    108–109
Owls, 19, 79, *81, 86,* 87, 94,
    129, 136
    capturing injured, 127
    feeding, 93–96
    force-feeding, 120–122
    freeing, 99
    nest, 83

Pelicans, 79
Petting and handling animals,
    63–64
Pheasant, 100, 103, 104, 133
    housing and feeding, 107
Pinfeathers, 82
Prairie dogs, 23, 146
Precocial birds, 100–113
    approaching the orphan, 101–
        102
    cage, 103
    feeding, 104–107
    special housing and feeding,
        107–113
    warmth and shelter, 102–104
Protected species, 19–20

Quail, 100, 101, 104, 107

Rabbits, 28, 38, 149

formula and feeding, 43–45, 58–59
use of antibiotics on, 68
Rabies, 22–23
Raccoons, 20, 22, 28, *33,* 35, 37, 72, 73, 149
formula and feeding, 41, 43, *48, 50,* 59, 61
Rails, 110, 147
Rare and endangered species, 21, 146–148
Rats, 20
Redwing blackbird, *80*
Regional Offices of Fish and Wildlife Service, 21, 144–145
Robins, 87, 133, 143

Sheep, 44, 149
Skunks, 22, 35, 37, 72
feeding, 59, 61
Snakes, 23
Song and Garden Birds of North America, 92, 105
Songbirds, 79
Sparrows, 20, 133, 143, 148
Squirrels, 28, *29,* 31, 39, 72
first aid, 73–74
formula and feeding, 41, 47, 49, 57–58
See also Flying squirrels; Gray squirrels; Ground squirrels
Starlings, 20
Stomach-tube feeding
animals, 53–55
birds, 117–118

Sunflower seeds, 123
Sweetener, 44

Temperature control; *See* Heat (warmth)
Tetracycline, 68, 129
Ticks, fleas and lice, 70–71
Titmice, 87, 143
Toads, 23
Toothpick formula feeding, 114–117
Turkeys, 100, 103, 104, 107

Unipet Powder, 95, 123

Veterinary assistance, 53, 55, 68
Vitamins, 61–62, 95

Warmth; *See* Heat (warmth)
Water birds, precocial
feeding, 107, 110–111
freedom, 112–113
housing, 111–112
Water for animals, 39, 74–75
Water for birds, 91–92, 96
Water, Prey and Game Birds of North America, 105, 110
Weaning baby animals, 51
Wildlife, 19–21
Wings, fractured, 137–139
Woodpeckers, 79

Zu-Preem Bird of Prey Diet, 96

ABOUT THE AUTHOR

William J. Weber, D.V.M., is Director of the Leesburg Veterinary Hospital in Florida. Dr. Weber's writing and photographs appear regularly in professional journals and natural history magazines.

To: The Heneelys

Love,

The Dean Tiptons

1979

Christmas

YOU & YOUR WORLD

Paul H. Dunn

YOU & YOUR WORLD

BOOKCRAFT, INC.
Salt Lake City, Utah

Library of Congress Catalog Card Number: 77-088131
ISBN 0-88494-327-5

3rd Printing, 1978

Lithographed in the United States of America
PUBLISHERS PRESS
Salt Lake City, Utah

Contents

Preface vii

I   Building Commitment
  1   A Call from the Prophet   3
  2   Meet Joseph Smith 13
  3   If a Man Begins to Build 19
  4   "Oh Beautiful for Patriot Dream" 26
  5   "He That Loseth His Life . . . Shall
      Find It" 32

II   Strengthening the Home
  6   My Wife's Husband 39
  7   Families Are Forever 45
  8   Preparing for Parenthood 51
  9   Being a Priesthood Man 67
  10 Parents, Teach Your Children 76

III   Gathering Souls
  11 The Worth of Souls Is Great! 85
  12 "Come Ye After Me" 89
  13 What Is a Teacher? 95
  14 "Strengthen Thy Brethren" 101
  15 Put on Your Spiritual Clothes 105

IV Refining a Testimony
16 How One Can Know That God Lives 119
17 Preparation for a Testimony 126
18 Living Prophets for Our Generation 143
19 The Meaning of Jesus Christ for
     Our Time 149

V Mastering Self
20 Know Thyself, Control Thyself,
     Give Thyself 159
21 Your Own Temple 167
22 What Is Courage? 179
23 "Follow It!" 183
24 Be Your Own Boss 188

Index 195

Preface

During my years as a General Authority it has been my privilege to mingle in gatherings of the Saints across the world, frequently bearing testimony to them as to the convictions that shape my life. Central is the conviction that Jesus is the Savior of the world, God is our literal Father in heaven, and the true Church has been restored in this age and is guided by revelation and a living prophet.

From these fundamental certainties spring other basic truths which are confirmed by day-to-day living and observation — principles of personal happiness, patterns for success in life, guidelines for the building of souls. These too form part of my conviction and thus of my expressions to people everywhere.

The publisher having suggested that a selection of these talks in the permanent form of a book might be well received, the book *You and Your World* was born. It contains mainly talks given at general conferences, with some also presented at Brigham Young University and other Church gatherings, plus some that have not appeared in print before.

This book is in no way endorsed by the Church, and I accept full responsibility for its contents. Specifically the Church and its leaders are absolved from any errors it might be found to contain.

It is hoped that these thoughts given in both formal and informal settings and styles will be of interest and help to readers.

I am grateful to countless friends and associates and particularly to family members who have encouraged me to put in printed form some of my convictions, feelings and philosophies of life.

I am particularly grateful to my wife, Jeanne, for her great support and encouragement in all things and for the balance that she gives in our life and relationship together; to my daughters, Janet, Marsha and Kellie and their respective families which include their husbands, Gary and Jeril, and their wonderful children for the zest and balance they give to life and for the great meaning and purpose they have added to mine.

A special tribute to my mother, Geneve R. Dunn, who yet reminds me of the good and positive things found in your and my world.

A special thanks to Sharene Miner for her outstanding secretarial assistance in typing and proofreading and to Paul Green and his associates at Bookcraft for their wonderful cooperation in so many ways.

Paul H. Dunn

I

Building Commitment

1

A Call from the Prophet

Latter-day Saints wherever you are, prepare yourselves! The world and the Church need you!

I say that very sincerely, because I believe I know in some small way the need for adequate preparation. It was Charles Lindbergh who said some years ago that "preparation precedes power"; and as you know, when he translated this formula into his life, the result was excellent, as it is in any field of endeavor.

Let me tell you why I feel this way, if I may, for a moment or two. One peaceful April day I was really minding my own business in California — part of it being my position with the Church institute program. As I have always done over the years, I sat transfixed in front of a television set while the general conference of the Church was being televised throughout the western part of the world, and I guess in many other areas of the world by tape.

I always take this opportunity as a father to gather my family around me. It gives me an excellent opportunity to teach my own children. Many times speakers do not always talk to the elementary or junior-high level. As a father and teacher, it gives me an opportunity to instruct further in the words of counsel and advice.

After the morning session was over and the picture vanished from our set, I remember my three daughters moving into other parts of the house to resume activities that were important to them. My wife graciously excused herself to go prepare an afternoon meal. I pulled a book down from the shelf to do a little reading and research which I had procrastinated for a number of weeks. All was well for about forty-five or fifty minutes. Then very quickly, and almost in an interrupted fashion, a knock came at our back door. My wife answered it. Standing there in the framework was the sixteen-year-old daughter of our bishop who lived just around the corner. (I think he moved there to kind of keep an eye on us.)

She was very excited. Even being one room removed, I could tell that there was some concern in her voice. "Sister Dunn, is your husband at home?"

I got up very quickly and came to the door. She was quite pale. "Brother Dunn," she blurted, "President McKay has been trying to reach you for over an hour. Your phone must be out of order. He has called my dad. You had better call him quick. Here's the number."

She was an energetic young lady, having palled around in the group with my oldest daughter. Knowing her as I did, I thought that she was just out a little early on one of these trick-or-treat businesses. I was ready to pass it off, but I could see that she was still serious.

I took the slip of paper that she had. On it was a Salt Lake telephone number. I got a little serious. I thanked her and moved into the other room. There I found out why the prophet of the Lord was having problems reaching me — my middle daughter was on the phone.

Not meaning to be the prying type of father, I stepped to the closet door — where she had gone into secrecy — to see just how long she would be. I only had to listen a minute to tell she was but halfway through her agendum. So I stepped back to the desk and wrote out a little note. I thought I would make it pertinent but not too faith-shaking, so I just said, "The prophet of the Lord is trying to call us." I slipped it under the door, and those two doors opened up about as fast as I have ever seen, and she came stumbling out and handed me the telephone. I took it into the other room — we have one of those five-hundred-foot cords where you get privacy at every point — and I sat down and dialed the number.

Sister Middlemiss, President McKay's secretary, answered the phone. I identified myself. She said: "Your telephone is out of order. I would suggest you get it checked." I did not dare tell her what my problem was. She continued, "Just a moment; the President would like to speak with you." Realizing I had just watched him on television a few minutes before, my heart started to pound. I wondered, "Well, what has he found out about me?"

The next voice I heard was that of President McKay. He spoke firmly, very kindly, "Brother Dunn?" I came to full attention. "Yes, sir?"

"How long would it take you to get to Salt Lake City?"

Well, I have a very peculiar mind. The way that my thought processes go, I tend oftentimes, without thinking any more than I do, to say things that need to be thought out more clearly. This was one of those occasions. I said: "President McKay, I am in Downey, sir. That's in California."

He then made what I thought was a very marvelous observation for a prophet. He came right back and said, "I know that." Again, very gently, he said, "I'm asking you, how long would it take you to come to Salt Lake?"

I said, "Well, without checking into the schedules, I believe I could be there sometime tomorrow."

"That would be fine. I'll expect you in my office at eight o'clock tomorrow morning."

Well, my mind is still the inquisitive type. So I started to pursue a little bit, because I could tell he was ready to hang up. I said: "Well, what should I bring with me? Do you need my institute of religion reports?" I thought, "What has he discovered?" By then every sin I had ever committed had gone by. I needed to know how to defend myself.

He said, "No. Just bring yourself."

"How about my wife?"

"That would be lovely, if you could bring her."

"Anything else?"

"No," he said, "I'll see you in my office at eight o'clock tomorrow morning. Have a nice journey. Good-bye." And he hung up.

That is a traumatic thing. How do you go back into the kitchen and tell your wife that the prophet wants to see you? I tried. She was just putting the final touches on the meal and was at the breadboard slicing the roast beef. Typical of all good American housewives, wanting to know what was the purpose of the call, she turned to me, and I will never forget that expression. She said, "Who was that on the phone, dear?"

"Oh, no one, just the prophet." She about cut the breadboard in two.

Then to show you how much faith she had in me, the next observation she made was: "Well, what did you do? What did you do?"

I said, "I don't know, but he wants to see us tomorrow morning at eight o'clock, and we had better get going."

Some of you who reside in Utah and the surrounding areas may appreciate the problem we sometimes have with the weather there. I finally elected to drive because it was the only sure way of getting there at the appropriate hour. What a trip that was! I pulled into Salt Lake about ten minutes before I was due. I left my wife with the Tingeys, very close friends of ours in Provo, because the prophet had asked to see me alone.

I knocked on his hotel door, standing there wondering what all this entailed. The door very quickly opened. One of the aides asked me to step in. Getting just inside the doorway I could see down the little corridor to my right into the room that had been made over into a little office for President McKay, where he could work in the hotel when his strength would not permit him to go over to the office.

He was sitting there very diligently at his work. He looked up and, noticing that I had arrived, very quickly got up and took his cane; and he hurried down that little corridor, laid his cane beside the wall, and extended his two hands in greeting to me. He said, as he looked into my eyes, "Brother Dunn, thanks so much for coming to Salt Lake to see me."

Imagine that! Talk about graciousness and respect! He was thanking *me* for coming to see *him*.

Then he turned to the other individual and said, "Will you see that Brother Dunn and I are not disturbed for the next hour?"

I remember thinking, "What in the world have we got to talk about for an hour?"

Then he very quickly and gently took me by the arm, cane in the other hand, and I was literally escorted back into his room. He was helping me; it was not the reverse.

As we got inside his office, he closed the door. Because I had a topcoat on, he turned me around — just moved me bodily — helped me off with my overcoat, put it over his arm, took it over and put it on the couch. He came back, and instead of putting me out in front in a typical counselee-counselor relationship, he asked me to take a chair beside him. Then he worked his way back around the desk and took his place in a little swivel chair. He turned it sideways so that we had this face-to-face contact, and he leaned back, just looking right through me as only he could do. With that wonderful smile on his face, he said, "Brother Dunn, tell me a little bit about yourself."

I couldn't even remember my name. I remembered vaguely I had a mother, so I started there and kind of worked back. I believe he enjoyed my fright and plight, just sitting there smiling very kindly.

After about twelve minutes of visiting — and did he have an ability to make you feel good, at ease, and like an equal brother and sister in the gospel — he said, "I guess you are wondering why I have asked you to come to see me."

The thought *had* gone through my mind. "Yes, sir," I responded.

"Brother Dunn, last December, as you know, we lost a great

Latter-day Saint in the passing of President Levi Edgar Young. I am calling you this morning to fill that vacancy."

When he said that, I had a feeling and an impression come over me like I have never experienced in my life. Spiritually I was just out of breath. Having played professional baseball for a number of years, I have been hit in the midsection my share of the time. You brethren who have been so involved — maybe some of you good sisters — know how difficult it is to get your wind. This is exactly what I was going through — just gasping for air. I believe he even enjoyed watching my struggle.

I then made another comment that came out before I thought about it. Don't ever say this to a prophet of God. "President McKay," I said, "in all my life I have never once doubted your judgment or inspiration — until right now."

He did not lose his sense of humor entirely, but he came pretty close. He raised his finger and started to shake it at me a little bit, and he cautioned: "Now, Brother Dunn, I don't want to hear of that any more. The Lord has called you to this position."

Then he went on for the next forty-seven minutes to interrogate and to investigate my soul through the process of diligent interviewing.

Oh, I wish it were possible for every Latter-day Saint to not only sit in the presence but to feel the ability of a prophet of the living God to search the heart and the soul and the mind of people. I got just about that much look into the eternities and a feeling as to what it is going to be like for each of us to one day give an accounting to the Savior. I know now, as I have never known before, the process by which we must account for those things which we have done or that we have failed to do in this state of our existence. I think if every member of the Church could just undergo that for a few moments, how it would revamp the thinking process and the kind of activity we often see in people today.

Well, I do not have the ability to relate all that goes on in an interview of that type, except that it is a spiritual experience one can never forget.

At the conclusion of it President McKay stood up, which was my indication that the interview was over. He again very warmly extended his hands to me to take. As I did so, without any warning, he very quickly threw his arms around me and kind of pulled me close and held me there, just the way a father would do his son, or a grandfather his grandson, and did not say a word. But, oh, the spirit that radiates from a living prophet as you are in close physical communication one with another! Talk about a testimony being verified!

Then as he broke the embrace — about as quickly as he started it — no words were exchanged; he had tears in his eyes, and I certainly did — he looked into my soul again and said, "Brother Dunn, I want to be the first to welcome you officially into the family." Then he went on to instruct me a little further on the mechanical process of how this would take place, not only that day but the rest of the week.

I knew about this call an hour before the rest of the Church did. As I sat being interviewed by a living prophet I commenced to appreciate all the more the value of preparation. I have thought back a number of times about the hours and the days that I have let go by because I thought I was too busy. I have thought of the number of meetings in my Aaronic Priesthood days when I could not quite catch the vision of all this religion; so I would go out a conveniently located door or window to the drugstore to read magazines. I thought of a lot of other problems that I created for myself because I lacked the spiritual insight and vision to catch hold of the opportunities that were mine as I prepared for life. And, oh, if I could only have that time back now to help me prepare spiritually and academically for this calling!

Well, President McKay kept his sense of humor right to the end — all the way through. He said: "When you get over to the Tabernacle this morning, you take a place in the congregation, because we have to sustain in this Church. You know that, don't you, Brother Dunn?"

"Yes, sir, I know that."

He continued, "The people of this Church will have an opportunity to raise their hands and sustain you in this position." Then he came around the edge of the desk and started to nudge me in the side with his elbow. "Do you know, they may not sustain you."

Well, I thought about that, too. As I was excused to go out, he said, "Now, you can call your wife and tell her, but no one else until this is finalized this morning."

That was a challenge, to be sure, because my wife was down at the Tingeys. This became quite a traumatic thing. Just as these things often work out in life, two weeks before that we had just finished remodeling our home, which we had been planning to do for eight years. Do you sisters know what I am trying to say? I had to phone her and say, "Fold up the tent; we're moving on." What a challenge!

I finally got the courage. When she came on the phone, I remember asking her, "Jeanne, are you standing or sitting?"

"I'm standing."

I said, "Sit down."

She did and then asked, "Well, what in the world went on up there?" I just got ready to tell her and she said: "Before you tell me, let me tell you something. I don't know what the prophet has asked you to do, but about ten minutes after you left I had the sweetest, most comforting spiritual influence come over me that I have ever known in my whole life." She added, "Regardless of what he has asked you to do, if it takes you anywhere in the world, even if it means we have to sell our home, I'm willing."

Can you imagine what that did for me? And not one moment since has she had a regret or a criticism. Only wives of that caliber can appreciate the problems and the challenges that are hurled upon a family in terms of this kind of commitment and responsibility.

The following Thursday I was privileged to go into the house of the Lord with the prophet and again sit at his feet for an hour and fifteen minutes as he gave me counsel and instructions relative to this assignment prior to the ordination. And if I only had the ability to convey to you what a living prophet can teach in an hour! Getting a bachelor's degree and a master's degree and a doctor's degree at some of the finest universities in the world was not one-half the experience in terms of eternal verities as one hour of instruction at the feet of a prophet.

Do you understand what I am trying to say? I am sure you can, because it is a spiritual thing that one must undergo.

As he concluded, President McKay leaned back in his chair — we were sitting there again in a very close physical relationship — and he said: "Brother Dunn, it has come to my attention that you have a very strong testimony of the gospel. Is that right?"

I looked right back at him and said, "Yes, sir, that's right."

I will never forget that expression. I can just see it every day of my life. He leaned back with a beautiful smile on his face. "Oh, that's marvelous. I'm so happy! Now Elder," he added, "in the presence of these witnesses in the temple this morning will you bear it to me? Bear me your testimony, Elder."

There was a challenge. As I said a silent prayer, I looked at him and told him how I felt in my heart — how I had struggled as a young person and how I had come to know in many ways that this Church had been restored and that there were living prophets, that God lived and that Jesus was the Christ, that the Prophet Joseph Smith was an instrument in the establishment of this Church again upon the face of the earth, and how I had come to know, with all the assurance that I had, that he himself was such a prophet.

President McKay did not say a thing. He just sat and looked. I guess it took two or three minutes, and then he leaned back and broke the silence with this observation: "Brother Dunn, the Spirit has just manifested to me that what you have said is right. We will now proceed with the ordination."

He stood up, had me take his chair, and he came around behind and invited others to do likewise, and, placing his hands upon my head, ordained and set me apart for this particular calling. As he did so, he gave me the special blessing and opportunity to bear witness to the divinity and reality of Jesus Christ as the Savior of the world. As he pronounced that blessing, the sure knowledge of what I am saying now came into my heart and soul to the point that I can testify to each of you, regardless of your station, position, or attitude, that I know that God lives, that Jesus is the Christ, that there are prophets called and ordained to lead this people. I had the privilege of so being in the presence and receiving that kind of instruction from one such, in David O. McKay, a living prophet.

2

Meet Joseph Smith

One hundred thirty miles north of Boston, Massachusetts, is one of the most beautiful places I have ever seen. Nestled in the rolling green hills of Windsor County, Vermont, is the birthplace of a prophet of the Lord — Joseph Smith. On the grounds of the original homesite stand two buildings housing a bureau of information and a religious display center.

Recently on one of our trips to the memorial we had our young daughter Kellie with us. She has been there many times and is always noticeably affected by the inner peace and spirit that prevails. She never leaves that building without signing her name in the guest book provided for visitors and giving her evaluation in the column provided for comments. (Incidentally, another column asks if you would like more information about the Church. We have received over forty referrals from her already.)

On this particular day she wrote: "The Church is the greatest thing in my life." My wife and I obviously were filled with joyful emotion. Why? Because the Church and the gospel with its ordinances is a "way of life," and by following its teachings we as a family are finding the true joy and happiness we all seek.

It was just over 150 years ago that a young lad with simple faith asked a very important question: "Which church is right?" That beautiful spring morning in 1820, God the Father and his Son Jesus Christ revealed themselves to a young boy whose name will never perish. That boy was Joseph Smith, the first prophet of this dispensation.

Having lived in New England, my family and I have spent a great deal of time at the birthplace of the Prophet. The Lord has hallowed that spot, and each time we gazed upon the granite shaft that pierces the sky over the place where he was born, our hearts filled with joy and the Spirit whispered to us, "He was indeed a prophet."

One of the best gifts I could give you is an opportunity to know the Prophet Joseph Smith a little better. I shall not undertake to explain to you the accomplishments of Joseph Smith, but I want to tell you about the man, the Seer, and the Prophet. I think it is important that we know the how and why of his life, for to do so is to increase our understanding and appreciation of this "prince of our present dispensation," even Joseph Smith, the man of whom Brigham Young said, "Jesus Christ excepted, no better man ever lived."

A life that has become a candle of the Lord is a life that all would wish to see more clearly. Such a life was Joseph Smith's — a life given in the service of others and a life of love. We declare that he was, without a doubt, one of the most noble sons of our eternal Heavenly Father.

He was a tall, well-built man, over six feet in height and about 210 pounds. He had a light skin, light hair, and blue eyes that could gaze into the heart of any man. He was as quick as a squirrel, strong as a lion, and mild as a lamb. One young man said of him that "he wore no whiskers, and that altogether, he presented a very formidable appearance, being a man of gentlemanly bearing." A young lady said that there were no pictures of him in existence that can compare with the majesty of his presence. His wife said no one could capture his true countenance because his expression and countenance changed with his moods.

As one looks more deeply into his personality, experiences, and character, one can see a remarkable blend of Christlike qualities. His peers spoke of his solemnity in sacred moments, yet were much pleased at his prophetic wit, his love of music, poetry, drama, and, very notably, his hearty laughter. They were continually amazed at his versatility in changing pace. He could move from studying the scriptures or any of his four foreign languages to playing ball, wrestling, jumping at a mark, and back again to studying. All people could recognize his easy jovial appearance when he was engaged in activities of fun, but they were quick to note his dislike of anything that was degrading or vulgar.

He could reprove betimes with sharpness and always showed forth afterwards an increase of love. "I am determined," he said, "while I lead this church to lead it right."

Joseph Smith was a rugged and free outdoor man. He delighted in physical work and taught that it was a God-given principle to keep our bodies strong. During the building of the Nauvoo Temple, he would often work in the rock quarry. Many people learned of the restoration of the gospel while working at his side in the quarry, in the forest, or in the hayfield.

Joseph Smith had a strong and abiding testimony of Jesus the Christ and never let an opportunity pass in which he could tell others of the knowledge he had. When he spoke, he seemed to shake the very earth, and the people said that he had the appearance of one that was heaven-borne while preaching. Not only did he speak with the Spirit, but the records show that at one time or another in his life he possessed every spiritual gift, and one of his most profound teachings was uttered in these words when he said, "I have made this my rule: When God commands, do it."

In carrying out God's commandments, Joseph possessed the rare Christlike combination of what Carl Sandburg called "velvet and steel," which can move people with gentleness, meekness, and love unfeigned, without threat or force. If the world would only learn God's commandments and live like Joseph Smith, what a wonderful world this would be.

President McKay often told us that we become like what we love. Joseph loved Christ and became like him. He said, "I want to become a smooth shaft in the quiver of the Almighty," "My voice is always for peace," and "Jesus Christ is my great counselor."

He was a man, like any of us, but unlike us today he endured unspeakable suffering and persecution. He was driven from four states, lost six children in birth, was tarred and feathered, was poisoned; yet he led his people with great courage and said, "I cannot deny what I know to be true."

Brigham Young said that he lived one thousand years in thirty-eight, and although he was mobbed and beaten, Lydia Bailey said, "His face shone with the mellow radiance of an astral lamp."

He led like Moses, spoke like Peter, and wrote like Paul. Wilford Woodruff said, "His mind, like Enoch's, expands as eternity, and God alone can comprehend his soul."

In knowledge and understanding of the gospel, he was unsurpassed. Joseph Smith left on record fifteen hundred statements that spoke of the future. Many hundreds of these have already come to pass, and in our own lifetime we will see the fulfillment of many more. You may pick at random any of his writings and find more about the last days than in the entire Bible. His writings, letters, and spoken words are so extensive that it seems almost impossible that one man could do so much in so little time. The Book of Mormon, the books of Moses and Abraham, and the Doctrine and Covenants, all of which he recorded under revelation, total 830 pages, and his own history, speeches, and minutes total over 3,200 pages.

We have been called the happiest people on earth, and much of our happiness comes from living the truths revealed to us by Joseph Smith.

If any man was taught by God and angels, Joseph Smith was that man. He was a spiritual amphibian, with one foot on earth and one foot in heaven. Edward Stevenson says, "He possessed an infinity of knowledge." And Wilford Woodruff said, "He seemed a fountain of knowledge from whose mouth streams of eternal wisdom flowed." Parley P. Pratt said, "He could gaze into eternity, penetrate the heavens, and comprehend all worlds."

Joseph Smith taught that this great nation of America was a choice land that came into being under the Lord's direction, and he bore a strong testimony of the divine importance of the work done by the Founding Fathers of this great country. He said: "The Constitution of the United States is a glorious standard; it is founded in the wisdom of God. It is a heavenly banner; it is to all those who are privileged with the sweets of its liberty, like the cooling shades and refreshing waters of a great rock in a thirsty and weary land. It is like a great tree under whose branches men from every clime can be shielded from the burning rays of the sun." (*Documentary History of the Church*, Vol. 3, page 304.)

He never asked for a light load, but rather he prayed for a strong back; and he was indeed a prophet, for his constant plea was, "Oh Lord, what shall I do?" Those who listened to his prayers marveled at the spirit he presented and learned in their own lives that the heavens could literally be opened. They understood what he meant when he taught: "It is the first principle of the gospel to know for a certainty the character of God, and to know that we may converse with Him as one man converses with another." (*Documentary History of the Church*, Vol. 6, page 305.)

Someone has said that the greatest of all discoveries is when a man discovers God. Joseph Smith made available to the world, with no exceptions, the true nature and knowledge of God, a personal and loving Father. He taught that God is our Father and that Christ is not only his Son, but also our elder brother. The Christian churches of the day said, "We believe in God," but Joseph Smith said, "I saw God and Christ and they did in reality speak to me." He was persecuted for saying that he had seen a vision, yet it was true. Not only has he made known to us that God exists, but also that he is ever willing to answer our prayers.

Prayer is the soul's sincere desire, says a great hymn, and if Joseph Smith gave us nothing else he set the example whereby we could have our desires fulfilled and our hearts made clean and pure. Thus, on his way to Carthage before he was martyred, he said: "My conscience is void of offense." "I am not afraid to die." He spoke as a man whose life could stand inspection before the Master.

On that fateful day in 1844, he was killed by a mob of about 150 men with painted faces. At the time of his death it was written: "The blow that subdued Joseph Smith has palsied the arm of Mormonism. They will now scatter in the four winds and gradually merge in the great mass of society." (*Boston Globe*, June 27, 1844.) This congregation today and the millions in our listening audience refute those words.

The enemies of God were sure that by killing the Prophet, they had destroyed the truth; yet it lives, greater and stronger with each passing year. It is indestructible, for it is the work of God, and knowing that it is the work of God, we know that Joseph Smith, who was God's chosen servant, is a prophet, holy and true, for he said, "I obtained power or the principles of truth and virtue, which will last when I am dead and gone."

It is my personal witness that he was and is a prophet. His mantle fell upon succeeding prophets and rests upon the shoulders of a prophet today.

3

If a
Man Begins
to Build

About two miles from our former home in California stood the framework of a house which had remained unfinished for several years. It was beautiful. It was in a very lovely location. The plan of the house was interesting, and the material out of which the framework had been built seemed quite satisfactory.

As I continued to drive past the house month after month on my way to work, I noticed that the lumber was gradually changing color — first a faded yellow, then a darker yellow; light brown, then darker brown; until at the close of the first year the framework appeared to be almost black.

Not only was the color changing, but with each passing day the skeleton of the unfinished house became more articulate, until one day it actually seemed to speak to me. So challenging was its message that I know I shall never forget it. Like the voice from across the centuries, the blackened structure seemed to ask: "Which of you, intending to build a tower, sitteth not down first, and counteth the cost, whether he have sufficient to finish it?

"Lest haply, after he hath laid the foundation, and is not able to finish it, all that behold it begin to mock him.

"Saying, This man began to build, and was not able to finish." (Luke 14:28-30.)

The message was being hurled directly at me and, I think, at all others who had sworn, regardless of cost, to build a completed life. Have we stood by this promise, whether the houses of our lives were large or small? Are our lives each day completed structures? Or have the tempting challenge of the crowd and the worries of depressing moments caused us to become slack in our work? Do our lives now stand before the world as half-finished skeletons of the beautiful houses we had sworn to build?

The voice continued to speak: "What king, going to make war against another king, sitteth not down first, and consulteth whether he be able with ten thousand to meet him that cometh against him with twenty thousand?

"Or else, while the other is yet a great way off, he sendeth an ambassage, and desireth conditions of peace.

"So likewise, whosoever he be of you that forsaketh not all that he hath, he cannot be my disciple. . . .

"He that hath ears to hear, let him hear." (Luke 14:31-33, 35.)

This voice of warning suggests, I feel, one of the most vital teachings of the Savior. If we really want to build well, the first thing we must do is to have faith in God and in his Son Jesus Christ, admit our weaknesses through repentance, and then seek baptism by those having proper authority in order that we might "come unto him."

But we must not stop there. Having admitted our present incompleteness, the next step is to put everything we have into the development of a great life. "And blessed are all they who do hunger and thirst after righteousness, for they shall be filled with the Holy Ghost." (3 Nephi 12:6.) "But seek ye first the kingdom of God, and his righteousness; and all these things shall be added unto you." (Matthew 6:33.) Once again, the principle Jesus advocates is truly as old as the hills. Other things being equal, he intimates that we get exactly what we seek if we seek it diligently enough.

Someone has said, "The longer I live, the more deeply I am convinced that that which makes the difference between one man and another, between the weak and the powerful, the great and the insignificant, is desire, invincible determination, the purpose once formed and then death or victory."

When Sir John Hunt stood at the foot of Mount Everest, he did not expect his team of mountain climbers to reach its summit by some sort of magic or in one leap. He had mapped the climb by stages, one day at a time. Each day the men ascended as far as they had planned for that day. The morning that two members of his party, Hillary and Tenzing, finally stepped upon the summit was the climax of many days' effort. The last step was the crowning one of many arduous steps to the top.

What you set out to do may not seem as difficult or spectacular as climbing Mount Everest, but you must apply the same principle. You must go step by step, with full desire and energy focused on the end you seek. Such is the law of success in every sphere of life. Why should it not be so in the building of a balanced, righteous life? "And blessed are all they who do hunger and thirst after righteousness, for they shall be filled with the Holy Ghost." (Matthew 5:6.) This challenging principle becomes ever more vivid when we study the conditions of Palestine and learn of the severe physical hunger and thirst that are experienced in that semidesert land.

It is not uncommon for bath water, for example, to be drained off and used for irrigation purposes. So very scarce was water that biblical writers frequently and effectively mention water in their figures of speech. I call your attention to only a few.

Perhaps the most poetic Old Testament writer, the Psalmist, yearns: "As the hart panteth after the water brooks, so panteth my soul after thee, O God.

"My soul thirsteth for God, for the living God." (Psalm 42:1-2.)

Isaiah, searching for words to describe the happy future of Zion, tells his people: " . . . for in the wilderness shall waters break out, and streams in the desert.

"And the parched ground shall become a pool, and the thirsty land springs of water. . . ." (Isaiah 35:6-7.)

When Jesus talks to the Samaritan woman at the well, he tells her that if she will accept the water of life which he has to give, she will never thirst again. "Whosoever drinketh of the water that I shall give him shall never thirst; but the water that I shall give him shall be in him a well of water springing up into everlasting life." (John 4:14.)

John the Revelator even goes so far as to compare heaven to a place containing a crystal spring of water where one may drink as much as he pleases without charge. "I will give unto him that is athirst of the fountain of the water of life freely." (Revelation 21:6.) "They shall hunger no more, neither thirst any more; . . .

"For the Lamb . . . shall lead them unto living fountains of water. . . ." (Revelation 7:16-17.)

Water, you see, is so hard to find in Palestine and the surrounding desert country that people almost go crazy from thirst. Food is so scarce that men and women are often compelled to live on a daily diet of no more than a few dates and a cup of milk, or even so little as a piece of hard bread. Under such conditions people naturally make the attainment of food and water their chief concern. Jesus contends that only when we are equally serious about attaining a righteous life, when we really hunger and thirst after righteousness, shall we be filled.

An outstanding teacher was once listening to his wife play a beautiful sonata on the piano. "I would give anything in the world to be able to play like that," he said.

"All right," she responded. "Let's see if you really mean that. You say that you would give anything in the world to be able to play as I have. I have given several hours a day almost every day for the last fifteen years. I have given up picnics and parties and many other kinds of entertainment in order to stay at my task. I have sacrificed the study of many interesting subjects; I have given and worked and worked and given. At times it seemed that I could not work another hour or sacrifice another thing. To play the piano as well as I do, would you really be willing to give that much?

"You've got me there," he admitted. "I thought I would give almost anything to be a great piano player. I realize now that while I would give up a few things, I do not want this particular ability enough to sacrifice much time or many pleasures for its attainment."

"But you are a great teacher," she reminded him. "You have succeeded in your profession because you have done with your teaching what I have done with my music. You made it the first consideration of your life, sacrificing where others have not been willing to sacrifice, studying, working, and planning where others have not been willing to make the effort. You have sought first the kingdom of teaching, and this you have been able to achieve."

So the Savior would have us realize that in the building of eternal lives, there is nothing mysterious or unusual about the illustration just cited. If we want to build mediocre spiritual houses, let us give a minimum of time and effort. If we want to build beautiful houses of life or to change the design of our present lives, if we wish to reach great heights in our upward climb toward eternal life, let us do away with all of the things and every thought that hinder our progress. A mere public announcement of faith will little hasten our progress. Simply joining a church and regularly attending all of its various meetings is no guarantee. Only when we put faith, repentance, and baptism first, and seek righteousness in our thinking, and without serious regret give up every conflicting desire shall we be able to reach the coveted goal, because the Savior has said, ". . . strait is the gate, and narrow is the way, which leadeth unto life, and few there be that find it." (Matthew 7:14.)

The reason, I suspect, that we have so many mediocre musicians in the world is that there are only a few people who are willing to follow the narrow road that leads to great musicianship. We have so few great artists, lawyers, doctors, and teachers because only a few are willing to get rid of the excess baggage that

prevents them from traveling the straight and narrow road.
Herbert Hoover once warned: "We are in danger of developing a
cult of the common man," which he went on to interpret to mean
a cult of mediocrity. The great human advances have not been
brought about by mediocre men and women; they have been
achieved by distinctly uncommon people with vital sparks of
desire.

In Palestine a person who always looked at others with envy
was referred to as one having a "bad eye." One who stole was said
to have a "long arm." Jesus, knowing that everyone would understand what he meant, told the people that it would be better for
one to pluck out his eye (envying others' wealth and honor) or cut
off his hand (being unjust and dishonest) than to keep these bad
habits and ruin the possibility of developing a fully rounded,
well-balanced life. (See Matthew 5:29.)

Does honesty always bring material reward? "Be good and you
will be wealthy." I suspect that many of us believed that as
children. Some wealthy people, however, are not honest, and
some honest people have never had many worldly possessions.
We miss the point of the Savior's teaching unless we realize that
the reward of righteousness is something bigger, better, and more
beautiful than material gain. Envy, dishonesty, and unfairness —
all of these are excess baggage, and as such are not worth what it
costs to carry them with us. Our Heavenly Father knows our need
and will bless us accordingly.

This principle, I think, is illustrated by an experience of a
young friend of mine. Married, with two children, and living on a
very small salary, he found it necessary to budget strictly. He and
his wife spent only a few cents occasionally for entertainment. He
traveled all over town to find reasonable prices. Often when I
asked him to go some place, he would reply: "Sorry, Paul, I can't
do it this week. I've used up my budget for gasoline."

One summer I found him a job doing some menial tasks that
would be classified as unskilled labor. Since he was a college
graduate and a high school teacher, I asked if he really enjoyed

doing such work, if he found satisfaction in the bondage of such a restricted budget. He replied, "Of course I don't enjoy it, but I do it because I'm anxious (hungry, if you please) to have a house of my own."

In conclusion, let me say that the house I mentioned earlier was finally completed. It is really a beautiful structure. If I were to take you past it without telling you its history, I am quite certain that you would never guess it had been black and unsightly, standing for months as nothing but the framework of a great purpose. Today it is a most attractive home. And it still talks to me, reminding me each time I see it that even adults who have failed thus far may still build beautiful eternal lives.

Perhaps we spent too much time worrying about the mistakes of our youth, forgetting that we as adults have the opportunity to continue building as the years go by. I suspect the Lord was thinking of all ages and classes of people when he said, "And blessed are all they who do hunger and thirst after righteousness, for they shall be filled with the Holy Ghost." (3 Nephi 12:6.) "Seek ye first the kingdom of God, and his righteousness; and all these things [whatever proves necessary for righteous people] shall be added unto you." (Matthew 6:33.)

Today throughout the world there are thousands of young men — we call them missionaries — who have been sent forth with a divine message to help the people of the earth "seek" in order that they might find the "strait and narrow path" of which the Savior speaks. May I invite you to open your doors and hearts so that you too might come to know and be filled with that same sweet, holy spirit.

4
"Oh Beautiful for Patriot Dream"

Some time ago in the summer heat of Boston, two men worked vigorously and perspired mightily to construct displays for the American Bicentennial. One stopped to mop his brow and asked the other, "Do we really have to go through this every two hundred years?" The correct answer, of course, is that we have not celebrated often or deeply enough the birth of this promised land, this choice and beautiful and still-young land, which we possess as the Lord's gift in freedom and joy — just as long as we serve him.

Boston is a proper place to begin; Boston, in fact, is "a very proper place." We who have prayed, preached, and tracted in lovely New England did not find it at all that formal. It is a charming place with friendly, wonderful people. On all sides you see the "where it happened" of precious American tradition.

Indeed, it has been just over two hundred years since a better-than-average silversmith on a black horse made history as Longfellow later recalled:

The fate of a nation was riding that night;
And the spark struck out by that steed in his flight. . . .
A cry of defiance, and not of fear. . . .
And the midnight message of Paul Revere.

That's the way it was, from Boston to Lexington to Concord,

as the war for independence and liberty began. Most of all, it was for people — men and women of courage and vision and faith, strengthened by God as a part of his plan, who struggled, froze, starved, and when necessary died, that these free states in union might be born, in Thomas Jefferson's incisive words, "to assume, among the powers of the earth, the separate and equal station to which the laws of nature and of nature's God entitle them." (Declaration of Independence.)

It was worth a lot to the new Americans of that hour to beget this nation — worth all they had, all they were, and all that they had dreamed. What is it worth today, to you and to me, and especially to us as Latter-day Saints, who alone *know* what the Lord is doing, to assert our free agency toward the fulfilling of his plan?

As you decide, let me suggest an exciting tour for you. Go, if you can — and if you cannot, then make the trip in your mind's eye from your study or your armchair or your library, but *go* — go to Charlestown and Breed's Hill, to Washington's Crossing, Brandywine Creek, Saratoga, to the great courthouse and a dozen more, and to King's Mountain and Cowpens and Guilford Courthouse on the road to Yorktown, where it finally ended. Ask yourself along the way who these people were, and where they got their vision, and listen intently for a drummer boy tapping out a song that is two centuries older than George M. Cohan.

Give a thought as well to a lad aged twenty-one who regretted that he had but one life to give for his country and a twenty-year-old French major general who came three thousand miles to secure the final victory. And if you are traveling and you come to one of those too-numerous claims that "George Washington slept here," and you kind of hope that if so the sheets have been changed and that modern plumbing has been installed, pause to remember that there really was such a man as George Washington, sometimes disliked, but respected, gladly followed and *superbly* there when we needed him most, to lead in carrying out the plan of the Lord in the founding of America. Childless, the Virginia planter today has 220 million living children. You and I are among them. God had set him apart and lifted him up.

Carry on with me then to Philadelphia to the year 1787. Gathered to frame a constitution in cramped and overheated quarters, delegates from most of the thirteen sovereign states struggled through the summer months to produce a document upon which a free nation might be built. Fortunately (and it has been said by those not of our faith), they achieved a Constitution and a Bill of Rights which far exceeded the best that could come from these men. *But it did.* More than that, it was and is a living document, capable of defending its basic principles but flexible enough to adapt to the needs of this changing and growing United States.

You and I are made aware, of course, that there is a better explanation of what really occurred. The scriptures tell us. The Lord "established the Constitution of this land, by the hands of wise men whom I raised up unto this very purpose, and redeemed the land by the shedding of blood." (D&C 101:80.)

The land was "redeemed" indeed by thousands killed and wounded along the way at Germantown, at Bemis Heights and Charleston, and at so many other places in the American Revolution.

President Brigham Young spoke for himself and for every living prophet who has addressed the question since when he said, "The signers of the Declaration of Independence and the framers of the Constitution were inspired from on high to do that work." (*Journal of Discourses* 7:14.)

An objective study of the delegates involved — their fears, their limitations, vested interests, and the like — makes it clear that they were not the sort of men we usually think of as prophets. Nonetheless they were inspired, and the Constitution they provided can be designated accurately as a divine document.

But even a divine constitution requires something further; it demands a kind of people who will, by their very natures, receive and respect such a constitution and function well within the conditions it establishes.

Again the Lord said: "Wherefore, this land is consecrated unto him whom he shall bring. And if it so be that they shall serve him according to the commandments which he hath given, it shall be a land of liberty unto them." (2 Nephi 1:7.)

As Latter-day Saints then, we know why some persons came to America and others did not. And as someone has said, "We haven't done badly for a nation of immigrants." We are immigrants, you and I, because the Lord made immigrants of us and brought us here. We have done as well as could be expected, and are richly blessed despite our shortcomings because the Lord has thus far held us in his hands and worked his purposes, his ultimate purpose, through us.

Can you understand, this is what America is all about? You and I know, and you and I *alone* really know, the reason for this blessed and beautiful land. In a world where men have given up on this most vital question, we know the purpose of America.

For this country did not end in Philadelphia, even if Horace Greeley did mean that city when he urged us to "go west." It was a new land, fresh, clean, unspoiled with a past. America included the frontier. In 1805 the Prophet Joseph Smith was born, and he grew up toward adolescence just like the new land. He fitted it. He was young, clean, unspoiled — a lad without a past, kneeling in a grove. This pristine land — this innocent young man — and thus the Lord reached out and kept his promise. He established his conditions over centuries; you see, God has time. His plan made it possible for the holy priesthood and the Church to be restored upon the earth — the restoration of the gospel of Jesus Christ — but only in America.

Can you understand the way God has worked? And if you do, will you join me this day in committing yourself to preach the message of the Lord's glorious achievement in America and to teach it as missionaries wherever the opportunity allows? This is a time when you and I can afford to be patriotic, in the best sense of that term. There is reason to be proud that we live in an established land that has been conditioned by the Lord so that his gospel could be restored. The purpose of America was to provide a setting wherein that was possible. All else takes its power from that one great, central purpose. May I commend to you Mark E. Petersen's book *The Great Prologue* (Deseret Book Co., 1975). Read it in connection with your scriptures and receive greater light on our history and its purpose.

As some of you know, I have never counted mathematics as my most exciting subject. Nevertheless, I believe that I can set in sequence the steps the Lord has used in his plan.

First, there was selecting and bringing the people. The next step was establishing a free nation. The third was inspiring a divine constitution. The fourth was opening the American frontier, new land, fresh and clean. The fifth step was calling young Joseph Smith to become a prophet in such a little time, God's prophet, seer, and revelator, and later his martyr.

Let me add one final stop to your American journey. The place: Arlington National Cemetery in Arlington, Virginia — the tomb of America's unknown soldier. Today the remains of three servicemen from three wars lie there. The inscription reminds us, "Here rests in honored glory an American soldier known but to God." There are in addition 4,724 other unknown servicemen buried in Arlington, and all across the nation and the world I have seen the crosses, row upon row, marking the places where lie America's honored dead, literally in the thousands. What did it cost them that this nation might remain "the land of liberty"? How shall we honor them, you and I?

In two ways, it seems to me: First, by striving to make our citizenry the righteous people the Lord requires of us. And second, by telling the story of what the Lord has done for you and me and this great Church, and why.

> Oh beautiful for patriot dream
> That sees beyond the years.

Thine alabaster cities gleam
Undimmed by human tears.
America! America!
God shed his grace on thee
And crown thy good with brotherhood
From sea to shining sea.

Katherine Bates,
"Oh Beautiful for Spacious Skies,"
Hymns, Number 126

May that be the song of our heart and our prayer for fulfillment.

5

"He That Loseth His Life . . . Shall Find It"

He was a big fellow, about six feet four inches tall, and weighing 220 pounds — an all-American boy from the physical standpoint. He was attending the University of Southern California on a four-year, fully paid football scholarship. And he had a right; he had earned it. Everybody clamored for him. I think he could have gone to any one of sixty colleges.

But he had one problem — he thought he was the only thing that existed. And as he walked around the campus he gave that air and authority. The only reason he came to the LDS Institute was that I taught a class at noon with twenty-eight girls in it and two boys. That was his motivation.

He used to time his entrance into the class to just follow the opening prayer. He would plop down on the back row, put his feet up on an adjoining chair, and then a sneer would form on his face which suggested: "Brother Dunn, I'm here. I dare you to teach me."

Did you ever see a student like that? It is a real challenge to a teacher, I promise you. Try as I would — I put on floor show after floor show for him — I couldn't penetrate his shell. He was just too hard, because he was turned in, selfish. The only time he looked interested was when we were honoring him at some event or banquet.

Talk about discouragement! I would go home and tell my wife:

"I'm through. I quit. I can't teach." That would usually be about Thursday or Friday.

And she would grab me by the arm and say: "You can! Go get him!"

By Monday morning I would charge back. "I'm gonna get that boy!"

By Wednesday, down in the valley of despair I'd go. "I can't, I can't!"

"Yes, you can!"

I guess I resigned every week for six weeks.

One day I got a telephone call from a very close friend of mine in Hollywood. His wife had had a little baby born prematurely and it wasn't expected to live. They had it in an incubator at the Hollywood Children's Hospital, and he wondered if I could hurry over and help administer to it and give it a name and a blessing before it passed on. I was honored. I hurried over, and in my anxiety to get to the floor where the incubators were located, I got off one floor too soon. And, lo and behold, I found myself standing in the orthopedic ward of the Hollywood Children's Hospital — thirty little beds lined up. Have you ever been up to the Primary Children's Hospital to see those little children, many of them confined there with crippled bodies? I don't know what it does to *you*, but it touches this dad deeply.

So, after completing the administration, I went back to take a second look at those little children, and again it affected me. This time I noticed that they had some volunteers working with them. And so I stepped up to the desk and asked the nurse, "What's going on here?"

She said, "We have a little program where two days a week people from the community come in and try to brighten the day for the children."

"How do you get involved?"

"It is easy," she said. "Sign right here."

Now I took the pen really wanting to put down my own name,

and I couldn't. I was inspired to put down my student's name —
old Bill. So I wrote his name in place of mine.

The nurse said, "Thank you," and called me by his name.

I had signed for the following Thursday at six o'clock in the
evening.

I didn't have the heart to go tell Bill what I had done. You see,
he was the type of a person who would have refused had I asked
him to volunteer, because we weren't honoring him. To do
something for somebody else? "Haven't got time, I'm too busy."
So I waited until five o'clock the following Thursday, which was
the date of our appointment. Then I rang him on the phone, and
his mother answered. I said, "Is Bill there?"

She said, "Yes, we're just ready to sit down to supper."

I said, "May I speak to him for a minute?"

"Certainly."

I learned a long time ago in World War II that the element of
surprise is necessary in combat.

Bill came to the phone and said, "Hello?"

And I just reared back and I said: "Bill! Will you help me,
please?"

He said: "Oh, yes, sir. Yes, sir. But who is it?"

"It's your institute teacher, Brother Dunn. Thank you, I'll be
by and pick you up in fifteen minutes!" And I just hung up.

Well, I wish you could have been in the car with me. I drove
over, and he was standing out on the curb. He had his letterman's
sweater on, all three stripes showing, and a half of an apple pie in
his hand, eating it. I pulled over to the curb and opened the door
and I said, "Get in, quick!"

He asked, "What's the matter?"

"Get in," I said, "and I'll tell you."

He got in and I slammed the door. I think he thought we had
just received a call to go back to Missouri. Then I just sped off,
knowing that when I did tell him, he would probably bail out. I
got around the corner doing about forty. He said, "What is all the
excitement?"

I said, "Bill, I really appreciate you."

He said, "For what? for what?"

"You're going down to the Children's Hospital and read to some kids."

"I'm what?"

He wouldn't talk to me for the rest of the trip.

We got to the hospital. I literally pushed him out on the sidewalk. I gave him a note — third floor and the name of the nurse — and said: "I'll be back in an hour and get you. The Lord bless you." Then I drove off and left him.

An hour later I came back, and out of that hospital door walked a new man. He got in the car, and he couldn't talk.

"How did it go, Bill?" I asked.

"I can't tell you."

I said: "I understand. Don't try. But when you get your composure, let me know." I turned on the car radio so the silence wouldn't be too obvious. We drove for about ten minutes.

Then he turned the radio off. He said, "Brother Dunn, that was one of the great experiences of my life."

"I thought it would be. What happened?"

He began: "They assigned me to a little three-year-old girl who was born without a spine, never known a day out of bed. And that little girl is happier than I am. What's the matter with me?" (I wanted to tell him, but that wasn't the place.)

He went on to say that he was given a chair, and it was brought up to the side of the bed. All the time he was reading she wanted to hold his hand. He read to her out of a giant pop-up Pinocchio book.

"You know," he said, "it is embarrassing to read to kids, particularly when people can hear you. But after I finished the first page, I didn't care who heard me." Then he went on to say that he finished the story and then another and another, and finally it was time to go.

"Brother Dunn, I made ready to go, and the little girl didn't want me to. She pulled me down, and you know her whole hand barely fit around one of my fingers. And then she gave me a kiss on the nose and asked me to come back next week. Brother Dunn, you might think I'm a nut, but I signed up for another month."

"No, I don't think you are a nut, Bill. This is what we have been trying to talk about in class. See, you can talk about theories and lesson plans all you want. But you found out what the Lord said, as Matthew records it, that when you lose yourself in the service of others, you find the real you. This is the greatness of the gospel."

Bill discovered it in his nineteenth year. Two weeks later a knock came at my door, and he filled the whole framework. I said: "What is it, Bill? What can I do to help you?"

"Well," he said, "I've really done it this time. I just resigned my scholarship — four years."

"Now, what did you do that for?"

"Just accepted a mission call. I'm going out and kind of lose myself."

I spoke at his farewell. Two years later he returned. He blessed me with a little visit. I am proud to announce to you that when Bill came back, he was still six feet four inches tall and 220 pounds, but now he had a spirit to match it. What a great contribution he will make to the world — to the Church — because he followed the admonition of the Savior:

He that findeth his life shall lose it: and he that loseth his life for my sake shall find it. (Matthew 10:39.)

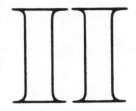

Strengthening the Home

6

My Wife's Husband

Every once in a while there comes into the life of each father and husband a tremendous challenge, and some time ago it was one of these challenges that brought me to a greater realization of my responsibility as both father and husband. I am sure my experience is not unlike some that many of you here today have had.

It all happened this way. In her interest to go shopping with one of her close friends, my wife one day asked if I would be kind enough to attend to the household chores for about four hours during her absence, besides tending our smallest daughter. I assured her I was most anxious to do what I could as a priesthood bearer and as a loving father and husband. And I will have to confess there was a selfish interest at heart, thinking as I did that perhaps here was an opportunity to catch up on some of my own projects.

Well, now, I want to tell you, that was a day I shall never forget. Let me just give you an accounting of my accomplishments on that afternoon:

I answered the telephone fifteen times. Thirteen of those calls were for our teenage daughters.

I shouted, "Don't, Kellie (she was then five), forty-three times.

I spread bread with jelly nineteen times. Some of my youngest daughter's little friends were visiting with her at the time.

I stopped nine different quarrels.

I wiped noses twelve times.

I tied shoes eight times.

I shut and opened doors fifty-three times.

I bandaged six different fingers.

I answered 117 questions.

And as well as I can figure at this point, I ran approximately two and a half miles without ever going out of doors.

Now, brethren, I ask you, how long has it been since you stood in the place of your good wife? For example, two or three days following this little episode, I took this same group of wild Indians to the grocery store and attempted, as all mothers and housewives do, to fill the grocery basket. There was another challenge, to keep one youngster from digging into the cookie box, while another picked up, dropped, and broke a jar of pickles, and the third in the meantime became lost and, in her anxiety to find her father, shouted so that all the neighborhood could hear, "Daddy, where are you?"

Brethren, fathers, priesthood bearers, I tell you that I sincerely believe that my day is as long and nerve-racking as any represented here. But I wouldn't trade my job, and I don't believe most of you would, involved as it might be, for that of a good wife who manages the home, supervises a family of children twelve hours a day and more at times, not to speak of a few other little responsibilities that engage her time from morning until night.

I wish today, brethren, that my wife's husband could remember every evening when he comes home that, no matter how tired he is or how hard he has worked, she has labored just as hard. And no matter how disappointed he may be with the things that have gone on during the day, she has an equal reason to be tired and discouraged with the load of her multitudinous and hectic responsibilities.

If my wife's husband could always realize this, I believe he would try even harder than he does to forget his own troubles and would try to bring into his home a spirit of love, fun, optimism, and assurance that would make every member of his family glad to be alive.

There are a number of other things that I wish my wife's husband would do as he views this lovely creature that he has taken unto himself as a bride for time and all eternity — that he would continue to court her and respect her as he has promised to do because of his genuine love and appreciation for her.

I wish my wife's husband would also remember at all times the responsibility he has to direct the affairs of his family, to be the loving father and the companion for his daughters that he basically wants to be but sometimes forgets to be because of busy schedules.

Thinking about the home and its importance and the role of a mother and father I am reminded of one of the finer studies that was made some years ago by Dr. Sheldon and Eleanor Glueck, a husband and wife sociology team at Harvard University. After much research and investigation of many cultures, they developed a scale which could predict delinquency, and they concluded that there were five basic ingredients that assured successful living and happy homes. Their discovery shouldn't surprise the Latter-day Saints because prophets of old, as well as today, have related these to us.

Briefly stated, they suggested that if you want to have successful family relationships in your home, the mother must show affection for her children. Now much has been said on many occasions concerning the role of the mother in the home, and I would be the first to wholeheartedly endorse all these words as to the influence of what that mother can be and the need for her to be constantly available to all young children. I think by nature the mother more normally tends to give this basic love because of her place in the home.

The second basic ingredient would be love shown by the father. And sometimes, dad, even though we have this basic interest and affection for our children, we fail to display it in a way that is meaningful in the lives of these young people. I am sorry to confess there have been times in my so-called busy life when I have neglected this very thing, thinking my dear wife would certainly fill in.

I was brought up rather short some years ago by one of my daughters when one Sunday afternoon she took from my coat pocket my appointment book, opened it up, and wrote her name; and as she brought it to me she said, "Dad, I'm wondering if I can have an appointment with you at two o'clock next Sunday." I think you might appreciate in some small measure how I felt, and it was at that moment I began to take a serious inventory of my own life and my responsibilities.

The second daughter on that same occasion chimed in, and she said in almost an echo form, "Dad, why is it that you always have time for other people's children and not for us?" Well, I am happy to announce that I have attempted to right my life as a father and as a teacher in the home, and I am finding as I found some years ago that what our prophets ask us to do is right. I bear fervent testimony of what this can do in any home in America today.

The third thing in this formula was supervision, which the Gluecks basically assigned to the mother but certainly included the father.

And the fourth: discipline from the father, which does not exclude the mother as a part-time disciplinarian.

Fifth: the point of cohesiveness, tying it all together, which depicts again the wisdom that has come from on high through living prophets concerning the Family Home Evening. This program affords mothers and fathers the opportunity to sit down and work out programs that will assist the youth of our nation and of the world to better ways of life, to a higher and more divine understanding of our very purpose in the world.

I am so grateful as a father and as a husband for these things which have been revealed to us in these latter days.

May I share with you from the pen of an unknown author "A

Father's Ten Commandments," which I think have modern-day application:

"Thou shalt love thy children with all thy heart and hesitate not to manifest interest in and affection for them. This is the first and great commandment.

"Second, thou shalt not make unto thee any graven images of thy business, thy career, or thy sports, or any likeness of pleasure, occupation, or pursuit in the heavens above, in the earth beneath, or in the waters under the earth. Thou shalt not bow down thyself unto them, nor serve them so that thou forgettest to be a pal and a chum to thy children.

"Third, thou shalt not take the name of 'Dad' upon thee lightly, for Jehovah will not hold him guiltless who has little regard for the responsibility of fatherhood.

"Fourth, remember thy children's portion of thy time and keep it holy. Many days shalt thou labor and do all manner of work that thou mayest provide suitably for all their needs, but in that portion of thy day which belongeth to them, thou shalt not do any work, neither shalt thou bury thy nose in a book, betake thyself to the golf links, or busy thyself otherwise according to thine own pleasure.

"Fifth, honor thy wife, for thy children loveth her dearly and cannot admire, respect, and love thee if thou display not loving kindness for her.

"Sixth, thou shalt counsel and advise with thy children in all things and share with them the secrets of thy heart.

"Seventh, thou shalt be firm in thy discipline lest thy children stray from the paths of righteousness for the lack of thy guiding hand. But thou shalt not hold the reins of thine authority too tight nor fail to understand that thy children desireth and needeth more and more of that independence of action which becometh a man.

"Eighth, thou shalt have trust and confidence in thy children and be patient and long-suffering with all their shortcomings.

"Ninth, thou shalt walk uprightly before men and make thy ways clean in the sight of thy God, for thy children doth follow after thy example. Moreover, take heed that thy children hath more discernment than thou sometimes thinkest and art more influenced by what they see thou really art than by what thou pretendest to be.

"And tenth, thou shalt not forget thou wert once a boy. Neither shalt thou be unmindful that times have changed very much since the days of thy youth."

I am grateful for knowledge of the gospel of Jesus Christ and for its meaning in our homes. May we be equal to the tasks as dads and husbands, as priesthood bearers, to raise up a generation that will bless the world.

7

Families Are Forever

I always refer to fellow Latter-day Saints as my brothers and sisters, for I have a deep and abiding conviction that we are all children of one Eternal Father. An experience I had during World War II deeply impressed this on me.

While serving in the South Pacific, I came upon a wounded Japanese soldier who had concealed himself in a cave. Though he was near death he made every effort to defend himself, but in his weakened condition he could not resist, and he soon surrendered. Since the two of us represented different governments, different cultures, and different philosophies of life, it was natural for him to suspect that I might take his life. He immediately withdrew into himself and even tried to hide his face behind his arms. It was obvious that he feared the worst. Though I could not speak his language, it took me several minutes to convince him that I was trying to give him help.

After cleaning out his wound and giving him food and water, I found an interpreter and asked him to assist me in communicating with this young soldier. To our surprise, we found we had much in common. Both of us had been drafted by our country to go to war. Both of us had families back home. Both of us were very homesick. Both of us had an interest in baseball and even idolized the same American baseball players. Had the decision to continue fighting World War II been ours to make, we would have shaken hands and gone home. We felt a common brotherhood. Truly as the apostle Paul said, "[God] hath made of *one blood* all nations of men. . . ." (Acts 17:26. Italics added.)

We are brothers and sisters, children of one Eternal Father!

It has not been too many years since I underwent surgery. During those precarious weeks and months, when life was in the balance, it gave me time for deep reflection and meditation. My thoughts, of course, spanned my lifetime, but where do you suppose those thoughts lingered most? It was not on any special attainment I may have been fortunate to have achieved; nor was it any material possessions that have come to me. My dominant thoughts were with a lovely wife, three daughters, and my grandchildren — my family. More than ever before, the truth brought forth to the Prophet Joseph Smith sunk deep into my heart; that families may be forever! This means that those sacred associations and the happiness enjoyed by loved ones here may be extended for all time into the eternities, only there, it will be coupled with a more pronounced joy.

There was an early apostle in this dispensation by the name of Parley P. Pratt. He had the occasion to be personally instructed by the Prophet Joseph Smith on the eternity of family relationships. He recorded this experience in these sublime words:

"During these interviews he taught me many great and glorious principles concerning God and the heavenly order of eternity. It was at this time that I received from him the first idea of eternal family organization, and the eternal union of the sexes in those inexpressibly endearing relationships which none but the highly intellectual, the refined and pure in heart, know how to prize, and which are at the very foundation of everything worthy to be called happiness.

"Till then I had learned to esteem kindred affections and sympathies as appertaining solely to this transitory state, as something from which the heart must be entirely weaned, in order to be fitted for its heavenly state.

"It was Joseph Smith who taught me how to prize the endearing relationships of father and mother, husband and wife; of brother and sister; son and daughter." (*Autobiography of Parley P. Pratt,* pages 297-298.)

Yes, families are forever, provided of course that certain conditions are complied with. Now may I briefly refer to three of those conditions by which your family may be a "forever family."

1. *First, a love between a husband and wife that is nourished.* Some people — even among Church members — have the mistaken notion that the initial attraction that brought a husband and a wife together will remain constant without attention. This, of course, is not true.

When I perform a marriage in the temple, I often counsel the young couple to write down the things that attracted them to each other. The bride and bridegroom are then asked to share this list with each other during the first week of their marriage. I then suggest to them that they periodically review this list, so that they can be reminded that their love needs constant attention.

President Kimball has counseled married couples with these words: "Your love, like a flower, must be nourished. There will come a great love and interdependence between you, for your love is a divine one. It is deep, inclusive, comprehensive. It is not like that association of the world which is misnamed love, but which is mostly physical attraction. When marriage is based on this only, the parties soon tire of one another. There is a break and a divorce, and a new, fresher physical attraction comes with another marriage which in turn may last only until it, too, becomes stale. The love of which the Lord speaks is not only physical attraction, but spiritual attraction as well. It is faith and confidence in, and understanding of, one another. It is a total partnership." (*Faith Precedes the Miracle,* page 130.)

2. *Second, a home that is sustained by the priesthood.* We must not forget that a spiritual love is begotten by the Spirit of God. That spirit comes "by the prayer[s] of faith." (D&C 42:14.) No family or individual is able to cope with the challenges, entice- ments and cynical voices which decry honorable marriage and

traditional family relationships without the aid of heaven. The priesthood is heaven's power to act.

President Spencer W. Kimball has said: "In the Lord's program for families, the parents and especially the father will teach the children. And it is available to the people of the world regardless of the church to which they might belong. It provides a formal meeting and a planned program and consistent teaching of the gospel of Christ with participation in the reading of the scriptures and in the program by the children and parents. Each child has his own scriptures. The organizational teachings may complement the home teaching.

"In the great home teaching program and family home evenings, the responsibilities lie first and properly on the head of the father. The wife will assist. What true father would shift the planning, organizing and conducting of such family programs? What dutiful father would evade this teaching opportunity and responsibility?"

3. *Third, a family union that is sealed by the power of God in holy temples.* The Lord has said: "In the celestial glory there are three heavens or degrees; And in order to obtain the highest, a man must enter into this order of the priesthood [meaning the new and everlasting covenant of marriage]; And if he does not, he cannot obtain it." (D&C 131:1-3.)

There are covenants, obligations, key words and priesthood rights which can only be conferred on a couple in holy temples. These covenants, when complied with, entitle a man and woman to enter an "order of priesthood" called celestial marriage. President Joseph Fielding Smith taught that the sons and daughters of our Heavenly Father "have access to the home where he dwells." But to have that access, he said, "You must receive certain key words as well as make covenants by which you are able to enter." (*Doctrines of Salvation*, Vol. 2, page 40.)

By these solemn, sacred ordinances, fathers and mothers receive the keys to their own little kingdom. May I share a touching account which illustrates this:

A number of years ago in Utah, a very impressive story was related by a sister at a meeting where many husbands and wives were present. This good mother had been asked to tell about the joy which had come to her when, with her husband and family, she had gone to the temple. She related how her husband as a young man had been careless. He had strayed away and taken up some bad habits, so that when the time came for him to be advanced in the priesthood he was not ready. When the couple fell in love and were ready to be married they were not prepared to go to the temple, but he promised he would soon take her there.

The years passed and five little girls were born to their union. Then some good brother — a member of the priesthood, a home teacher — with patience, understanding and love, encouraged this wayward brother to come back into activity.

The day finally arrived when that husband took his wife to the temple. She now related the story of that day. She told how she was sealed to her husband across a sacred altar in the temple by a man of God in authority. Then the doors opened and in came five little girls in white dresses. They all gathered around the altar and that same man of God pronounced them a family for eternity.

She told this story beautifully with much emotion. Before her sat her husband in the first row or two. She leaned on the pulpit and seemed to forget anyone else was there but just the two of them. She said to him: "Daddy, I don't know how to tell you how the girls and I feel about what you have done for us. I guess all I can say is: Thank God from the bottom of our hearts for you, Daddy. Except for you who holds the priesthood which is *the key to unlock the door to our heavenly home,* not even the girls and I could be together in the hereafter. From the bottom of our hearts we thank you, our Daddy." (Harold B. Lee, "Preparing to Meet the Lord," *Improvement Era,* February 1965, page 124.)

Yes, we can be a forever family. Just as we are children of our Eternal Father and constitute his family, so may our family associations lawfully and eternally endure when his conditions are met. Our Heavenly Father's grand objective is to exalt his family —

those who will come — to the joy he now possesses. Would there ever be a heaven without our family?

A love nourished by a husband and wife, a home sustained by prayer, fasting and family teaching, and a family union sealed by the power of God in holy temples — these are the conditions that make "forever families" possible.

I witness to you that our family is our greatest possession. It is the one thing you can take with you when you leave this life, provided that the Lord's conditions are met. I thank God for the restoration of this glorious truth through the Prophet Joseph Smith. I thank him for a living prophet who holds these keys to seal families together today. I testify to the truth that families may be forever as we meet the conditions that the Lord has given to us.

8

Preparing for Parenthood

I would like to direct my remarks to you young people as if from your youth, your future children. I think it fitting that I see beyond your faces and eyes of today. I see in your places your children and through them to their families. As I envision this picture before me, I see the incalculable effect of what we are doing now upon the vision of tomorrow. I'll try to imagine what your children might have me say to you if they were blessed with the power of articulation to say it. For just a few moments, may I represent your children to you?

I would hope and pray that you are preparing yourselves not only physically and mentally, but also spiritually to meet the challenge that lies ahead. James Adams said on one occasion: "There are obviously two kinds of education. One teaches you how to make a living; the other, how to live." I spend most of my time as a General Authority trying to help people learn how to live. I see in you the answer for the generations yet unborn. There are just four things I'd like to speak about as I represent your children and the generations unborn.

First, I think your children would have me direct to you and would have you remember the infinite worth of a soul. You're going to be charged — all of you — with precious souls from our Heavenly Father. No greater institution than The Church of Jesus Christ of Latter-day Saints has as its greatest goal the infinite worth of a soul. The Lord, speaking to a prophet, said, "Remember the worth of souls is great in the sight of God." (D&C 8:10.) It was the Prophet Joseph Smith who taught us the true definition of a soul: "The body and the spirit constitute the soul."

I think there is a tendency in today's world to put a greater emphasis upon the physical and not enough upon the spiritual. The children you will bring into this world will have a great need for spiritual emphasis. I'm the father of three daughters, and, of course, I have a wife. It is interesting to note the great emphasis they put upon their physical attraction. I don't want to denounce that; I think it's terrific. When my wife leaves the car, she's made certain that everything is in its proper order. I learned a long time ago never to walk by an open bathroom door, with three daughters in there using hairspray. I made that mistake one time and got lacquered to the wall.

Having gone through a little physical challenge last year myself, I'm sensitive to that aspect of my life. In almost every magazine or newspaper I open up I see an ad wanting me to donate my body to some health spa, to get into shape and to look proper. That's fine, but I hope we put an equal if not greater emphasis upon the spiritual and the mental.

How much value would you put upon a soul? The Lord said it's of great worth. Could you attach a dollar-cent price tag to it? When I was back in Boston a few years ago, a very interesting account came to my attention. Most of you are familiar with that old historic site, Boston Harbor, where Paul Revere caught the signal from the Old North Church; where the old wonderful battleship "Ironsides," *U.S. Constitution*, is anchored. On the Mystic Bridge just above it there was a gentleman, as the news report gave it to us, walking one March day. It was a cold day but with something of an early spring in the air. He happened to look over the bridge and saw a little dog out on a cake of ice in the harbor. The ice had thawed enough that it had broken up, and the little dog was stranded, yapping and barking. The man, taking note, walked to the other side of the bridge and made a telephone call to the Boston police department. Policemen rallied to the call but surmised quite early that they did not have the facility to retrieve this dog, so they called the Boston fire department. As things will often happen in communication, some eight ladder companies answered the call. You ought to see a ladder truck trying to get down a Boston street. Well, when they got there, they couldn't quite figure out how to get this dog, literally floating out to sea, off the cake of ice. So they called for some additional emergency equipment. One enterprising reporter, sizing up the situation, did some fast calculations and surmised that in about a six-hour effort the city of Boston had paid $8,250 of the taxpayers' money to get one mongrel dog off a cake of ice. Well, I'm not going to debate the value of a dog. My daughter would tell you that it was worth it. We have a dog.

Question: What is the worth of a soul? Permit one other little "for instance." This is quite tender to me because I remember it vividly. I was near the scene where it happened, and, more particularly, I had a little girl exactly the same age when it occurred. The reporter tells it better than I.

"At 4:45 on a Friday afternoon in April 1949, a laughing three-year-old child was playing with her small friends in a grassy vacant lot beside her home. Suddenly she disappeared. She had fallen into a long-abandoned well. Fifteen minutes later her mother called the police and reported that her daughter was wedged in a rusty old shaft. Half an hour later firemen were pumping oxygen into the small opening. At the end of an hour, efforts to raise Kathy with a rope had failed, and at 6:00 power equipment began digging a parallel hole. During this brief time the girl called back bravely to the familiar world above her. She always answered those she loved with courage: 'Yes, I'm all right.' She wanted to please. 'Will you try to grab hold of the rope, Kathy?'

" 'I am. I am.' Then her voice ceased, but she had spoken long enough to convince those above her that she was unhurt by her fall.

"By the time I reached the lot, it was no longer vacant. Under a blaze of light, men and machines began to battle with Mother Earth. Men by the hundreds began to volunteer their help. Circus midgets living in the vicinity arrived and risked being lowered by their feet into the crumbling old shaft. There were boy scouts, long thin men, acrobats, engineers, firemen, and contractors. They were men with dark skin, with red hair, with fierce accents and waving hands. Some wore patched pants; others, well-cut business suits. All were drawn by the human drama, wanting to help. By daybreak people throughout the world were invisible spectators. Newspapers, radios, and television put aside war and international news to headline the story of a desperate rescue attempt.

"Bill Yancy, a thirty-eight-year-old contractor who was one of the nation's underwater demolition men who often cleared the water of mines in the fortified beaches long before the first troops landed, was on the scene. He was the last man out of the hole. At one stretch he moved back five back-breaking feet of earth in less than half an hour.

"An ex-sandhogger and boilermaker left his home in San Fernando Valley the minute he heard of the accident. In spite of the stabbing pain of a hernia this man stayed at his dangerous job beneath the ground until he himself collapsed and was rushed to the hospital.

"The father of five children sneaked out of his own home to volunteer his help, although he had not done any deep excavation work for a long time. 'I didn't want to worry my wife,' he said, 'but I have good reasons at home.' There were so many more.

"The parallel hole reached the fifty-seven-foot level early Saturday morning. The parallel hole had been started the night before. By Saturday night a steel casing had been completed in the new shaft, but workers hit a sand pocket and water had flowed into the tunnel. Pumping began desperately. Seldom had so much prayer power been focused on one person or on any one rescue. Exhausted gray-faced men continued their dangerous work around water, sand, and cascades of rock.

"And what was happening around the world! Men on a lonely

watch on a ship far at sea followed the progress and took up a collection. Hard coalminers in Denver had offered help, a neighbor brought a chocolate cake, the only offering she could think of. One unidentified man brought over seven hundred gallons of coffee and stacks of doughnuts for the workers.

"Meanwhile, sitting side by side in a parked car during most of these frantic operations were the girl's white-faced mother and father. Beneath the giant machines and rigging, bright lights, and microphones booming directions lay a tiny figure whom none of these gallant rescuers had ever seen. Was all well with her? Was there water where she lay? Did she know moments of consciousness and fear?

"Fifty-three hours later, after a total expenditure of a half-million dollars, Bill Yancy was lowered into the rescue shaft on a bucket fastened to the end of a cable. The trapped girl's own doctor, clad in a blue jacket, aviator's cap, and dungaree trousers, began his descent while the world waited above. Then the answer came up. Men had lost. Kathy Fiscus, the little girl whom the whole world had come to know, was dead. She had gone shortly after she had last spoken.

"And that was all the facts I had to report but not the end of the story. I knew there was something to explain the frantic, futile fight. I looked around the city room. There were the usual reports — wars, strikes, famine, family in trouble, racial problems — and suddenly I saw the contrast. There on the vacant lot in San Marino, California, the whole world had united for a few hours over the life of one little child. Men had *not* lost. The little girl had got people loving one another. No distinction of color, race or creed, rich or poor rose to mar the efforts of men and women who fought to save one who was made in his image. That was the story, that was the miracle, of little Kathy Fiscus."

Was that effort worth it? What price would you place upon the physical well-being of a soul? Well, I don't think we'd argue the case in point. I suppose the parallel question is what price would you place upon the spiritual soul of an individual. I am representing your children, remember, and I would like to ask you this question. Are you preparing spiritually to teach me, the whole person, when I come into your care and keeping? I remember the incident in the life of Horace Mann, the great educator. He was speaking, as I recall, to a dedicatory service for a new school. In the course of his remarks he said, "The great investment we have made together [and it was in the multi-thousands of dollars in those days] for this building will be worth it all, if we save but one child." Following his address he was approached by one who challenged him: "Didn't you overstate that just a trifle?"

"Not if that one child were mine," he replied.

Second, would you remember that I have needs to be met and a soul to be nourished? There's a tendency of parents and educators to forget what it is that they are about and to concentrate upon their own needs. I see in you the great challenge to refocus that attention on the lives of the young people whom you will influence.

I'm reminded of the experience a teacher had who had taken a few history classes at the university and then brought back his cynicism into the junior high school by debunking the religious faiths of his students. One mother went to the teacher and reminded him of his responsibilities. She said, "Remember, we hired you to teach our boys skills, not to undermine their faith." Oh, how educators, parents, and you young people need to have burned into your souls the words of Edward Markham:

> We are all blind until we see
> That in the human plan
> Nothing is worth the making
> If it does not make the man.
> Why build these cities glorious
> If man unbuilded goes?
> In vain we build the world, unless
> The builder also grows.

Let me just make a couple of suggestions. As you prepare to enter into the covenant of marriage, you have a tremendous opportunity not only to put your own houses in order and train up the young people that will be sent to you, but also to take active involvement in community and church affairs. What we need today is a group of delightful young leaders like you who can set society correct.

I was impressed by a young Texas housewife. Let me share her little story showing what one person involved in proper values can do. More than ten years ago Mrs. Gabler decided that something was wrong with some of the books used in Texas schools when one of her sons asked some questions about the Constitution of the United States. "It seemed to me that my children were not learning it like they ought to," Mrs. Gabler said. "What really bugged me was that the textbooks seemed to divide the children from their parents — especially the social studies, which appeared to teach a child a philosophy quite foreign from that of the parents." Mrs. Gabler questioned eight paperback civil government books from a noted publisher. For fourteen-year-old pupils, the books took up a large amount of space on how to apply for welfare. This series could not do as it claimed — motivate children for citizenship — because the texts were based on a false premise. They were almost completely negative in that they explained the bad and emphasized it. They had nothing of beauty or encouragement to challenge students to become better men and women.

Mrs. Gabler said she and her husband, with the help of mothers (and she was the rallying effort), caused the state of Texas to reject the education commission recommendation on such books, to reject the fifth-grade history that had a sentence or two on each of five different pages about George Washington but a six-page spread about Marilyn Monroe. She also objected to passages in the text which she claimed separated the young people from a religious way of life. One placed a farm leader, Cesar

Chavez, and the late Martin Luther King on a par with our Lord and Savior, Jesus Christ.

These are real influences in our life. Consider the Idaho community where young people like you got together because the parents of your generation would not close down an X-rated theater. I'm always reminded of the simple lesson that President Kimball so often teaches just by his very presence. He related to the General Authorities a little experience that occurred to him one day at the hospital. He was going in for a very close check, perhaps an operation on his throat. We were aware of that and were quite concerned. Being somewhat medicated in preparation for surgery, he was being wheeled down the hospital aisle by an orderly on one of those transporting tables. In trying to maneuver the table with President Kimball on it to the elevator, the orderly caught his finger between the table and the elevator door. He let out a string of words among which he took the Lord's name in vain. Let me ask you a question. What would you have done? Just passed it by because that's what people do? The President of our Church, sick as he was and partly medicated, raised his head and said to the young orderly, who was perhaps even a member of the Church, "Please, please, young man, don't talk that way about my best friend." Well, you can imagine the lesson that was taught to the young boy by the prophet of the Lord.

Now you go into the locker room or in the dressing room; you are even around Latter-day Saints who sometimes forget their standards and quality. Can you be counted upon to stand up and gently and lovingly set society in order? That's what will be needed as you take your places as parents and future leaders in our great society. As you consider the needs of your young people, would you also not forget to educate the spirit along with the body? Do you remember what Theodore Roosevelt said on one occasion? "To educate a man in mind and not in morals is to educate a menace to society." John Dickey put it this way: "The end of education is to see man made whole both in competence and conscience, for to create the power of competence without creating a corresponding direction to guide the use of that power is bad education; furthermore, competence will finally disintegrate apart from conscience."

Third, would you remember (and I'm still speaking for your children) how to keep me inspired and reminded about my worth, my responsibility, my potential? The home plays a vital role here, and I think so vital. Understanding, as you and I know, is perhaps one of the greatest of all ingredients in God's wonderful plan.

Permit one other little story in this connection. A man was putting up a sign in a window: "Puppies for Sale." Before he had driven the last nail there was a small boy standing at his side. That kind of sign seems to attract small boys. The youngster wanted to know how much the puppies were going to cost. The man told him that they were very good dogs and that he did not expect to let any of them go for less than thirty-five to fifty dollars. There was a look of disappointment and then a question: "I've got $2.37. Could I look at them?" The man whistled and called, "Lady."

Out of the kennel and down the runway came Lady, followed by four or five little balls of fur and one lagging considerably behind. The boy spotted the lagger and, pointing, asked, "What's wrong with him?" The reply was that the veterinarian had said that there was no hip socket in the right hip and that the dog would always be lame. The boy's immediate rejoinder was: "That's the one I want to buy. I'll give you $2.37 and 50¢ a month until I get him paid for." The man smiled and shook his head. "That's not the dog you want. That dog will never be able to run, jump, and play with you." The boy very matter-of-factly pulled up his little trouser leg and revealed a brace running down both sides of his badly twisted leg and under the foot, with a leather cap coupled over the knee. "I don't run so well myself," he said, "and he'll need somebody that understands."

I don't suppose there's any greater attribute you can take into marriage and into parenthood than real understanding. Mrs. James Parker, president of the National Congress of Parents and

Teachers, made this statement: "Boys and girls are not delivered as raw material to the school door; they are products of four or five or six years of processing in their homes. More and more we can realize what the school can do is to develop a child's potential, but it's limited by what the home has already done and is doing for him or her."

What can the home do? Well, I think that this audience, of all audiences, knows; for that has been our theme in the Church since the restoration of the gospel. The home provides the child's positive or negative self-concept, the child's propensity to work or just get by, the child's ability to get along with others, the love of learning, attitudes toward community and church leaders, and goals to achieve such as Church service, missions, happy marriage, and worthwhile, contributing operations and occupations.

How are these attitudes learned? Well, I remember what my father-in-law taught me many years ago. He wasn't even a member of the Church. He said, "Paul, will you remember, *remember*, that you don't teach anybody anything: you help them find it within themselves." And then he made this very distinct statement: "Religion is caught, not taught." And I've never forgotten it. You and I catch a lot of truths by what we are and what we are trained up to be. In my experience there is no such thing as an identity crisis or a poor self-image to the youth. There is no such thing; I just don't believe it. I think every young person knows from instinct that he is a child of God, and you and I need to reinforce that as parents in the home.

May I just say a word about our collective self-image. We are engaged today in a national self-assessment, and we don't like what we see. We have become our own self-accusers. We have seen our prestige slip, and we are starting to believe what others are writing and saying about us — that we are second-rate. What a wonderful opportunity for you as the leaders of this country, as parents in your homes, to reassess that thinking and redirect it in the lives of young people who will come under your influence.

Now, I get pretty tender on this point. I served as a lonely soldier in a great conflict some years ago. I just think somehow you and I and your children have got to get the lump back in the throat when we see the flag, when we hear our national anthem, when we read about our history and review the great contributions of this country and its preparation by the Lord himself. I recall helping to shoot a lock off of a concentration camp in an island in the Pacific. I won't attempt to describe the filth and the misery, the pain and the muck I saw there. Three thousand people had been incarcerated for over three years. Over thirty babies had been born that year alone — all with terrible malnutrition and disease.

As I was helping to evacuate these natives back to a safe part on the beach where medical aid and comfort could be given, I was interrupted by a thump on my boot. I looked down, and wallowing in the mud was a human being. I later learned he was a sixty-seven-year-old Protestant minister who had been trapped on that island during the invasion. He was six feet one inch and weighed eighty-five pounds. We got him on a stretcher and cleaned the mud off his face, and I asked what I could do to help. As we were preparing for evacuation (I'll never forget this lesson in American history), he said, "Soldier, do you have a flag?"

I said, "I don't have one on me, but I can get one." We secured one from a local jeep, I handed it to him, and he held it on his bosom and welled up with tears. He said to me (I was nineteen years old at the time), "Thank God you came."

I have often thought, as I looked through my daughter's history book, "Where is that kind of feeling — that 'Thank God you came'?" I saw one battle in which I took part described in a U.S. history book for eleventh grade, and it gave us two lines. That kind of hurts my feelings — not because I was so important out there, but because I saw the price that some of my buddies paid for those two lines in that history book. I hope you have the sense to instill in your youth, your children, the desire for patriotism in defense of this country and love of God with it, because it's important. I think your precept here will be important, and how you do it and the way you do it will make the difference in the outcome of this great nation of ours.

Please, my beloved young people, make your home a gospel-centered home. I hope you are taking time in your classes now to prepare to give for the future. I know school is school, and sometimes (with all due respect to your wonderful teachers) you have to sift through the chaff to get the grain. You may wonder, but it's there. I challenge you to find it and prepare. Don't waste a minute in these vital years in your education.

I was touched by a little poem that came to my attention some time ago. As a teacher I try to collect these. Louise Strobeck put it this way:

> As I pass up the aisle between the rows of desks,
> Sometimes a little hand creeps out to touch my dress,
> Not because the fabric is rich or fine,
> But just because it happens to be mine.
>
> There was another garment long ago,
> And other hands reached out to touch His hem —
> A gesture of reverence and love and gratitude,
> For tender thoughts of them
> Makes me very humble, and I see
> A little hand reach out to touch me.

Now, there are thousands of little hands that will reach out to touch you, and I hope and pray that you will have the courage and the strength and the preparation to reach back in a way that the Lord would have you do.

Finally: as you go through life in preparation for these great honors that will be bestowed upon you, be enthused! Get excited about what this life is and what this Church offers. If I have one concern as I travel around the world, it's in seeing a Latter-day Saint who doesn't have that vision. We ought to *bounce* through life. My dad taught me a great lesson many years ago. He said:

"Paul, when you grow up, if you aren't careful, you'll be a little disappointed. You'll look around the Church, and you'll see a lot of Latter-day Saints who have gone to seed. That isn't everybody, and I don't want you to do it. Remember life is a journey process; too many Mormons are camping. You move, boy, and move fast." I have been trying to move ever since. Life *is* a journey, not a camp. You and I have got to break camp. We've got to do it enthusiastically.

You know, when you travel around this Church you see Mormons everywhere. You can't get on a plane without being with one or two of them. They see you and you see them. It's kind of fun. I find that people kind of test you in these situations. I like to test them. I got on a plane the other day in San Francisco going home. The stewardess brought me a cup of coffee and said, "Here you are, sir."

I said: "Good heavens, you've got me confused with somebody else! I didn't order that."

"I know," she said, "but I'm just testing you, Elder Dunn."

Well, I like to test you. When I get on a plane, and when I find that I'm not recognized, I have a little fun in reverse. Once I was coming back from New York, and then I got on a transfer at Chicago. I had just gotten seated and was strapping myself in the seat. Lo and behold, on the plane comes a returned missionary. We can spot them everywhere. They may not think so, but we can, and I caught his eye and nodded at him. He nodded, but there was no recognition, so he went on back to the other cabin, took his seat, and we got airborne. I thought I would just check him out and see if he really knew, so I walked back and forth two or three times, and it didn't register. Then I noticed that there were two open seats beside him, and so I thought, "I'm going to really give him the whole test." I got a magazine and said, "Pardon me, young man, is that seat taken?"

I knew right then what kind of missionary we had because he said, "No, sir, sit down." And that was all I needed to know. I sat down, opened up my magazine, and got real involved. I watched out of the corner of my eye his approach, and I saw him gird up his loins, fresh courage take. He cleared his voice and said, "Pardon me, sir, what do you know about the Mormons?"

"Oh," I said, "I know a little bit."

"Would you like to know more?"

I said, "I believe I would." Now, that isn't a lie, is it? Before I could get another word out, he opened up his briefcase, took out one of those portable flannelboards, and put it on the seat between us. Out came his flipcharts, and in the next 2½ hours I got four complete lessons. He was terrific! He was enthused. He was excited. He knew what it was all about. I thought, "Now I'm going to give him the supreme test." So I asked him every miserable, hard question I have ever been asked. He looked at me and said, "Ah, sir, you're missing the point."

I said, "How am I missing the point?"

"You're not listening with your heart; you're arguing with your head. Now listen," he said. "I'm going to bear my testimony, and you'll know what I know." He bore his testimony. It was sweet and wonderful. I wanted to be rebaptized. Well, he was great. As we finished the fourth lesson, we circled over the Wasatch Range and headed into Salt Lake Valley. All of a sudden without any notice he closed his book and said, "I've got to quit."

"What's the matter? This is getting good."

He said, "I'm home."

"Where's home?"

"Right here."

"Well," I said, "Where have you been?"

"I have been on a mission for the Mormon Church."

"Was it worth it?" I asked.

He teared up and said: "Was it worth it? It was the greatest time of my life."

I said, "Anybody here to meet you?"

He nodded, "I think my whole genealogy is here." The plane landed, taxied over to the runway, and there was the sign that you could see had been made in family home evening — about twenty feet long. "Welcome home, Elder So-and-so." The plane stopped, the door opened, and he said, "Would you mind if I got out ahead of you?"

I said: "Not at all. I love to watch a successful missionary come home anytime." What a scene that was! Down the ladder he went. You didn't have to tell me who his mother was. She had broken security. As she ran over to him, she swept him off the bottom rung of that ladder and spun him around. Behind her came the little five- or six- or seven-year-old brother, proud of his big brother. He grabbed hold of his brother's thigh, held on, and all I heard him mumble was "my brother." Behind him was the sweet little thing who had waited. You elders ought to know that they *do* once in a while. She wanted to be proper. You could tell she had come from the right kind of environment, so she put out her hand to shake his. That didn't quite seem to fit, so she pulled it back and then she kind of looked to see if heaven was looking. Finally she let her womanly instincts take over, grabbed that kid, and introduced a whole new technique. When that boy came up, he was looking for President Kimball and all the Brethren. Behind her came the father. You can always tell a father, can't you? Kind of proud, puffed up, but he doesn't want to show it. He had his hands in his belt, kind of sauntered over, and his look said, "That's my boy." They embraced as dads and sons do, patted each other on the shoulder, and I knew exactly what kind of home that was. So I tried to get out of there, made a right-hand run, but while the dad was patting the son he saw me. "Elder Dunn," he said, "Were you on that plane?"

And the boy said, "Elder who?" Well, he turned and came over, and I walked back and said, "It's true, and I just want to say this, Elder: Thank God for young people like you." And I thank that family.

I thank God for young people like you — great, wonderful youth who have a tremendous future and who have so much responsibility and obligation put upon your shoulders. I'm not really worried how you will turn out. You've got a few challenges.

Who hasn't? That's what you and I were sent to this world for. You've been blessed by having people placed in your midst to give you that reassurance, to know with assurance that Jesus is the Christ and that God lives. I know that God lives and that Jesus is the Christ. I have great faith in you — great trust. You're terrific. Now go out there and show the world how to do it.

9

Being a Priesthood Man

In a recent conference, our prophet stirred our souls with a profound message concerning our young people, and it caused me to do a great deal of thinking, some soul-searching in my own life. I went home with his thoughts on my mind and reread a letter that had appeared in the *Deseret News* just a few nights before. I thought it was significant as it applies to father-son relationships. May I just share a part of it with you.

A young navy man wrote to an advice column in the paper. He said: "Before I came into the service, I felt I knew just about everything. I was sure my parents no longer needed me, and all that I could think of was the day that I could be on my own. The first time I realized how much my parents cared for me was the day they took me to the train station to see me off. When my father said good-bye to me, he broke down and cried. I have never seen my father cry before, and I shall never forget it as long as I live. I have had a lot of time to think. I never told my father that I loved him. I gave both my parents a hard time when they tried to guide me for my own good. Now I write home every chance I get, and I am trying to make up for the heartaches I must have caused them, and for my failure to be a better son. When my next leave comes up, I am going straight home and really get acquainted with my wonderful parents. I have written this letter in hopes that other thoughtless teenagers will wake up before it is too late. Thanks for letting me get this off my chest."

Contrast that, if you will, with an experience I had just a few weeks ago as I came through the Los Angeles terminal on my way to Salt Lake City. While waiting for my flight, I was approached by a former acquaintance from Southern California. As we exchanged greetings as you do on such occasions, he hurried to tell me that he was seeing his boy off. His son was entering the army. When he learned that I was to be on the same plane, he said, "Paul, would you be kind enough to sit with my son as far as Salt Lake?" I told him that I would be more than pleased to do so.

So it was, and I got reacquainted with the young man, who had matured considerably since we had last met. As we sat together we talked about the little things that mean a great deal to young people, and he commenced to tell his story of what his mom and dad had meant to him and what a great influence his home life had had on him.

He said: "You know, Brother Dunn, going back to Fort Dix doesn't really worry me. I know I will be lonesome, and I will be homesick, but what my folks have taught me will see me through." He said: "You will never know what a thrill it was to have had my own father place his hands upon my head and give me a father's blessing. I believe I will be able to withstand all the temptation in the world."

While we can rejoice with the first young man upon his finally catching the vision and realizing the efforts of well-meaning parents, I think we also realize that many like him who have received the advantages of close relationship with their parents are never fortunate enough to make his discovery. How much more desirable, in our understanding of the gospel, that our children constantly receive through their growing years the added strength, security, comfort, and closeness of our love and concern! Let's look for just a moment at some of the ingredients we could build into our lives that more nearly bring the desired results.

When a young couple is married by one of the Lord's appointed leaders, a new Church unit is officially organized. The man becomes the leader of this new and basic unit of the Church. Just as a new bishop is given divine authority to preside over a ward, so is the new husband given divine authority to preside over his home and family. A bishop is given the responsibilities of presiding over meetings, of directing the affairs of all the ward auxiliaries, and of watching over the spiritual and physical welfare of all ward members.

The husband is given similar responsibilities within his family. It is his calling, among other things, to preside over the family, to look after their spiritual, moral, and physical well-being, to conduct family home evenings, to hold family prayers. Like the bishop, the father's priesthood aids him in this great calling, and it gives him wisdom and inspiration that he is entitled to receive from heaven.

Unlike the bishop, who will some day be released from his responsibility, the husband, and later the father, is never released. His position is an eternal one, and it cannot and should not be delegated to another. I say "should not" because in some cases this great assignment is lost by default. This is contrary to the Lord's will. President Joseph F. Smith said on one occasion: "This patriarchal order has its divine spirit and purpose, and those who disregard it under one pretext or another are out of harmony with the spirit of God's laws as they are ordained for recognition in the home. It is not merely a question of who is perhaps the best qualified. Neither is it wholly a question of who is living the most worthy life. It is a question largely of law and order. . . ." (*Priesthood and Church Government*, page 83.)

To this Elder John A. Widtsoe added: "In the Church no adjustment can be made. The priesthood always presides and must, for the sake of order. The women of a congregation [and I must add family] — many of them — may be wiser, far greater in mental powers, even greater in natural power of leadership than the men who preside over them. That signifies nothing. The priesthood is not bestowed on the basis of mental power but is given to good men and they exercise it by right of divine gift, called upon by the leaders of the Church. Woman has her gift of equal magnitude, and that is bestowed on the simple and weak as well as upon those who are great and strong." (*Priesthood and Church Government,* page 90.)

The husband and father is the one the Lord has appointed as the leader of his family. For him to allow his presiding right to fall upon his wife's shoulders is no more in accord with the Lord's government than for a bishop to allow someone else to preside over his ward.

Thus we see, brethren, that as priesthood holders we have the right and obligation to direct our families. Those of us who are already husbands and fathers have the opportunity to exercise that right. Others who are younger will someday have the same opportunity. We must be aware, however, that like all great rights this one of leadership over the home is coupled with great responsibilities, and it is only by fulfilling these responsibilities that we as husbands and fathers can lead by love and understanding rather than by force or dictatorship.

Certainly a bishop who carries out his responsibilities brings great blessings to the ward over which he presides. Fathers should also bring such blessings to the members of their families. It occurs to me that there are three definite ways, among many, by which a husband can bless his particular family.

First, the father can be a blessing to his family by the way he lives, by his attitude, and by his example. Family life, as we all know, often gets disrupted. It is amazing what can happen in a home because of a lost shoe, a telephone conversation that lasts too long, or an ungranted request for the family car. Yes, families do face crises from time to time. The question we must ask is: What is our role as the family leader in these situations — how can our attitudes set the pace for other family members?

One father reports that each night when he returns home from work he pauses just before entering the front door and offers a prayer something like this: "Heavenly Father, may my presence in this home bring faith and a cheerful good evening to those that I love. May my homecoming strengthen my family and bring us closer together. Keep my voice even, calm, that I may build confidence and respect of me as their father, husband, and friend."

This man realized his role and also his responsibility. Being a blessing to our families by attitude and example is not always easy. Certainly part of our prayers should be for strength in this vital area.

One of the best ways to teach your sons respect for womanhood and its associated virtues is to respect your wife and their mother. One teenage son reported to a teacher that his highest standard while dating was the way he had observed his dad always treating his mother — by example, which is the best and the greatest lesson. He had learned that womanhood was worthy of his greatest respect.

Let your children know of the love that you have for your wife. Just the other day one of my daughters was a little bit upset at her mother. She came to me to point out what she thought were some of her mother's shortcomings. I listened to her for a moment and then I broke in, and I said: "Now just a minute. I suppose you know whom you are talking about. Remember, your mother is my sweetheart, and I have chosen her to be my partner forever." Needless to say, the criticism stopped rather abruptly. Now, in relation to our children: The best way to set an example is to do the things that should be done. I read recently a modern parable called "The Prodigal Father." In this parable a father admits the fact that somehow other things became more important to him than his son — his work, the country club, and various other activities. When he realized the errors, he returned to the son, but the son did not want him back; it was too late.

It is a busy life we lead. One father said he would like to spend more time with his family, but he would have to be released from other duties first. Such a father should ask himself, "When was I released as a father?" Let's not wait until it is too late, brethren; let's be a blessing to our children by spending some quality time with them now.

Second, a father can be a blessing to the family by teaching his children gospel principles. Parents, by their very nature and the responsibility given to them by the Lord, are teachers. Today, for example, one of the great challenges facing all parents is to teach their children how to live a well-balanced, spiritual life in a materialistic world.

One of our leading authorities stated recently that whereas in the past there were only two institutions outside the family that influenced our children, the school and the church, now there is a third one — advertising. We have heard a great deal about this in our conference. Advertisers would lead our young people to believe that nothing we desire should be withheld from us. A priesthood father has a real responsibility to teach his sons and daughters the true nature of things and their proper value.

Let me share a brief experience of a priesthood father, my own. When I was about two years old, my family moved to the southern states, and there I spent the early part of my life. This was during the depression, and things were hard; but, fortunately for us, the Dunn family had it reasonably easy. My father was well-paid for his labor. I remember, as a young, aspiring athlete, wanting to approach Dad on one occasion for a new ball glove; and being the child psychologist that I was, I knew that timing was everything. I plotted and schemed for the right moment to approach him, and it finally came.

I heard him come into the driveway and slam the car door and enter the house quickly. He entered the house whistling. That was always a good sign. My mother unknowingly had helped me to set the stage by fixing one of his favorite meals.

After dinner was over he had occupied his usual rocking chair and picked up the paper. I let him get through the heavy part, knowing that that was not a good time to interrupt, and then I tiptoed in at the appropriate moment. I had an old worn-out mitt that wouldn't see me through another game, and I thought certainly he would understand my needs and would give the money without question. Well, I held the glove behind me, and as I stood looking at my father, I said, "Dad, how are you feeling?"

He assured me he was in good shape.

I said: "You have always taught your boys that whenever you do a thing in this life, you ought to do it right. Is that correct?"

He said: "That's right. I am glad you know it."

I said: "You have always taught us that when you do a job, you need the best equipment. Is that right?"

"That's right. I am glad that got through."

And then I said: "Whenever your boys perform, you have taught us to give it the best we have. Is that right?"

He said, "That is exactly right."

"All right," I said, "That is the reason I am here, sir. I want to show you something," and I brought the glove out.

He said, "Good heavens, what is it?"

I said: "It is a ball glove, and I need a new one. It will only cost $7.50 and I need the money right now. I have a big game Friday night and I am to pitch. If you will give me the money I'll be on my way and we'll both be happy."

He reached in his pocket and took out his pencil and his little notebook, and then I knew I had lost the battle. He went to work figuring. The going rate at that time for a boy my age was, I think, something like ten cents an hour. He said, "Why, Paul, that will only cost you seventy-five hours of labor." And I thought, how can a man be that cruel?

And so we went to work figuring out projects, and sure enough some four or five weeks later when I turned in my work slips, I was handed the $7.50 that I had earned. I remember going down to select that ball glove and as I put it on my hand, I patted the pocket for just the right fit. I bought a ten-cent can of linseed oil in order to put it in proper shape.

I learned a great lesson that day. Of all the gloves I had ever owned, that glove was never left in the rain or for someone else to care for. I was a proud young man, but more specifically, young priesthood bearers, I began to see the point of a "welfare" dad and the principles he taught. The time has now come when my father isn't with me anymore, but the principles he taught remain, and I will always be able, I think, to stand and look the world in the eye because a dad cared.

I think the third point or way that a father can bring blessings to his family is by using his priesthood to bless in times of need. When I say in times of need, I do not mean just in times of illness.

One father told me just the other day that before each of his children enters school for the year he calls them into his study where they have a personal talk about the coming year and their particular role in it. In concluding the discussion, the father asks each child if he or she would like a special blessing concerning the important time that lies ahead. Each child has readily agreed to such a blessing, and the father remarks that on few occasions is the Lord's Spirit ever more evident.

You will note that this father asked the children if they wanted a blessing. This is in order, as it should be. The father knows of the importance of such blessings, whereas the child has yet to learn. It is through receiving the blessings that the child comes to know of their importance.

One father's son was going to leave for the army the next day. The father noticed all the preceding day that his son had something he seemed to want to say, but somehow he couldn't muster the courage to say it. Finally, in the evening the son spoke, "Dad, I don't know how to say this, but I would sure like a blessing."

The father was, of course, thrilled, as you would be, but it is too bad that the son felt so hesitant in making the request. Let's make it easy for our families to ask for blessings by giving them regularly in times of need — such times as when children are leaving for summer camp, when they take important tests, when they give talks, when they leave for college, when they leave for missions or for the service, when they embark in marriage — all times when a priesthood and father's blessing could be a comforting and strengthening influence.

Brethren, I challenge each of us to do several things: First, assume the responsibility of leadership in our homes. Second, bring blessings to our homes by honoring our wives, by being courteous and kind. Spend quality time with our children. By quality time, I mean time when we are with our children in body, mind, and spirit. Just being home is not enough. Third, let us take every opportunity to teach our children correct principles as we assume our rightful roles as teachers in the home. Finally, let us make priesthood blessings more a part of the family experience.

Just the other day another father told me of a great experience. He said he was sitting in his living room, visiting with his family late Sunday afternoon, when his little eight-year-old son asked him this question, "Daddy, are you going to sacrament meeting tonight?" The father replied, "Yes, son." The son then asked, "Why?"

And while the father contemplated what profound answer he might give to the question, the little seven-year-old sister who was sitting also at the father's knee said very quickly and simply, "Because he is a priesthood man, that's why." The father could not have been more proud.

And may I say, brethren, that more important than being a Princeton man, a Yale man, a Harvard man, or any other kind of man, is the honor of being a "priesthood man."

10

Parents, Teach Your Children

One of the basic tenets of The Church of Jesus Christ of Latter-day Saints is that we believe in continuous revelation. It is our testimony to the world that God communicates to prophets today the same as he did in ancient times. God's revelations in times past have been sustained and revered in holy scripture. New revelation is the mind and will of the Lord through current prophets, and when they speak when moved upon by the Holy Ghost it is "the *will* of the Lord, . . . the *mind* of the Lord, . . . the *word* of the Lord, . . . the *voice* of the Lord, and the *power* of God unto salvation." (D&C 68:4. Italics added.)

President Spencer W. Kimball some years ago made this observation:

"Sunday night, April 7, the great Tabernacle was closed, the lights turned out, and the record machines stopped, the door locked, and another historical conference became history. It will have been lost motion — a waste of time, energy, and money — if its messages *are not heeded.* In the seven two-hour sessions and in the several satellite meetings, truths were taught, doctrines expounded, exhortations given, enough to save the whole world from all its ills — and [he concluded] I mean from *all* its ills. . . ." (Spencer W. Kimball, "In the World But Not of It," *Speeches of the Year,* 1968, pages 2-3.)

I would like to direct some thoughts to parents everywhere, and I pray that my message will be heeded.

An oft-quoted passage of scripture and revelation of the Latter-day Saints is contained in the Doctrine and Covenants:

"And again, inasmuch as parents have children in Zion, or in any of her stakes which are organized, that teach them not to understand the doctrine of repentance, faith in Christ the Son of the Living God, and of baptism and the gift of the Holy Ghost by the laying on of hands, when eight years old, the sin be upon the heads of the parents." (D&C 68:25.)

I don't know how many times you have heard this passage of scripture, but certainly no counsel could be more timely or pertinent to the problems besetting families throughout the world. How many times have parents said to themselves after hearing this message, "I know it's true and I know what the Lord expects, but how do I *do* it?" In other words, how do I become an effective teacher of the gospel to my own children?

As I have thought about this, it has been my observation that most parents really want to be good parents. Most want to do a better job. May we consider then four things that parents can do that will help them to better achieve success in rearing their children in righteousness?

First, I would itemize the power of parental precept. Parents teach two ways. The first is by precept — or what we say by way of teaching correct principles to our children.

I am reminded of the father who, in gathering his children together one morning, asked, "What would you learn of me?"

The reply came: "How shall we care for our bodies? How shall we play? How shall we work together? How shall we live with our fellowmen? How shall we pray? How shall we know God? For what ends shall we live?"

And the father pondered these words and sorrow was in his heart, for his own life and teaching touched not these things.

You may recall the old farmer who had quite a reputation for being a philosopher. He said, "You can no more teach what you ain't got than you can go back to where you ain't been."

I recall as a young man when I first heard our text quoted from the Doctrine and Covenants, I went to my own mother and exclaimed, "Well, Mom, how does it feel to have all my sins on your head?" Then she taught me the lesson of that passage. She said: "Ah, Paul, you forgot to read carefully what the Lord said. He said that the sin be upon the head of parents if they do not teach their children the principles of the gospel. And you've been taught!"

And I had been taught! Thank the Lord for parents who realize their responsibility to instill in their children the principles of the gospel and who follow the counsel of the Lord's prophets. Parents in the Church today have been counseled to regularly, consistently, and inspiringly hold family home evenings and to take advantage of other great teaching moments to so acquaint their children.

The second way would be the power of parental example. Ralph Waldo Emerson said, "What you do thunders so loudly in my ears I cannot hear what you say." Will you remember this little couplet:

> Parents can tell but never teach
> Until they practice what they preach.

I'm grateful for the example of a father who, as a busy executive of a great supermarket chain, still found the time to demonstrate by his concern that groceries were less important than his boy.

Like many young men, I once had a paper route; and I had to get up early in the morning to deliver them. One morning I woke up and looked outdoors to see one of those torrential Arkansas downpours. I thought we were in for another flood! As I prepared to go out in that rain, my father came into the room dressed in his business suit. "Get in the car, Paul," he said. "I'll drive you around your route this morning." This meant that he would have to go without his own breakfast.

On that morning, in addition to the heavy rain, the papers came late. By the time we had them delivered, it was considerably past the hour that my father had to be to work. And on this particular morning he had scheduled a very important board meeting. He arrived at the meeting late, walked into the board room, and announced, "I'm sorry I'm late, gentlemen, but I had to deliver my papers this morning."

Do you think that there was ever any doubt in my mind as to my father's greatest concern? Interestingly, I don't recall too many lessons my parents verbally taught, but their example is still a part of me till this day.

Third, remember the power of parental love. Recently I came across a little article by Doris Jehnke entitled "Saturday with a Teenage Daughter." It seems all too typical of parent-daughter relationships these days. Let me share it with you.

"Are you going to sleep all day? . . . Who said you could use my hairspray? . . . Clean the dishes off the table . . . Turn down the radio . . . Have you made your bed? . . . Your skirt is much too short . . . Your closet is a mess . . . Stand up straight . . . Somebody has to go to the store . . . Quit chewing your gum like that . . . Your hair is too bushy . . . I don't care if everybody else does have one . . . Turn down the radio . . . Have you done your homework? . . . Don't slouch . . . You didn't make your bed . . . Quit banging on the piano . . . Why don't you iron it yourself? . . . Your fingernails are too long . . . Look it up in the dictionary . . . Sit up straight . . . Get off the phone now . . . Why did you ever buy that record? . . . Take the dog out . . . You forgot to dust that table . . . You've been in the bathroom long enough . . . Turn off the radio and get to sleep now.

"Another day gone, and not once did I say, 'I love you.' " (*Especially for Mormons*, Vol. 1, page 141.)

Too often it is easier to criticize, to point out the faults, than to praise or give love. Mothers and dads, when was the last time you told your children "I love you"?

A good friend of mine makes it a point every day to find

something positive that he can compliment in his children so that he can truly say, "I love you." Will you make the opportunity soon?

Finally, utilize the power of parental prayer. The Book of Mormon provides a great example of a father who recovered a lost son by the power of personal prayer. The conditions of his time are akin to our own day.

"Now it came to pass that there were many of the rising generation that could not understand the words of king Benjamin, being little children at the time he spake unto his people; and they did not believe the tradition of their fathers.

"They did not believe what had been said concerning the resurrection of the dead, neither did they believe concerning the coming of Christ.

"And now because of their unbelief they could not understand the word of God; and their hearts were hardened." (Mosiah 26:1-3.)

One of these of the "rising generation" was Alma the Younger. He was "a man of many words, and did speak much flattery to the people," leading away "many . . . to do after the manner of his iniquities." (Mosiah 27:8.)

We are further told that he was "a great hinderment to the prosperity of the church of God" because of the dissension that he caused. (Mosiah 27:9.)

I suppose the tendency then, as it often seems to be today, was to "write him off." But you know the miraculous story of how an angel of the Lord appeared to that young man and how he became one of the greatest missionaries in the church of Christ. What was it that caused that great change to occur? The angel testified to Alma the following: "Behold, the Lord hath heard the prayers of his people, and also the prayers of his servant, Alma, who is thy father. . . ." (Mosiah 27:14.)

Think of it! The power of parental prayer! As we consider the challenge of rearing children in a world fraught with temptations, false ideologies, and materialistic enticements, do you not feel the need for guidance and inspiration beyond your human capacity? There is no greater help or strength that a father or mother can obtain than through securing that help from the Lord.

Just the other day I had a sweet experience. I stood in the presence of a mother and a father who had just greeted their long-lost son home from the wars — I mean the worldly wars. What a tender moment! I can tell you that their prayers were heard and answered.

Remember what Alma said: "Counsel with the Lord in all thy doings, and he will direct thee for good. . . ." (Alma 37:37.)

I testify to all parents in Zion everywhere to the efficacy of these great principles in rearing our children righteously: the power of precept, the power of example, the power of love, and the power of prayer.

Gathering
Souls

11

The Worth
of Souls
Is Great!

Someone once said, "I am intensely interested in the future because I expect to spend the rest of my days there." I get excited about the young people of the Church because they project that kind of a positive future. We love and trust them.

I am reminded of a short story from Mt. Kisco, New York, reported in the *Reader's Digest*:

"Once upon a time, there was a little red schoolhouse with one big room for twenty-seven children. The teacher sat with an American flag on one side of her and a blackboard on the other. The children sat in rows facing her, the littlest ones in front. The youngest was seven, and she was very little. The biggest was sixteen, and he was six feet tall. The youngest was smart, and she could read with the other children. The biggest was dumb, but he was strong and could help the teacher carry in wood. In bad weather, he carried the littlest girl across the puddle in front of the schoolhouse. And sometimes she helped him with his reading.

"Then one day the state built a big highway, right past the schoolhouse door. And the State Education Department came by and said: 'Great things are happening in education. There are special teachers for arithmetic, reading, art and music. If you combine with other schoolhouses, you could have a great big school where your children could have all the advantages. And big yellow buses could carry your children over the new highway right up to the school door.' So the parents voted to consolidate, and the little red schoolhouse was abandoned.

"At first things went well in the big school. But after a while, the State Education Department said that it wasn't providing the children with enough meaningful experiences. And some parents complained that the children were not learning to read and write and figure as well as they had in the little red schoolhouse. 'We will try some new things,' said the educators. So they tried the ungraded primer, where fast readers were not slowed down by slow readers, and where children who had trouble with numbers did not get moved on to the next grade before they could add 3 and 5. This helped, but not enough.

" 'We will try something more,' the educators said. 'We will tear down some walls at the new school, so the children will be working together in one big room. That way, there will be less peer-group competition.'

"Finally, an important educator came along, looked at the school and said, 'This is good, but it is not good enough. It is too big, and the children are losing their identity. There are not enough interpersonal relationships in the infrastructure. What we really need is a one-room schoolhouse. And since red is a cheerful color, I think we ought to paint it red.' " (From Mt. Kisco, N.Y., "Patent Trader," *Reader's Digest*, March 1973, page 68. Used by permission.)

The educator in this story did not mean that the consolidated school, the special teachers, or the ungraded primer were not advantages. The point of the story is that along with the wonderful new discoveries in education, the emphasis must still be placed upon the individual and upon his needs and relationships with others.

This philosophy applies just as importantly to Church organizations as it does to the little red schoolhouse. In a revelation given to the Prophet Joseph Smith just prior to the organization of the Church, the Lord said:

"Remember the worth of souls is great in the sight of God;

"For, behold, the Lord your Redeemer suffered death in the

flesh; wherefore he suffered the pain of all men, that all men might repent and come unto him.

"And he hath risen again from the dead, that he might bring all men unto him, on conditions of repentance." (D&C 18:10-12.)

Our Lord's response to the Pharisees' question, "Why do they on the sabbath day that which is not lawful?" was, "The sabbath was made for man, and not man for the sabbath." (Mark 2:24, 27.)

I understand from what the Lord has revealed to us through the prophets that *people* are his greatest concern. We are somebody. We are his children, and he continually reveals himself through the prophets so that one day we can be like him.

Programs, then, wonderfully inspired programs, like the Sabbath, exist to help people. If we are not careful, it is very easy to put the mechanics of the program ahead of the person. Jesus was constantly trying to put the spirit back into the letter of the law. Our first priority, I feel, as parents, leaders, and teachers should be the individual within the home or Church program.

I remember some years ago an experience I had while directing one of the religious education programs of the Church in Southern California.

One of my responsibilities as a coordinator was to secure property, eventually erect an institute building, and then provide a religious program for our college youth. We had secured a wonderful institute site adjacent to the Los Angeles State College. Shortly after the transaction was consummated, the state of California indicated to me that they wanted to take the property by right of eminent domain, which was their prerogative. I checked with my superiors and they said, "Look into the legal side and see if we still have a chance." I did. We went into court for a hearing. The judge was impressed with the program of the Church and what we do for youth and people. We were sent back to do some additional homework and gather added information.

The day came for the final hearing. I had about eight hours of work to do in four when at about ten o'clock one morning a knock came at the door. Because of my frustration I almost said (but I didn't), "COME IN!" Instead I said, "Come in." And in the framework of that door stood a nineteen-year-old USC freshman student who had refused our offers to come and join our group on four previous occasions. His head bowed, hands in his pockets, he said, "Brother Dunn, I have got to see you, *now*." And I almost said (but I didn't), "Can't you see I am busy?" Because I was. Fortunately I had the presence of mind to invite him in; and as he took a chair, several questions went through my mind.

Question number one, "What are you going to court for this morning, Paul?" "Well, to try to save a piece of property." "What do you want the piece of property for, Paul?" "Well, to erect a building." "Well, what do you want a building for?" "Well, to teach some students." "What just knocked on your door?" "Oh, a student." And wouldn't you know, he took the whole four hours.

The time came for legal counsel to arrive, and we went to court. I don't know all of the ramifications. We lost the hearing and eventually the piece of property, and it took us two years to secure another site. You would be happy with what the Church has done at Los Angeles State College, but more important, we saved the boy. Had it been your son, I think you would agree that we made the right decision.

God grant us the vision as leaders, teachers, and parents to put people first. Remember the worth of souls is great in the sight of God.

12

"Come Ye After Me"

We have been challenged to return to the fundamentals. If only the world would heed this counsel and get down to the things that matter most.

This reminds me of a little experience I had in Vermont. I was attempting to find a short-cut to the little town of Rutland, and I took one of those exciting back-road routes and soon became hopelessly lost. I came to a fork in the road. I noticed a farmer standing in the field, so I wound down the window and I asked, "Say, fella, does it matter which road I take to Rutland?" He said, "It doesn't matter to me at all." I think sometimes the world has that problem.

In the upper part of New England we sometimes get snow-bound, and once after a rather heavy storm I followed a snowplow into Saint Johnsbury. The town had been isolated for some eight days. Again, I was lost. In seeking help I went into a little country store, and sitting there on the typical cracker barrel was another Vermonter. I asked, "Tell me, sir, what do you do all winter when you get snowbound?" He said, "We just sit and think, mostly sit."

I think that might be a major problem in the world: we are sitting rather than thinking and acting.

Those of you who take an active interest in sports and know of its importance in turning boys into men, cannot forget that great football coach and builder of men, Vince Lombardi. Here was a man who came to a last-place team comprised of men who had forgotten what winning was — a team with no spirit, no confidence, and no respect — and in three short years he turned them into a team of world champions. But being a champion once didn't satisfy Vince Lombardi. He and his team went on to win again and again, game after game, title after title. The Green Bay Packers soon became the winningest team in professional football. Here was a man who could be as mean as a lion, yet gentle as a lamb. A man who said that God and family should come first. A man who taught that not only physical toughness is important, but spiritual and mental toughness are also essential to success, and a man who said to all those who have problems and sometimes get discouraged, "Winning isn't everything, but wanting to win is."

I submit to you that we as a people, member and nonmember alike, can learn some meaningful and timely lessons from the life of that great man.

One of the great attributes of the Church is that we too are building men. As a mission president in New England, I had under my direction some 175 of the finest young men and women anywhere in the world. I had great faith and confidence in them and the things they did, and I have great confidence in the missionaries serving today. We appreciate you fine parents who sacrifice so that your sons and daughters can fulfill missions. You are doing them a great service, and you in turn are being blessed. In private interview and in testimony meetings, missionaries often express love for you and for their families. You may rest assured they are very happy.

I might just say here parenthetically that one of the challenges of a mission president is to keep a physical balance in missionaries as well as the spiritual and mental. I saw two of my assistants upon my return home, and I noticed they had taken off about thirty pounds. (The Saints are good to them in the field.) These same two assistants, in trying to help a little ninety-seven-pound weakling put on a little weight, on one occasion approached him and said, "Elder, it looks like you've been through a famine." And this sharp little elder came right back and said, "And you two look like you caused it."

Since the days of Joseph Smith, over seven hundred million dollars have been spent by parents to send their children on missions. One mother recently said to me, "I agree with you, Brother Dunn, that the accent is on the youth, but the stress is still on the parents."

Sister Dunn and I recently visited with a Harvard professor and his wife who had had some contact with the Church and the missionaries. This learned man, holder of many degrees, and his charming wife had noted something special in these two young men who had borne their testimonies of the reality of God, the divinity of Christ, and of the restoration of the Church in these latter days. As we spoke, this professor said: "Mr. Dunn, what is it that gives these young men such a strong conviction? What is this missionary work really doing for people? What motivates them to give up two years of their lives? Why do you go to those who are already Christian? Wouldn't two years of college be of more value?"

To answer these questions, we turned, as do all missionaries today, to the scriptures, both ancient and modern. We read, for example, in Isaiah and Ephesians of the restoration of all things. We turned to Mark and read the words of Jesus, "Come ye after me, and I will make you to become fishers of men" (Mark 1:17), and "Go ye into all the world, and preach the gospel to every creature" (Mark 16:15).

As the evening progressed, Sister Dunn and I were able to explain to this couple the very purpose and the fruits of missionary work. We told them that a mission helps a young man to find out who he really is. It helps him to set patterns, attitudes, and habits that will carry into his adult life. I just personally believe it is easier to build a boy than to mend a man. We told them that for our young people a mission is life in miniature; it's a journey, not a camp.

We answered their inquiry when we explained to them the visitation of the Father and the Son to the Prophet Joseph in 1820. Although we realize the great good that other churches are doing in the world, the Lord said, and I remind you: "... they teach for doctrines the commandments of men, having a form of godliness, but they deny the power thereof." (Joseph Smith 2:19.)

A mission most of all provides the chance for people to accept the gospel and to take upon them the name of Christ through faith, repentance, baptism, and the gift of the Holy Ghost. The reason we go to those who are already of a Christian faith is because we believe that the *was* in Christianity still *is*. We believe that Paul on the road to Damascus is no different from Joseph Smith in the grove — now called sacred. God speaks today!

About knowledge: We read from Moses that "the glory of God is intelligence." This great educator was much impressed with the Mormon philosophy of education that includes the whole man. College and money are important, and I don't want to minimize them, but in making a living don't forget to make a life. The words of the Savior, filled with truth and wisdom, sounded again as we read, "... what shall it profit a man, if he shall gain the whole world, and lose his own soul?" (Mark 8:36.) A mission teaches that spirituality is important.

I related to this educator and his fine wife how acceptance of the gospel and the way of life can provide the opportunity for people to change attitudes, and thus their lives.

During the past year I have watched one of society's outcasts, an ex-convict, rise from the depths of a prison cell to become a responsible citizen, a worthy Latter-day Saint. This man's life was changed because two of our missionaries brought him a message of hope and of salvation. He had thought because of his past all was lost and his chance had passed. But these two young elders brought him the gospel and a new way of life.

Unfortunately there are some in this world who continue to ignore or invalidate the principle of true repentance and say,

"Once a thief, always a thief," or "Leopards don't change their spots." Need I remind you who say such things that we don't work with leopards; we work with men, and men change every day.

Our missionaries knock on each door knowing and believing that a basic premise of this Church is that when men and women are motivated by the proper spirit, they can and do change their lives. President McKay said that the purpose of the gospel was to make bad men good and good men better.

This same ex-convict whose life was once tattered and scarred with sin sat in our living room not long ago and said: "Brother Dunn, I thank God every day for the elders who brought me the gospel and had the patience to teach me. I know the gospel is true for I have lived it; and although I'm not what I ought to be, and I'm not what I'm going to be, I am *not* what I was."

Such are the fruits of missionary work. Again the words of the Savior ring through the ages to the convert, to the missionaries, to the college professor, to you, and to me. It was Jesus who said that when we lose ourselves in the service of others, then, and only then, can we find ourselves and possess true joy and happiness. Gratitude is the memory of the heart, and if a missionary did no more than to help one convert like this catch the vision of the gospel, his two years would be well spent.

The Lord told us that if we labor all our days and bring save it be one soul to him, great shall be our joy with him in the kingdom of our Father.

As the evening passed, Sister Dunn and I gave this couple from Cambridge a brief history of the missionary system of the Church. We told them of the day when Parley P. Pratt stood in a river for six hours, baptizing people one after the other. We told them how Wilford Woodruff converted eighteen hundred people in eight months. We reviewed the proselyting program of the Church from Samuel Smith in 1831 up to the present day, and we noted that close to one thousand of their New England neighbors would join the Church that year.

The visit ended. We closed with our personal testimony and

extended an invitation to this couple to come join with us. What a spiritual thrill to see distinguished, capable, academic giants humble themselves before the Master and accept his simple gospel teachings! Yes, missionary work is a calling in which one may find many rewards, for true joy comes in giving and teaching the gospel of Jesus Christ.

The first prophet of this dispensation, Joseph Smith, who lived and died a missionary, gave us his summary of the importance of this work when he penned the following to John Wentworth: "Our missionaries are going forth to different nations, and in Germany, Palestine, New Holland, Australia, the East Indies, and other places, the Standard of Truth has been erected; no unhallowed hand can stop the work from progressing; persecutions may rage, mobs may combine, armies may assemble, calumny may defame, but the truth of God will go forth boldly, nobly, and independent, till it has penetrated every continent, visited every clime, swept every country, and sounded in every ear, till the purposes of God shall be accomplished, and the Great Jehovah shall say the work is done." (*Documentary History of the Church*, Vol. 4, page 540.)

13

What Is a Teacher?

I have been thinking a great deal about teaching and great teachers. Elder Marion D. Hanks tells about the situation concerning his departed cousin, a Brother [Ivan] Frame, who had a deep impact on humanity. He mentions that one of the great tributes paid at his funeral was that every boy should have a Brother Frame in his life. I have thought about that, and I thank God repeatedly for such an individual in my life. He was a seventy-eight-year-old man who was assigned to be a priests adviser to six of us who were in our struggling teens and challenged with the future. His name was Charles B. Stewart.

I don't know what you thought about a seventy-eight-year-old man when you were sixteen, but some of us questioned the wisdom of our bishop, for we thought he had literally brought Moses back.

I remember the first day I reported to my class in that rickety old upper room of the Hollywood Ward. There was that kind, gentle man to greet me. He took me by the hand as he had the other boys and said, "You're Harold Dunn's son, aren't you?"

I said, "Yes, sir."

He talked a little bit about me, my family, and showed a great personal interest. And then he said: "Paul, one of the requirements for being a member of this class is to think a new thought every day. Do you have one this morning?"

Well now, I hadn't had a new thought in years, and he could

see my plight, and he said: "All right, I will teach you one. Listen carefully. 'Attention is the mother of memory.' Now can you repeat it back?" And I tried and finally gave it back to him. He permitted me to enter.

We had a wonderful class. It ended; as I went to leave he said, "I forgot to tell you — before you go home you've got to give me another new idea." I thought, I won't go home. I didn't have one, and so he said, "Now listen very carefully and I will teach you one that you'll always remember." He said, " 'Oh, what a tangled web we weave, when first we practice to deceive.' " I've never forgotten it.

Another week passed, and we went through a similar experience. I still didn't have a new thought. He said: "Listen very carefully. 'There's an odd little voice ever speaking within, that prompts us to duty and warns us from sin. And what is most strange, it makes itself heard, though it gives not a sound and says never a word.' " And I've never forgotten that one.

I started to go home and found he wouldn't let me go until I cited another. When I couldn't he said: "Listen carefully. 'There was a wise old owl who sat in an oak, and the longer he sat the less he spoke. The less he spoke, the more he heard. Oh, Paul, why can't you be like that wise old bird?' "

I've thought a lot about that since. Still another week and another great thought. He said: " 'Remember, young man, example sheds a genial ray which men are apt to borrow. So first improve yourself today and then your friends tomorrow.' " And I haven't forgotten that concept either.

Time won't permit a number of others. Two years later I found myself in the fighting forces of our country. I was on the island of Okinawa. I received a letter from Mrs. Stewart, and it told me of the sad news that my kind friend and adviser had passed away. In it she had attached a half-written letter from Brother Stewart to me, and he said: "Dear Paul, I've been thinking about you in that far-off country, discouraged, I'm sure, and somewhat depressed; and in order to build your spirits, I have included some additional gem thoughts." There were twenty-five new ideas, and I have never forgotten them.

Thank God for people who care, for the Frames and Stewarts. I have since counted on my hand five such teachers who have influenced me for good. I would agree with Elder Hanks; there ought to be a Brother Stewart and a Brother Frame in every boy's life.

What is a teacher? The teacher is a prophet. He lays the foundation of tomorrow.

The teacher is an artist. He works with the precious clay of unfolding personality.

The teacher is a friend. His heart responds to the faith and devotion of his students.

The teacher is a citizen. He is selected and licensed for the improvement of society.

The teacher is an interpreter. Out of his mature and wider life, he seeks to guide the young.

The teacher is a builder. He works with the higher and finer values of civilization.

The teacher is a culture-bearer. He leads the way toward worthier tastes, saner attitudes, more gracious manners, higher intelligence.

The teacher is a planner. He sees the young lives before him as a part of a great system that shall grow stronger in the light of truth.

The teacher is a pioneer. He is always interpreting and attempting the impossible, and usually winning out.

The teacher is a reformer. He seeks to improve the handicaps that weaken and destroy life.

The teacher is a believer. He has an abiding faith in God and in the improvability of the race. It was James Truslow Adams who said: "There are obviously two educations. One should teach us how to make a living, and the other how to live."

We are engaged in teaching people how to live.

That was the genius of the Savior. He taught us divine

principles we could apply to ourselves and thus solve our personal problems. The Savior had no peer as a teacher.

For just a moment, let me walk you through the fifteenth chapter of Luke, wherein this great master teacher tells us how to solve problems that we all face. Luke records that there drew near him a great multitude, the publicans, the sinners, the Pharisees, the Sadducees, and he spake unto them this parable, saying: "What man of you, having an hundred sheep, if he lose one of them, doth not leave the ninety and nine . . . and go after that which is lost."

Then he tells about the rejoicing moment when the sheep is found. And then, without even a pause, he goes into a second parable like unto it, which says: "Either what woman having ten pieces of silver, if she lose one piece, doth not light a candle, and sweep the house, and seek diligently till she find it." And she too rejoices with her neighbors. (Luke 15:4, 8.)

And then he goes into that parable of parables, the Prodigal Son: "A certain man had two sons: And the younger of them said to his father, 'Father, give me the portion of goods that falleth to me.' " And we recognize how with his agency he squandered it all. (See Luke 15:11-12.)

I used to wonder, as a teacher so-called, why the Savior would spend time citing three parables about things that get lost. And then one day it dawned. People do get lost in various ways, and here in this great chapter of Luke we find the Savior counseling how to recover them.

Permit me this observation: The Savior might say to us today, if he were to teach this parable again, that sheep (or people who get lost) are not basically sinners by nature or even choice, but people, like sheep, get confused in what's important. In other words, they have misplaced values. And I am sure the Savior would say to the teacher in the classroom, to the adviser, "If you want to retrieve this kind of person, put a higher value in place of the one he now elects." Family, service, brotherhood are all greener pastures for today's sheep. Feeding here brings them home.

Next, he talks about lost coins. These precious coins that become lost are our young people. And there are those of us who are the responsible agents who, like the woman of this great teaching parable, let these priceless gems slip through our fingers. Certainly we wouldn't recover this kind of lost article the way we would a sheep. He would say love, care, and attention would be the process used to recover lost coins (or people).

And then the great parable of the Prodigal Son, with the Savior saying that there are those who get lost by choice; and in the concluding of that parable, he says: "And when he came to himself he [the Prodigal Son] said, How many hired servants of my father's have bread enough and to spare. . . ." (Luke 15:17.)

There are those who get lost because their free agency takes them down that path. We can't do a lot at some points to recover this kind of a person except open our arms and our church doors and let them know they are wanted. Teachers and advisers are really needed here. But note: he came to himself. He repented, sought forgiveness, and came home. Many people are like the Prodigal Son.

Let me just say that this is a *positive* gospel. We ought to be the happiest people in the world. The gospel of Jesus Christ is a great building force. It teaches people to be happy and to always wear a smile. But sometimes we neglect the simple things that mean the most. Most people in the rush of modern life never know real friendship and the warmth that the gospel and even a smile can bring.

An acquaintance of mine recently said to me as we walked down the street and noticed a man with a sour face, "He looks like he was weaned on lemon juice and a dill pickle."

I also heard about a mother and her young daughter who were listening to a public speaker when the child said to her mother,

"Isn't that man happy?" The mother replied, "I guess so." To which the girl remarked, "Why doesn't he tell his face?"

I think our Heavenly Father would be most disappointed if he saw the expressions of some of us who have all that the world contains and fail to incorporate it into our lives and share it with others. The meaning and purpose of the gospel of Jesus Christ to me is that it brings joy and happiness, peace and contentment.

We all have problems. The world is sick with problems. And yet in these sacred words in the standard works are the solutions to the problems we face. Let us encourage the world to know the word of God.

There are forty-three other parables in the New Testament that teach us how to help people. Search the scriptures, for in them ye shall find the way to eternal life.

My testimony is that the gospel is true and that it works.

> I gave a beggar from my store of wealth
> Some gold. He spent the shining ore,
> And came again, and yet again,
> Still cold and hungry, as before.
> I gave a thought, and through that thought of mine
> He found himself, the man, supreme, divine —
> Fed, clothed, and crowned with blessings manifold
> And now he begs no more.
>
> (Adapted from "The True Gift,"
> Author Unknown)

14

"Strengthen Thy Brethren"

The other night I was somewhat amused as I looked through an evening copy of the *Deseret News*. I noticed a picture depicting a problem that one of the Baptist churches in the South was having. It seems that their parking lot was being used by an adjoining establishment for commercial use, and the enterprising minister put this sign up at the entrance to the parking lot: "Warning — Violators will be baptized."

I couldn't help but think of that as I read the real warning of the Lord in the Book of Mormon. When the Lord appeared to the Nephites he said, "And again I say unto you, ye must repent, and be baptized in my name, and become as a little child, or ye can in nowise inherit the kingdom of God." (3 Nephi 11:38.) That was his real warning.

Many years ago I entered Chapman College in Southern California as a student. I came under the wonderful influence of Dr. Guy M. Davis, philosopher, educator, and teacher. Recently I had the privilege of witnessing this magnificent man, a man with so brilliant a mind, become as a little child as he entered the waters of baptism and became a member of the Church.

I thought of another scripture as I witnessed that baptism experience of my friend. The Lord, admonishing his chief apostle Peter, as Luke records it, gave this simple counsel and direction: ". . . when thou art converted, strengthen thy brethren." (Luke 22:32.) I pray the good bishop, the home teacher, the congregation of the ward to which Guy and his family have now been assigned will strengthen my brother.

Permit a personal experience for just a moment. Strengthening one's brother, I think, comes closer to home when we think of fellowshipping and friendshipping our family. Some time ago when my youngest daughter was faced with the reality of attending a different school, she looked forward to the new experience with great anticipation and excitement but with the usual anxieties and concerns. Her mom and dad tried to make her experience meaningful, and one that would be positive, and we spent several hours attempting to prepare her mind for the new experience. We even planned a time when we could shop for new clothes and other special school supplies.

Finally, the long-awaited day arrived. A special evening was planned to help give spiritual comfort and guidance. Later she put her clothes out in anticipation of the next day. As she retired to her bed, seemingly all was well, but about an hour later she appeared at my study door where I was making some preparations.

"Dad," she said, rubbing her tummy, "I don't feel very well."

You know the sign; and I thought I understood it, so I invited her in and sat her on my lap. We put on a little music that we liked to listen to together. I rubbed her tummy, and she soon fell asleep. I took her back upstairs, placed her in her bed, tiptoed toward the door; and she broke the silence with the announcement, "I am not asleep yet."

I went back and laid down on the bed with her, stroked her head, gave what fatherly counsel one could under the circumstances, and reassured her. Finally she fell asleep. The next morning she appeared at breakfast in her petticoat and said, "Dad, I don't think I had better go to school today."

"Why not?" I inquired.

She said, "I think I am going to get sick."

You know what she was trying to tell us, don't you? I don't know how to handle a new situation, Dad. Will I make friends?

Will my teacher like me? Will I fit into the social group? Will I be accepted? These are the concerns that all of us experience, as we find ourselves in new and different social situations.

She knew what my answer would be and agreed to have me drive her to school. As we got in front of the school building, the warning bell sounded. The tears started to come to her eyes. I got out of the car and assisted her. We walked about ten feet, and she grabbed hold of my leg. It was as though she were a tackle on some football team. And then, as only a child can do to a father, she looked up at me and said philosophically, "Dad, if you really love me — if you really love me — don't send me in there."

I said, "Honey, this may be beyond your comprehension, but it's because I do love you that I am taking you in there." And I did. When we got inside the door, she grabbed hold of the other leg and held on. Numerous students came and went, and finally the little miracle happened that changed everything.

From I don't know where came a delightful, wonderful *friendshipper*, a *fellowshipper* who knew how how to lose herself in serving others; one who would now take the admonishment of the Savior to strengthen her friends. With the exuberance of youth this little girl said, "Kellie, how are you?"

"Fine."

"What is your home room?" And she told her. "Tremendous. I had that home room last year. Come on, and I will take you to it."

And before Kellie knew it, she had let go of my leg and had gone about ten paces away, then realized what she had done. I will never forget her expression and the sermon she taught as she looked back. "Oh," she said, "Dad, you can go now; I don't need you anymore."

Thank God for the little people as well as the big people who know how to friendship and fellowship.

Thousands of people are coming into this Church every month. I pray that we have the genius to follow the counsel of the

Lord to strengthen our brethren. I pray that a great bishop and a wonderful home teacher and other members are taking care of my friend, Guy Davis, and the thousands of others who need someone to take them by the hand and show them the way.

15

Put on Your Spiritual Clothes

I love the Christmas season. I'm a little boy at heart. I love the spirit of Christmas in the air, the feeling, the goodwill that seems to emanate. I had an interesting experience one Christmas season. I had an opportunity to be in a stake conference down in President Kimball's home country in Arizona. One of the things I like to do each Sunday morning before going in with the parents in the general session of conference is to visit in the Junior Sunday School. The children are exciting and refreshing and challenging, as you know. It perks up their spirits to think that the General Authorities know they exist, and I like to involve them where I can.

I was doing just that this particular Sunday and, knowing that President Kimball had come from their area, I thought I'd try to set the stage by asking some simple questions. I said, "Can any person in this Sunday School this morning tell me what person who is very special to all of us comes from this community?" One little fellow, about four, shot his hand up. I said, "Tell us, young man, who comes from this area that's very special and lives in Salt Lake?" He said, "Santa."

Well, I knew where his mind was, and it prompted me at this time to brush up on some interesting comments from other young people — all very real, perhaps not members of our faith, who each year write real letters to Santa Claus. The post office receives thousands of these every year. Here's a little collection of these letters. Think about them now, the refreshment of youth:

"Dear Santa Claus, how can you tell who are the good children and who are the bad? Please tell me as quick as you can."

"Dear Saint Nick, could you send me a snorkel and some flippers? I'm learning to be a deep-sea diver in the bathtub."

"Dear Santa Claus, I love Christmas because at Christmas there is pretty white snow, and everybody is nice to everybody, even grownups."

"Hi Santa! Could you leave a nice doll for my sister so she will have something to play with? My mother always makes *me* play with her."

"Dear Santa, can you give a pretty present to my teacher, Miss Lewis, and tell her it came from me, Jeffrey? I think it would help a lot."

"Dear Santa Claus, I think you should leave a big present for my grandma. She knew you when you were a kid."

"Hello, Santa Claus, I wrote to you last Christmas that I wanted a surprise, and you left me a book. I don't want any more surprises."

They're refreshing, to be sure — honest and sincere at heart.

I hope, particularly on this date, our minds are remembering another great occasion. Many of you may be too tender to recall personally, but historically I'm sure you can identify with December 7, 1941. On that fateful Sunday morning little did I realize that that event would involve me personally. Without walking you through all the details, several months later I found myself fulfilling General MacArthur's commission when he said that he would return to the South Seas. I went in two days ahead of him. Several weeks later on the island of Leyte, I learned a great lesson as a young Latter-day Saint in combat. I belonged to the Seventy-seventh Infantry Division. At the time, we were fighting General Yamashita, who was the General MacArthur of the Japanese infantry. Theirs was a crack outfit. We had just taken the Valencia airport and secured it on the island of Leyte, about two days before Christmas 1944.

In making preparation for the final assault on a rather large mountain near the airport, we were commissioned to dig in our foxhole at the base of the hill. There were about one thousand of us in our particular garrison. We did not know it at the time, but the enemy, holding the top of the ridge, numbered approximately three thousand. Whenever you take the offensive in combat, just as in football, you need a little greater power. But we didn't have that intelligence at our disposal at the time.

In that situation my heart and my mind naturally drifted back home. I was a nineteen-year-old boy, and Christmas had always been very special in our home. So I was naturally thinking of mom and dad and my brothers and my girlfriend and what they would be doing on that special occasion. As Christmas Eve approached, a slight drizzly rain set in on the mountainside. It was cold and shivery for those of us who knew better circumstances, but dig in we did.

I was bold enough to keep a family tradition going. A thirty-seven-millimeter antitank gun was located near my foxhole position, and I hung my stocking on the muzzle and settled in for the night. The rain continued. It turned to bitter cold, high in the mountains. We knew, because of the characteristic of the enemy, that about midnight they would invade our lines. They would often send in suicide squads to weaken our front and then follow with infantry attacks. And so we were preparing for the inevitable.

About eleven o'clock that evening, Christmas Eve 1944, out of nowhere on the side of the mountain a young tenor, whom I had never met before and still haven't, from somewhere on our infantry line in a beautiful voice sang a solo: "It came upon the midnight clear, that glorious song of old." By the time he got to the second verse, one thousand American soldiers had joined him. Why, you would have thought these hard-crusted old infantrymen were the Mormon Tabernacle Choir! He next sang "Hark, the Herald Angels Sing," "O Come, All Ye Faithful," and a great medley of songs that are very dear to us. Then he concluded with "Silent Night, Holy Night." We all joined in chorus with him. I guess, because of the circumstances, I haven't been touched quite like that before or since.

Twelve o'clock came, and the enemy didn't come. For the first time in my combat experience they had not acted according to schedule. One o'clock, two o'clock, and all night we sat ready with our weapons. But the enemy still didn't come. The next morning, as Christmas dawn broke, we very carefully came out of our foxholes, gave each other an exchange of greetings, talked about home, girls, the things that mattered most. The day passed. We had an interesting Christmas dinner, as you can in a front-line situation, and then on into Christmas night. Finally, about five minutes to twelve, as Christmas was fading into another day, the first enemy mortar crossed our lines, and World War II had commenced again. But for twenty-four hours I was a personal witness that peace on earth, goodwill toward men, can actually occur when people are touched by a true spirit.

I couldn't help but think, as I watched this marvel unfold before me, if a simple Christmas carol will do that between a Christian and a non-Christian nation, what will the gospel of Jesus Christ do for people everywhere? If only you and I, imbued with that same sweet spirit and testimony, could go forth (as our prophet has challenged us to do) to touch the hearts and minds of people in all nations. Well, I think we already know what would follow. We're seeing it happen: the greatness of the gospel in transforming the lives of people. I think that's significant, particularly at Christmastime.

Now, I guess I'm as Santa Claus-oriented as anybody, and I think it's a great tradition, although I hope and pray that it never overshadows the true purpose and meaning of why we celebrate Christmas. While we know it's not the exact birthdate, it's a date that we've set apart to commemorate the birth, and I think even more particularly the mission, of our Lord and Savior. People everywhere I find, like you, really want to know the gospel. They don't know how to find it occasionally, or they are a little confused sometimes when it is presented. Maybe they don't quite relate to it, but you and I have this tremendous opportunity to share. As a part of everyone's educational process they should sufficiently learn the gospel so that they might, in their own wonderful way, transform people everywhere throughout the world. I give you that challenge.

Some time ago I wrote a book, and I appreciate that what the world does not need is another book. But I like to write because it forces me to think. (My schoolteachers could tell you that I was not much of a thinker.) I've thought of some of the passing records I made when I was in high school. The greatest passing record I hold was getting *out* of high school, and I think that still stands. But be as it may, the important thing as we get our education is to keep that spiritual balance so that we might do the things the Lord has basically asked us to do.

One of the books I have written is on the Osmond family. Now, I'm not here to debate whether you think they're great or not. They're tremendous missionaries. They're the most popular singing group in all the United Kingdom. They're the most popular in France, they're the most popular in Scandinavia, they're the most popular in the Orient, and they're not too far from the top in the United States. They're opening doors no other Latter-day Saints could through a medium that, while some may have a question or two, is softening and touching many hearts. I thought their true story should be told from a personal point of view, and I wrote the book as a missionary tool.

This book is having an interesting reaction. Many hundreds of letters from non-Latter-day Saints come to me each month in response to it. Quite a few, of course, are from the teenage level, but surprisingly many of the letters are from those in their mature years, grandmothers and grandfathers who identify with a great family who are doing so much for so many. Would you like to hear a typical letter from an Osmond fan not of this Church? One came from Tokyo the other day. (Keep in mind that the writer, twelve years old, is not a Christian.)

"Dear Mr. Dunn:

"Thank you for writing the book on the Osmonds. They're my favorite people. I understand you're a General Authority for your church and therefore you work with a prophet. I would like to know about prophets. Would you please write me back as quick as you can?"

One comes from a young girl in England:

"Dear Mr. Dunn:

"Thank you for writing the book on the Osmonds. They are wonderful people. They've touched my heart very much. I understand in your position that you must know God. I would like to know God, too. Would you write me soon and tell me how I can get to know him?"

People all over the world are seeking what you and I have to give. Now, I often think as I read those letters that hopefully you and I are prepared in our own right, first as parents, next as members and leaders of the Church, to give honestly the answers that people seek. That's one of the great purposes I see in education, to prepare us academically, but also spiritually. It's that spiritual realm that concerns us the most, as you well know. I've often wondered what kind of parents these young people have. I could make some guesses. These youth are seeking to know, not knowing where to find.

I couldn't help but think at Christmastime of a great parable that Jesus taught many years ago. You know, one of the exciting things about religion is that it solves all problems. There isn't a question you have academically, personally, financially, or otherwise but what the Lord has given you an answer through a prophet. The question, I guess, is do you know where to find the answers to your problems? When you do, you resolve the challenges in your life accordingly.

Jesus was asked a certain question about God many times. It is perhaps one of the greatest single questions asked in the New Testament times, and I'm sure he also answered it while visiting this continent. The question is: "What is the kingdom of God like? What is it like to be with God?" Jesus, in Matthew, gave the answer.

Let me first set the stage for you. Matthew, of course, is a great teacher. He draws frequently upon the great parables to convey a heavenly principle in an earthly way that the people can understand. A multitude has gathered. The classroom for the Savior, in most cases, was by the seashore, the mountainside, in the village. He was asked: "What is it like to be with God? What is the kingdom of God like?"

"And Jesus answered and spake unto them again by parables, and said, The kingdom of heaven [the dwelling place; in modern vernacular, the celestial kingdom] is like unto a certain king, which made a marriage for his son." (Matthew 22:1-2.) People in Palestine understood kingdoms, because that's what they were part of. Today, he might have used the words *democracy*, or *governments*, or *Congress*, or *president*. *King* they understood. In England the people there understand *royalty*, and it's very easy for them to identify with this parable. The king represents the highest authority. The king made a marriage for his son.

Keep in mind that in the time of Jesus, as it is today, a marriage is perhaps the single greatest event. He's saying to his multitude: "Think of the greatest, most important event that can happen in your life. That's what it's going to be like to be with God in his dwelling place." (I can identify with some of this because I've married off two daughters.) Weddings in those days lasted a little longer than they do today. It wasn't uncommon for them to go three, four, five, six, seven days. Can you imagine standing in a reception line in a tuxedo three days? I can't. My wife couldn't even keep her shoes on for two hours. But the people in Jesus' time went about this in great celebration.

Could I just confide in you for a minute? I'm a very practical person, or at least I try to be. We sat down with both of our daughters at the time of their marriages, and we talked about cost and image. You know, the things that you're trying to do you do because you want to do right by your children, but not to overdo it. We finally settled on a caterer that would cost dad fifty-two cents per head. As the guests would come through the line, they'd take those dainty little cups, cakes, and juice — at fifty-two cents per head. I think everybody in Salt Lake City got in that line. You know, I think some people just saw the line and got in it to see who was at the end of it. Well, I could handle it for about two hours, but at the end of the third hour I was becoming frantic. You know, I was doing this, "Hello, Tom, Bill, Jim, thanks for coming." Then I was thinking, "There's 52¢, $1.04. . . ." So I can identify with the practical side of a marriage celebration.

Jesus was saying: "Think of the greatest event that can happen in your life. That's what it's going to be like to be with God." Continuing the parable, Jesus said, "And then the king sent forth his servants to invite the guests." There was no printing press in those days, and so they had to send invitations out by word of mouth.

Have you noticed the color and variety of announcements we have these days? I got an announcement the other day from one of my former missionaries. He was clever. His announcement had a picture of the couple on one side, and the words inviting you to the reception on the other. The picture showed the bride chasing him around a tree. I knew the elder, and I appreciated that picture, but there was no printing press in Jesus' day. They sent out invitations by word of mouth.

They were all invited to the great palace, and you can imagine what kind of festive affair it was. "And when the king came in to see the guests, he saw there a man which had not on a wedding garment." (Matthew 22:11.) In those days, when you went to a festive occasion, particularly a wedding, you got dressed up and you went properly dressed. What the king said to this man, I think, is one of the great, great lines in scripture. Don't tell me the Savior doesn't have a sense of humor. Watch this one: "Friend, How camest thou in hither not having a wedding garment?" (Matthew 22:12.) Look, the guy shows up at the palace dressed in his levis. I mean, he's got his Saturday grubs on, and he's standing there in front of royalty. The king says, "Friend, how come you came to my palace, this great reception, in your levis?" (That's not a modern translation. I'm just interpreting it for you.) Now notice the next line. It's terrific. "And the man was speechless." You got the picture? Can you see him standing there without a word, thinking, "Well, you got me there, king"?

Could I make a modern analogy for you? If I invited you up to see the prophet for a special interview (this would be great and I'm sure both sides would appreciate it if we could work it out, but I don't know how we could mechanically), I think you wouldn't need to have me tell you, "Put on a tie or a Sunday dress." I think you'd just do that. You dress up automatically for certain occasions, don't you? But there are some people who might be a little dense, who wouldn't get the message.

The parable continues, "Then said the king to his servants, Bind him hand and foot, and take him away, and cast him into outer darkness." (Matthew 22:13.) Boy, what a penalty for wearing levis!

Well, what does all that mean in plain old twentieth-century language? The king is our Heavenly Father; wedding guests, you and me coming back into his presence; wedding garment, getting spiritually prepared to meet God. The time of mortality is the place to prepare, which is an eternal gospel principle. Can you imagine if you and I did not prepare, not only academically but spiritually, and we reported back home improperly dressed? Can you get an idea of how you might feel, standing in the presence of God, not being spiritually dressed? I think we'd be speechless. Now that's not a threat; it's a basic law of the gospel.

You know that basically there are only two things you can take with you out of this world. Think about it a minute. (I thought for a long time that I'd take my ball glove, but some teacher told me I couldn't.) There are certain physical possessions I like, but I can't take them. Only two things will I take with me when I depart. You see if I'm not correct. One is my character, which would include in a Mormon setting my intelligence. The other is my personal relationships with my friends and my family. That's it.

Now let me ask you a very honest question: Why is it you and I spend most of our time accumulating things we can't take, at the expense of the things we can? Why do we do that in this world? That's the problem in the world today. And the Lord is saying to us that the time will come when we will have that opportunity to stand in his presence. Hopefully, we will be spiritually dressed for the occasion.

Now, you're preparing to get dressed for the greatest event that will ever occur in your lives. I thank God every day for great men and women, for great leaders who do so much to help us know how to put our spiritual clothes on. I thank God for them. The scriptures, then, become the process of learning how to get dressed. You know what the challenge is from our prophet to learn the scriptures. All the General Authorities have had a challenge to try to teach this more emphatically to members all over the world.

I ran across a little verse that I think is significant:

> Old Brother Higgins built a shelf
> For the old family Bible to rest itself,
> Lest a sticky finger or a grimy thumb
> Might injure the delicate pages some.
> He cautioned his children to touch it not,
> And it rests there with never a blot,
> Though the Higgins tribe were a troublesome lot.
>
> His neighbor, Miggins, built a shelf.
> "Come, children," he said, "and help yourself."
> Now his book is old and ragged and worn,
> With some of the choicest pages torn,

Where children have fingered, and thumbed, and read,
But of the Miggins children I've heard it said,
That each carries a Bible in his head.

I would hope and pray, my brothers and sisters, in this great
moment of your life as you obtain knowledge of the world, that
you will place above it all the holy, sacred scriptures and the
counsel from prophets that will assist you in becoming better
dressed in the Spirit.

I love you and I sustain you. I bear witness that these things
are true. I pray at the Christmas season — as we sing our carols, as
we exchange our gifts, as we share mutual admiration, feelings of
love and affection — that, above all else, you and I with our faith
and testimony, like the lonely twenty-year-old tenor on the island
of Leyte, will transform the lives of millions. Can you imagine, if
one tenor on a battleline could stop a war for twenty-four hours,
what twenty-five thousand Latter-day Saints turned loose on a
sick world could do with your knowledge and your testimony?
Now I challenge you to go do it.

Refining
a
Testimony

16

How One Can Know That God Lives

I remember one spring day when my little six-year-old daughter, Kellie, came rushing up to me and, throwing herself into my arms with all the exuberance that only youth can display, she said, "Daddy, did you know it is only three more days until Easter?" I assured her that I did. Then she, with an anxious look, wanted to know just what it all meant, and so we took a moment to visit. As we discussed the eternal verities of the gospel of Jesus Christ on a six-year-old plane, I commenced to think about the real meaning of Easter, as we do on these occasions. It reminded me of the delightful poem that Grace Daniels has recorded for us. Let me share it with you:

EASTER IS COMING

"Easter is coming," I said to a boy,
A wee little lad, by the way;
His eyes were bright and he smiled with delight
As he quickly looked up from his play.
"Oh, yes, I know Easter, for that is the time
When the bunny brings eggs red and blue,
And inside they're just like what old chickie lays,
But some are real candy, too."

"Easter is coming," I said to a maid,
With brown eyes and shining brown hair.
I looked in her eyes and not with surprise
Saw the dreamlight of youth resting there.
"Yes, I know it is coming," she shyly replied,
"And if you never will tell,
There's a wedding that day and I'm going away
To a dear little home on the hill."

"Easter is coming," I said to a man,
To whom middle-age brought no reprieve.
His silvering hair told of worry and care,
And his voice held a note of peeve.
"Don't talk about Easter, that's all I can hear,
Easter hats, Easter gowns, Easter shoes,
And for ruffles and frills, old Dad pays the bills,
Do you wonder I'm down with the blues?"

"Easter is coming," I said to a man
With bent form and beard white as snow.
His dim eyes grew bright with a wonder light
And his withered old face was aglow.
"Ah, friend, 'tis a message I fain would proclaim
To striving humanity.
To me it means life, resurrection of youth,
To endure through eternity."

I pondered their answers for many a day,
For each with its meaning was fraught,
And each one so different, yet, right in its way,
But what was the answer I sought?
Must pleasure come foremost, whatever the cost,
While life, youth, and love have their day?
And must the true meaning of Easter be lost
Till we come to the end of the way?

As springtime approaches with beckoning hands
And the promise of things "born anew,"
And Easter draws near with its myriad of plans,
Just what does it mean to you?

I am sure to many of us it means new clothes, perhaps a vacation from school, spring at last, or the beginning of baseball season. These are all quite wonderful and vital to us, but they are not the real reasons we celebrate Easter.

I recently stood beside the casket of a very close friend who had been taken in the prime of his life, leaving a young widow and four tiny children. And as we stood in that sacred room while the family said their last good-byes, it tugged at my heartstrings to watch a little four-year-old boy slip his hand into that of his mother and, wistfully looking up at her, ask the question, "Mama, will we ever see Daddy again?" I am sure this scene has been repeated many times throughout all the world, because death brings us face to face with the question of the ages. To quote Job as we frequently do at this time of the year, "If a man die, shall he live again?" (Job 14:14.)

On another Easter morning several years ago a great armada of ships assembled in the bay off the island of Okinawa. And on that Easter morn as I looked upon the faces of those who were to take the beach, one of the great, great questions of all the ages seemed again to be registered by those men. "What hope is there in the future?"

The answer came to me, I believe, in the midst of one of my darkest hours. As I pushed ashore with my buddies, I crawled a few feet into the sand, and there I found a young soldier in the last moment of this life. I didn't know his name, nor could I tell you to which faith he belonged. As I tried to give him a little bit of comfort, his last words were these: "Out of this filth, death, destruction, will come a new world and a new way of life." In the face of what seemed to be his defeat, he saw the real victory. And almost in a providential way, just a few yards from where he lay was a patch of Easter lilies, signifying to those who would observe the new birth and the new way of life. It was later I discovered that Okinawa was the Easter lily capital of the Orient.

It is when we encounter experiences such as these that questions are often raised that one wants to know, and rightly so: How can we know the reality of the resurrection? Is it true? One of the great educators of our Church, Dr. Lowell Bennion, listed for us four ways by which we can come to know truth or reality. First, by accepting it on the authority of someone else; second, by thinking; third, by experiencing; and fourth, by feeling, which we in this Church would call inspiration or revelation.

Let me just discuss for a moment each of these channels by which we come to know.

First, *authority.* There was a time when a prodigious mind, such as that of Aristotle and Herbert Spencer, could survey the entire field of human knowledge and draw conclusions. But with the great accumulation of knowledge that has been derived through specialization, no single person can grasp all of the learning that is now available to mankind. For this reason man is compelled to rely upon the experience or authority of others for some of his information. Each of us turns to the doctor, the dentist, the lawyer, the teacher, the mechanic, the spiritual leaders, and many other persons for guidance in particular problems. The student of chemistry, for example, does not begin from scratch to rely upon his own experience. He uses the efforts of the teacher, the text, the reference book, and other sources of authority. To bypass such a vast accumulation of knowledge would be folly indeed.

Likewise, in religion we have preserved for us the sayings and teachings and testimonies of Moses, of Amos, of Paul; of Alma in the Book of Mormon; of Joseph Smith in his life and teachings; and of course, of the Christ. These were not persons who were eccentric, but individuals who were significant in stature, living in real-life situations, claiming wisdom from God, and bearing personal testimony that these things that are recorded in our scriptures are indeed true. They too deserve an honest hearing.

Second, *reason* or *thinking*. In man's search for truth, the mind plays a leading role. Man, as a child of God, was created in the image of his Heavenly Father, the glory of whose intelligence is reflected in the beauty and orderliness of the universe. Why should man, God's child living in his world, not trust his own mind and use it earnestly as one avenue by which he can come to know the truth about reality — in this case, the resurrection?

The mind has the ability to weave the separate experiences of life into larger and more unified views. Each day the mind is bombarded with numerous ideas, impressions, perceptions, and feelings from without and from within. These enter the mind in a disorganized and miscellaneous fashion, but the human mind has the ability to bring a measure of order out of chaos by establishing meaningful relationships among phenomena that it experiences.

Reason alone, however, is not a sufficient guide to truth. For, as Goethe has said, "Human life divided by reason leaves a remainder." Through reason alone one cannot choose a mate, find God, or determine all things of greatest value.

Third, *experience*. One of the most trustworthy avenues to truth lies along the path of experience. Each of us has a rich amount of it, for it is common to all. In the affairs of everyday life, we learn to trust experience. We learn sweetness by taste, softness by touch, colors by sight, and joy and sorrow, love and hate directly in life situations. There is no substitute for experience, and without it we cannot know the truth.

Two types of experience have been described: that which is based on science and its discoveries, and that which is common to all of us in everyday life. The latter, which is a nonscientific experience, is just as real and may also be a valid source of knowledge, but it is often either more general or more unique and, therefore, somewhat more difficult to communicate to others.

Experiences of this type play an important role in religion. Many religious principles can be practiced and experienced in everyday life. The validity of religion does not rest on faith alone. We feel and observe the effects of selfishness, greed, lust, and hate. We also observe and feel the opposite effects of unselfishness, generosity, purity of heart, and love. Faith and repentance and forgiveness are not abstract principles but are real parts of life. Prayer and worship are religious experiences for those who participate in them with faith.

And finally, *revelation.* Despite the great emphasis on reason and the experience of science, inspiration (or intuition, as some have preferred to define it) also plays a very important role in discovering truth. Scientists have testified that some of their most profound insights have come to them, not in the labored process of logical thought, but as unexpected, unpremeditated hunches, possibly as flashes from the imagination, the subconscious mind, or even from God. They, too, recognize inspiration as a source of knowledge.

Revelation is communication from God to man. It is another avenue to truth, to a correct knowledge of reality. Revelation includes all the other avenues.

A prophet is not without experience in human life, for he lives among men and with himself. He is not insensitive to good and evil, right and wrong, joy and sorrow, life and death. Questions and problems come to his mind. He thinks, he reflects, and he searches for the answers; and then — and this step is distinctive in the life of a prophet — he turns to God in humility and faith. When the answer comes, it is usually not in an audible tone, although it can be and often has been in both former and latter days, but more often it comes through the "still, small voice" of the Comforter. This Comforter, the Spirit of Truth, clarifies the mind of the prophet and causes his bosom to burn within him so that he knows the will of God. Then he declares it to man. The testimony or reality of these things can be the personal experience of every honest, seeking individual in the world. Through these channels man has come to know the reality of Christ's life, divine mission, death, and eventual resurrection.

In answer to the questions: "If a man die, shall he live again?" and "What hope is there for the future?" I summarize the words of President David O. McKay:

To sincere believers in Christianity, to all who accept Christ as their Savior, his resurrection is not a symbol but a reality. As Christ lived after death, so shall all men, each taking his place in the next world for which he has best fitted himself. With this assurance, obedience to eternal law should be a joy, not a burden, for compliance with the principles of the gospel brings happiness and peace. "He is not here," said a witness many years ago, "but is risen." (Luke 24:6.) Because Christ does live, so shall we.

17

Preparation for a Testimony

I can't help but remember when I had to give my first talk in church. Do all of you remember your first talk, those of you who have had this chance or a similar opportunity? Well, I grew up in the mission field of the Church, and I had never had an opportunity to go into a ward until I was almost sixteen years old. That was the first time I had ever visited a Latter-day Saint ward. I hadn't been there five times when the bishop called on me to give a talk the next Sunday. There's a challenge for you — never been in a ward and all of a sudden they want you to talk.

I went home and announced the bishop's request to my parents. They were shocked, not only because had I never done this before in my life but obviously because their family name was at stake. They could see all sorts of problems arising.

At the time, my father had a little grocery store, and I used to report there every afternoon during the winter, when ball season wasn't around, and put in three or four hours before doing my homework. This was part of the family obligation. Knowing that I was to represent him as well as the entire family in church the following Sunday, he saw to it that we sat down together and worked up a little format on what I would say and how; that I would have sufficient time to prepare during the week while working in his store.

For about fifteen or twenty minutes each afternoon as we'd hit a little lull in the business, he'd say, "Okay, Paul, to the back room and start practicing." He would line me up in front of a section of surplus cans and say: "Now you'll be in privacy here. You just talk to those cans like you would the congregation next Sunday." (You know, I've since learned that's great counsel. I've noticed that there's a similarity between the expression on those cans and a lot of congregations I've had to talk to!)

There I was one Wednesday afternoon. I had my thoughts pretty well in mind, and as I was giving it all I had, almost unannounced and unnoticed a little lady customer stepped in the back room. I guess it shocked her to see the clerk standing there talking religion to a bunch of cans. She listened about as long as she could before interrupting me. She just said, "Young man, young man, could you tell me where I could find the Campbell's soups?" Well, now, you don't interrupt a young man like that without him having some problems making that immediate adjustment. So I turned to her, and in my anxiety to help her I just said, without thinking twice: "Yes, ma'am. It's in the forty-seventh section of the Doctrine and Covenants." Well, she looked a little surprised and went away unaided.

I think back on those days and can't help but compare myself as I was then with the tremendous ability, the spirit and capability of you young people today as I watch you operate. And we do watch you with great interest. Sometimes you may think you're kind of lost in the shuffle, but you're not. The Brethren in our Church offices are very much aware of who you are and what you're doing. Now, I won't take time to reveal to you all the ways and means they have of finding out just who you are and what you are doing, but they know, and they know very realistically how you measure up in terms of your commitment to this great gospel plan.

I have another little experience, if you don't mind my sharing it very quickly with you.

Back in 1959, about the time I completed my doctoral degree at the University of Southern California, and feeling, I guess, somewhat proud and resourceful, I was busy in my study preparing some materials for the next day. One of my daughters brought a little neighborhood friend into the house and immediately they went to her bedroom to play. Being an interested father as I try to be, I took great concern about the activity that was going on in there; while I was preparing my work I kept a listening ear to the activity in there. (You're aware, aren't you, young people, that Mom and Dad tend to do this by nature?)

I couldn't help but overhear a conversation that was going on. The little girlfriend, who was just new to the neighborhood, said to my daughter Marsha: "Say, I understand that your father is a doctor. Is that right?" (My doctorate happened to be in the field of education.)

Marsha answered, "Yes, that's right."

Then the little girl asked the second question. "Well, what kind of a doctor is he?"

There was a short pause. By then I was greatly interested in what words of wisdom my offspring would give her, so I listened very attentively. "Well, he's the kind of a doctor that doesn't do anybody any good."

Well, I hate to admit it, but I think she called the right shot on that occasion; yet I do hope and pray that the moments I have with you will be significant in terms of your placement in society, as we view some eternal principles in the gospel plan.

I think I can best share with you my thoughts and feelings by way of a personal experience or two. I used to play baseball with the St. Louis Cardinals. Now, it takes a lot of preparation to become a big league ballplayer. In fact, you have to prepare if you want to go anywhere in this life. The thing that concerns my heart and soul today as I watch the youth of America, is whether they are preparing themselves for what they eventually want to do. Yet frequently they wonder why at age twenty-one or twenty-two the world doesn't grab them up. Well, it's very obvious that they have failed miserably to incorporate the basic ingredients of preparation into their lives so that they will be a product that someone wants.

I started to prepare to be a professional ballplayer at age three, and I never took my mind off it, and that was one of my problems. I didn't think that public school or church had anything to do with becoming a ballplayer; and because of my poor vision, in terms of values, I had to learn a very hard lesson. And so everything I did from age three until I was eighteen when I signed that first professional ball contract was oriented toward the ball field. I ate, slept and drank baseball. That was all I could think of; but it was necessary in terms of my preparation. My only problem was that I got overbalanced in it. (I collected more boxtops from a certain highly advertised breakfast cereal than you can ever imagine, because I thought there was some correlation between eating that cereal and being a better ballplayer. That was another false premise on which I was building my life, but I learned too late, and I almost got so groggy eating the cereal that I couldn't run.) Nevertheless, it was all part of my basic program.

The time came when I could see the fallacy of my being too concerned in one field. For example, during my first twelve years of public education I never took a book home to study. I'm not proud of it; I'm sorry, and I've tried to repent. I'm spending the rest of my life paying the price of the void that I created by that silly practice. I used to sit in my algebra or English class and think: "Of what value is this to me if I become a great pitcher? I can throw a curve ball just as well without algebra and English as I can with it." So I quit it. See? I used to go home and say: "Yep, I'm all prepared for life. I can throw as hard as anybody and run just as fast and hit just as far, so don't bother me." I've lived to see the fallacy of that one.

When it came time to go to church on Sunday, I took it as a personal affront to me. How could church help me to be a better ballplayer? You see, that's the way my mind worked. So I used to crawl out of the window as a deacon and as a teacher and go down to the drugstore and look at baseball and sports books. I spent three years of my Aaronic Priesthood life doing that. That's a real contribution to the world, isn't it? But that was my vision. I thought that baseball was the most important thing in life. I've since lived to regret that program. While I guess I can never make up the lost energies that I so foolishly wasted, I'm doing all I can now to fill in the gap.

The reason I mention this is not that I'm proud of it but that I think I can appreciate in a very personal way the individual who tends to get lopsided in the affairs of the world. What a tendency there is in our lives to do that today — to put second things first! Now, I'm not saying that becoming a great ballplayer or lawyer or doctor isn't important; it is! It's necessary for temporal salvation, but it isn't the most important thing that we're sent to earth to do. It's the eternal things that really count when we leave this earth. It's the sharp, intelligent young person who catches this vision early and does something about it, be he member of this Church or not.

Way back at age three, I had never calculated that by my eighteenth birthday, World War II would be on the scene. You see, I hadn't put that in my program. I didn't know about it. Little did I know that Uncle Sam would tap me on the shoulder and say: "C'mon, buddy, follow me. You just forget that baseball for a while and come and help me kill people. That's what you're going to do for the next three years." I didn't want to go, as millions like me didn't.

I had signed my first professional ball contract just three months earlier. Do you know what that meant? Well, you ladies might not; but can you fellows appreciate it in some small measure? Here you plan for fifteen years to be what you want to be. You have eight major league scouts tracking you down. You finally graduate from high school (and I use that term loosely when I think of my preparation), and are permitted by your parents to sign that contract. You put your name on that dotted line and receive a pretty good bonus. Do you know what kind of a thrill that is for a teenager? I wish I had the ability to tell you. Then you report to that first team. You get off of the bus (and it was a bus in those days, not a plane), and they outfit you with that brand new suit, and you step into that dugout wearing a shiny new number. Can you imagine what a thrill that is?

Then you get a letter two or three months later that says: "Forget that, brother, and follow me. We've got other plans for you." You see? That's what I hadn't counted on. That was the uncertain product of my life that I had never planned for. Well, I was whisked off to basic training, and it was a terrible way to live. I could see then in some small measure, even though I hadn't the foundation I should have had, the value of the other things that I had neglected: schooling, training, religion. I got shoved on all of the dirty work because I couldn't qualify in any field of endeavor, couldn't do anything — could hardly spell my name. I hadn't thought that important.

Only as I commenced to undergo the temptations of the world did I begin to appreciate in a small measure the other side, the religious and moral, the spiritual side of life. Well, as I thought and I experienced, things began to be questioned in my mind. To make a long story short, about eleven months later I found myself on a troop ship out in the Pacific Ocean. Maybe a lot of you sisters again, even by way of television and the movies, can't appreciate what I'm attempting to say. But picture, if you can, a boat out there on the water, one of many in a convoy, heading toward an island for that first combat experience.

Crowded onto this particular ship that you have in your mental image were three thousand American soldiers, all going into war for the first time. These were men who represented all walks of life. They were lawyers, doctors, teachers, merchants, bums and criminals, the works. There were even a few ballplayers thrown in. We were mixed together with a common charge to defend this country at all costs.

The first two or three weeks out there weren't too bad because, while war was very much in our mind following the training and the films and all the other things that teach a boy to be what he ought to be in war, it was still not real. Interestingly enough, the army and navy — because they are always interested in the well-rounded personality — used to hold a general church service on board every evening where we could come and sing a common religious song, whether we were Jew, Catholic, Gentile or Latter-day Saint. It was something that could bind us together in a religious feeling. The chaplain would talk to us for four or five minutes and then we'd just visit and talk about home and girls and all the other things that seem to be important to men at that stage of their lives. Then we'd be dismissed.

For the first two weeks of the voyage there were thirty-five or forty of us, out of the three thousand troops on board, that used to go to this little one-hour service every day. Thirty-five or forty — that's typical of life, isn't it?

Then we entered the third week, the last week. Now the tempo began to pick up a little bit. We came to two or three little atolls in the water, and ships would stop there. We'd make some practice landings just exactly the way we were going to do it two or three days hence.

Being close to the last hour, suddenly we didn't have a room large enough to hold the group that wanted to come to the church service. So we held the meeting topside on the bow. And there, brothers and sisters, was one of the most interesting studies of human life I have ever watched in my life. Do you know what happened that day, July 21, 1944? Three thousand men came to church. How about that? You see, on the eve of combat three thousand soldiers kind of got excited about the higher values in life. When the crisis is really on, watch people get religion. It's then they sense inside, when the chips are down, the need for higher aid — whether they be merchant, criminal, ballplayer, or anything else.

I'll never forget that church service, conducted by a marvelous Protestant chaplain. I don't even know what faith he represented. But, bless his heart, he was honest and sincere and came straight to the point. I'll never forget that calm day. The sea was almost like glass, and we were sitting out there three thousand strong singing that opening song, "Abide With Me." Can you imagine a chorus of three thousand male soldiers letting their souls go, probably in many cases for the first time in their lives? Can you imagine what that sounds like? You could even hear other ships echoing the same type of activity. There was a brief opening prayer, and then that chaplain got as serious as I've ever seen a man. He said: "Men, I'm not going to kid you tonight. You've been training for the last year for what you're going to do tomorrow morning. You know full well what's before you."

"Now," he said, "army statistics tell us that on an invasion like you're going to experience tomorrow, a lot of you aren't going to make it. We've got to pay a price to get this island." He continued: "If our records are accurate, about half of you will lay your lives down sometime before eight o'clock tomorrow morning. What I'm saying, men, is that one-half of you will be standing before your Maker tormorrow morning at eight o'clock. Are you ready?"

Now what would you say, you young people? I was eighteen years old at the time. If we locked all of the doors now and said, "Tomorrow morning at eight o'clock you give an accounting to the Savior for your life and your attitude and your activity," how would you feel? That's the thought that went through my mind. I was sitting out there thinking of all of my great, glorious days of ballplaying. Do you see how insignificant they appear to be all of a sudden? Contracts, millions, fame and fortune — a lot of nonsense, isn't it, when you get right down to counting what really counts? For the first time I wanted to know concerning the validity of religion. Does God really live? Why am I out here? Why should I take the life of a person I've never even seen before? Thousands of questions like this started to rush through my mind. Why? Why? Why? And these are the questions we ought to ask ourselves right now. Why? Why do we do any of the things that we're doing in this existence of ours?

That church service ended, and there wasn't one person among us that slept that night. There wasn't much talking going on. You just held your rifle and reported to your boat team station. At five o'clock the next morning when that whistle went off, we prepared to embark. I was assigned to the seventh wave that morning. Unfortunately, and yet I suppose fortunately for me — depending on which way you look at it — the first six waves didn't even get ashore. They were completely blown out of the water. Thousands of lives were sacrificed for you, for me, for the defense of this country.

I remember going ashore on that little coral reef. By then the tide was in, and I had to wade ashore with water clear up to my chest, holding my rifle extended. I had to push through the dead bodies of my friends and those with whom I had trained and associated. Don't tell me I didn't ask questions! Why is this wonderful kid, nineteen years old, face down in the water? *Why?*

As I crawled ashore and finally made a little progress along the beach — about ten feet — I dug a small foxhole. I then took off my helmet and started to ask the Lord *why?* "Why, Lord? Why should I be out here?" Can you appreciate in some small way what I'm trying to tell you? Well, I'd never prayed like that before. I'd been a Latter-day Saint all my life; I'd watched my mom and dad get on their knees in family prayer. May I confess again, my attitude was that of a typical sixteen- or seventeen-year-old: "Let's get this over with folks. My gosh! My folks are fanatical. Oh, do we have to pray tonight?" Perhaps you know those feelings. I remember kneeling a number of times with my father and listening to him pour out his soul to his Heavenly Father. My dad was a sharp, capable businessman, respected by the community, a great leader that others sought counsel from. And yet, in his own humble way, he would often kneel and say: "Lord, here's my problem. Help my boy Paul and my sons Bob and David. Here's a difficult area in my business. What's your counsel, Lord?" Time after time, I watched my father get off his knees with a tear or two in his eyes and look heavenward and give thanks and appreciation.

While I had never known a God up to that point, there was one thing that I did know as I waded ashore on that fateful day — that my dad knew that God lives, and my dad got answers, real answers, to prayer. So as I dug in, I knew that I could do exactly what my dad did. I'll be eternally grateful for his guidance and teachings.

As I knelt down with my head bared, even in the danger of crossfire, I asked my Heavenly Father very simply: "Do you live? Are you real? Is Jesus Christ really a Savior? Was Joseph Smith a prophet of the Church like I've heard all of my life and can't understand?" And then it came, that sweet, inner commitment and verification, spirit touching spirit saying in a silent voice, "It is so." So complete was that feeling within my heart on that July day that I could have actually gotten up out of my hole, I felt, and walked unharmed across that battlefield. The peace and the security was that wonderful.

Can you understand even in a small way what I'm trying to say? A testimony was born because I asked with real intent to know. I had prayed a thousand times before, just the mechanical way because the pressure was on from the family and the Church. Now I really wanted to know. Are you there, Lord? Will you tell me? And he did! Since that day, I have given my life to him. I have had verification upon verification that this Church is true, that Joseph Smith was called and ordained to restore the gospel of Jesus Christ. Now, I haven't taken it just on the basis of one testimony because my mind won't permit me that luxury. (And I don't think most minds will.)

I came back from that war and used my GI bill and went to college. What a struggle that was because of the void that I had created in high school! To involve you in somewhat of a shorter story, I happened to have married outside of the Church because of my mixed values in those days. I think I have some idea of how youth struggle in this world today. And while I was fortunate enough to help my wife become converted and to see her join the Church and become one of the strongest Latter-day Saints you'll ever know, as I reflect back now, what a risk I took!

My wife came from a very strong Protestant family; and in order to handle myself effectively, or at least as effectively as I thought I should, I attended a Protestant theological school of their faith and graduated with their ministers because I wanted to know, spiritually speaking, whether the Mormon Church could stand the test of the world. How happy I am to report that not only did I get a testimony when I asked as Moroni indicated, but I put it to the test for four years in one of the best theological schools of the West Coast! It's true, brothers and sisters. Are you willing to really find out? Do you really want to know whether this thing is what we say it is? Then invest the time and the energy and the commitment in prayer and see if I'm not right. I have tried it, and I'm the type of person that frequently cannot just accept a thing because someone says so. I need to learn within myself that it is so.

At the prompting of my father, I had received a patriarchal blessing prior to my going into that combat experience. A patriarchal blessing is an opportunity to have revealed to us the spiritual gifts, opportunities, and actual capacities that are within us. These are revealed to us in such a way that we can actually formulate our lives for the future as we apply the principles of the Church.

I don't want to burden you with much of its contents, but that patriarchal blessing stated in a number of paragraphs that I would live to be what we might term in the vernacular a "ripe old age," that I would have a wife and a family and certain experiences in the Church. It concluded, as they often do, with the conditional clause, "if thou art willing." You see, there's the condition. If you're willing, Paul, these things will come to pass. One of the paragraphs indicated divine intervention in conditions of combat.

Well, I didn't have to wait long when I waded ashore on that beach to see the realization of that promise. I had committed myself in the foxhole that morning. I promised the Lord that if he would see me through the ordeal ahead, I would do everything in my power to serve him. Now, there were one thousand of us in my combat team that left San Francisco on that fateful journey and just six of us came back two and a half years later. How do you like that for odds? (And of the six of us, five had been severely wounded two or more times and had been sent back into the line as replacements.)

There had been a thousand incidents in which I should have been taken from the earth by the enemy but for some reason was not. Let me just give you another illustration. During my second night in combat, we pushed some two or three thousand yards into the island of Guam and dug into a very intense area of jungle. Of the same thousand men that I mentioned, this one night alone we lost 289 men. The enemy had very cleverly secluded three tanks in a wooded area that we didn't know about. The island of Guam is a solid coral-rock island. It has volcanic ash covering the surface. You go down a few inches and you hit this solid rock. It's like digging a hole in the sidewalk — about that easy. What I'm saying is, if you're digging a foxhole you don't go very deep in the solid rock.

We dug into our foxholes, pushing that volcanic ash up high enough so as to give us a little cover from machine guns and artillery shells. We used to dig in a perimeter effect similar to the Indian and pioneer fighting techniques you see on television where they get in a big circle. This kind of defense was the only way you could protect your flanks or your front, since during the night the enemy would completely surround you. They'd do this constantly.

Unbeknown to us the three enemy tanks were hidden in strategic locations. About eleven o'clock that night their motors started churning. We couldn't imagine what it was. (We could hardly get a jeep up there and they had tanks. How they got them there we don't know yet!) But all of a sudden, here they came. They rolled right through the perimeter, and small rifle fire doesn't do any damage to a tank. You couldn't throw any heavy stuff because it could bounce off the tanks and drop into the holes of your buddies. You could literally annihilate your whole force if you weren't careful. What the tanks were trying to do was create a panic, and they did a very good job of it.

The enemy realized as they came into the perimeter that we weren't deep enough in our holes to have protection, so they ran the tanks back and forth over the holes, crushing men below them. You could hear the screams and the pandemonium from one moment to the next. This went on for fifteen or twenty minutes.

There were two tanks out to my right and to the flank, and I was watching them with great care, although it was a dark, rainy night and I couldn't see five or ten feet in front of me. Occasionally a flare or bullet or ricochet would go off and I'd just glimpse a shadow. Because of the terrible noise (you couldn't hear yourself think), I was unaware that the third tank had come clear around behind me. Before I realized it, I heard this motor and I felt dirt crumbling in on me. I looked up and the tank track, or the heavy part of the track, was coming right over my hole. Fortunately, it was at an angle. If it had come straight in, I wouldn't be here to tell you about it.

My hole was just on the edge of a little hill; and as the tank went up and was about ready to drop down, for some reason or another it stopped. The heavy track caught my helmet and pushed my head into the bank to where I couldn't get it out. That's an interesting thing, isn't it, to have an enemy tank sitting on your head!

The track was edged so that no matter which way I went I was just stuck there; and if the tank had moved an inch or two either way, it would have just snapped my helmet and that would have been it. The machine sat there for what seemed to be a good four or five minutes, and our men were firing at it with everything they had. And then, for some reason, that tank backed off and went the other way instead of spinning or turning as it had been doing previously. The enemy could always feel when their tank was on an opening or a hole. The minute they sensed they were on top of one of our foxholes, they would just turn the tank, and it would crush anything beneath it. But in my case alone, they backed off.

The next morning as we measured the fight and followed the track marks, the sergeant said to me: "Boy! You sure are lucky, aren't you?" Yes, lucky — and I pulled out my patriarchal blessing and read a little bit of it. "If thou art willing, Paul, there will be divine intervention in thy behalf."

Not many battles later, my squad got the assignment to go out and find the position of the enemy's ammunition and supply belt, which was an assignment that was rather frequently given to an infantry squadron. (We used to rotate this assignment. Contrary to John Wayne, we didn't volunteer as you see on television. We just had to assign these on a rotation basis, and each man took his turn.) This assignment required an all-night scrimmage where we were to go out and spend one complete day and night and come back the next morning.

You can't always predict a battle, and this was one of that kind. By the time we got behind enemy lines, secured the position of their ammunition dump, plotted it on our map, and started back, the battle line had changed. Where we had been the day before, the enemy now was. They had pushed our forces back a quarter of a mile in a counterattack.

We came around the hill into a valley, thinking it was our territory. But the enemy now held both hills, and we were right between them in a valley. That's a thrilling experience, let me tell you, when you learn all of a sudden that both hills don't belong to you. By the time we discovered it, they had annihilated one or two of our squads and the rest of us took cover in a rather deep shell-hole right in the center. Our position was not too good because of the location of the enemy and the fact that it was close to late afternoon.

We knew we had to be out of there by nightfall for the enemy would move in and just squeeze us out, the fighting being what it was in that sector. So we sat there, eleven of us, plotting what we'd do and how we'd do it. We were still 350 to 400 yards from our lines. (In fact, we had even heard our fellows yell when they saw our plight, but it was too late.) So we kept calling back over to them, informing them that we were going to make a dash for it. Surveying our situation, we decided that right at dusk we would go as a team. We realized that some wouldn't make it; but it was the only way to get the rest of us out of there.

After a long inventory-taking episode, it was determined that we'd go at 6:15, because it would be just dark enough so that we'd be less of a target but light enough so that we could make our way. We called over to our fellows to give us as much cover as they could with fire power and to remind them that the eleven men they saw scampering would be us. They hollered back that that's what they'd do.

We stripped down our rifles, since we couldn't take them with us, and gathered all the heavy weights, the ammunition pouches, the grenades and disassembled them as much as we could so that the enemy wouldn't benefit from them. We sat there meditating, talking, and waiting. The others asked if I would kneel and lead them in a word of prayer. We promised to do certain things for each other if one made it and the other didn't, in terms of family and welfare and all the rest. I remember looking at my watch at 6:05. I always carried my blessing with me, and I now opened it up and studied it again. In essence it told me that I would live to see certain things come to pass, "if you're willing, if you're willing."

There wasn't a human way out of that situation. You would have to have been there to appreciate what I'm trying to tell you. The zero minute came and we shook hands. After that word of prayer you never saw eleven men scamper so fast. I wish I'd have had the track coach there. I think I set a new world's record right there as I made my way to the American lines. Three or four of the men didn't get above the surface of the ground. They were cut right down with machine guns. One of my good friends who was with me was almost cut in two with a burst. I stopped to try to help him but could see it was hopeless. So I started on. It had been raining hard and the ground was slippery and muddy. We would fall almost as many times as we took a step, trying to get some traction. As I ran, I moved this way and that way and I could tell I had a sniper with a machine gun right on me because the dirt and the mud just kicked right up behind and around me.

Well, by this time it was everybody for himself. As I scampered within fifty yards of our line, the sniper got a direct bead on me and the first burst caught me in the right heel and took my combat boot right off; it made me barefooted that quickly, without touching me physically. It spun me around and I went down on my knee. As I went down, another machine gun burst came across my back and ripped the belt and the canteen and the ammunition pouch right off my back, again without touching me.

I got up to run and another burst hit me right in the back of the helmet. It hit in the steel part, ricocheted enough so that it came up over my head, just burned the top of my head and split the helmet in two, but didn't touch me. Then I lunged forward again and another burst caught me in the loose part of my clothing at the shoulder, so that I could take both of my shirt sleeves off without removing my coat. And then one more lunge and I fell over the line into the arms of one of the dirtiest sergeants you ever saw. He had watched the whole encounter.

"Paul," he said, "you sure are lucky." I was the only one of the eleven that had even made it the first hundred yards.

Lucky? Oh, you call it what you want. But I've had verification after verification, and I have only told you two of a thousand such incidents that occurred to me in two years of combat experience. I can testify with quite a bit of assurance, brothers and sisters, of the divinity of these things that I have come to test, to know, through personal experience. I only relate these things because I feel that young people everywhere — in and out of the Church — need to commence a serious investigation of their own souls and status in this life. You're at a time now when you can prepare and do those things that you ought to do.

We placed an inscription over the Seventy-seventh Infantry Division cemetery on the island of Okinawa. In memory of thousands of brave soldiers, the inscription reads, "We gave our todays in order that you might have your tomorrows."

Now, young people of this Church, you have a moral obligation to prepare yourselves in countless ways if you are to repay in part the sacrifices that have been made for you. May you do this, as you find the true values of this life in search of sacred things. I bear you the witness which is mine that God lives, that Jesus is the Christ. I have come to know these things. I haven't always known them. There has not been in this world or this Church a greater skeptic than I. But now I know the truth of what I'm saying. I challenge you to come to find it yourselves, and as you do, you will be as excited as I am to share it with the world, because it's the most important message there is in this life.

18

Living Prophets for Our Generation

I am grateful for a happy church, a church that brings security and understanding and faith in the lives of its people. This is a church that is not only optimistic but also has a firm foundation. It has been reiterated many times already.

The optimism of this church brought to my mind the little experience of two Vermont farmers. It seems that in Vermont there falls a great deal of rain, and the hills are green as a result. One day a farmer was walking down a back road, and it was very muddy. Suddenly he came upon a large puddle, and in the middle of the puddle he saw a straw hat. He thought he recognized it. He tiptoed over and lifted it up and, lo and behold, under it was his friend Zeb. He was right up to his neck in the mud.

He said: "Zeb, it looks like you have a problem. Do you need some help?"

Zeb said, "No thanks, Zeke, I'll be all right. I have got a good horse under me."

Well, I have felt that kind of optimism throughout this church. Spiritually speaking, we have some great horses under us, and I am grateful for that kind of faith and testimony.

Sister Dunn and I had a sweet experience while in the mission home in Cambridge. A very wonderful couple sat before us investigating the Church, seeking answers to searching questions. In the course of our conversation the question was raised, Has God really spoken to man today?

I would like to answer that question again for other honest, seeking people.

It was Tuesday — three days before the crucifixion. Standing in the courtyard of the temple, the Savior looked down upon the dark faces of those who were plotting to take his life. Said he:

"Woe unto you, scribes and Pharisees, hypocrites! for ye are like unto whited sepulchres, which indeed appear beautiful outward, but are within full of dead men's bones, and of all uncleanness." (Matthew 23:27.)

And while he was on the subject of dead men, Jesus pointed out to these people that they had no capacity to honor God's prophets, until they were dead. He said again:

"Ye build the tombs of the prophets, and garnish the sepulchres of the righteous,

"And say, If we had been in the days of our fathers, we would not have been partakers with them in the blood of the prophets."

But then Jesus added: "Wherefore ye be witnesses unto yourselves, that ye are the children of them which killed the prophets." (Matthew 23:29-31.)

A moment later from the heights of the temple Jesus looked down upon the city and poured forth the sorrow of his soul:

"O Jerusalem, Jerusalem, thou that killest the prophets, and stonest them which are sent unto thee, how often would I have gathered thy children together, even as a hen gathereth her chickens under her wings, and ye would not." (Matthew 23:37.)

Here is an amazing paradox. Jesus was emphasizing one of the lessons of history, that the majority of the people have never been able to recognize a living prophet. In each generation they have idolized the prophets of the past, while they stoned the living prophets of the present.

Can you believe with me that God could speak to men who were the common clay of our generations? If you do, you are unusual, because the rest of the people follow the human tendency to look back and honor only the prophets who are dead. And look at the way they usually honor them:

They place these prophets of the past on imaginary pedestals.

They make a selection from their teachings that suits their own particular fancy.

And while honoring a few popular phrases that identify them with these great servants of God, they smugly go along their own way.

But you cannot do this with living prophets. Why? Because living prophets will denounce those who profess allegiance to God, but follow the rashness of their own selfish lives. They will not allow men to pick their teachings to pieces and construct a crazy quilt pattern of personal interpretation that suits fashion and private folly.

Perhaps that is why prophets are never very popular while they are alive to defend the teachings that God has given them.

Do you know what your task and mine is? It is to discover whether or not God has raised up living prophets for our generation.

The Bible teaches that whenever prophets are raised up, things will begin to happen. Doctrines will be made clear. New truths will be revealed. Prophecies will be pronounced. The kingdom of God will be revitalized — and every honest seeker after truth will be able to see the power with which the prophets of the past and of the present carry out their missions.

You see, that is what convinced Israel, when Moses came down to them. This is what aroused Judah when Jeremiah appeared in their midst. Even in the days of the Savior, the antagonistic teachers of the law were "astonished at his doctrine: For he taught them as one having authority." (Matthew 8:28-29.) And those who followed Jesus observed great power in his ministry.

This is also the way to find out whether or not there are living prophets of God on the earth today. If there are, things will begin to happen. There will be new revelation, the power of prophecy, the authority of the priesthood, and the capacity to revitalize the faith of every honest soul who hungers for a message from God for our generation.

Do you think it is difficult to be a prophet? As you read the scriptures, you cannot help but be impressed with the fact that the calling of a prophet is a most difficult assignment. In fact, you will be astonished to find that when some of the prophets first received their callings they pleaded with the Lord not to send them forth. This was the case with Moses, who said, " . . .they will not believe me. . . . I am not eloquent." (Exodus 4:1, 10.) This was the case with Enoch, who said, " . . . all the people hate me; for I am slow of speech; wherefore am I thy servant?"(Moses 6:31.) And this was also the case with Jeremiah, who said, ". . . behold, I cannot speak: for I am a child." (Jeremiah 1:6.)

These men felt incapable. They felt there were others who would be more readily accepted. But in spite of their own feelings to the contrary, they went forth and delivered their messages because God had called them.

The same principle applied when Jesus selected his twelve apostles. He said to them, "Ye have not chosen me, but I have chosen you, and ordained you." (John 15:16.)

And here's the *clue* to the way prophets are raised up! In the holy writ you will not find a single instance where God ever selected a professional holy man to be one of his prophets. In every case, the call came like a bolt out of the blue, often to men who considered themselves weak and incapable, and were amazed that God should honor them with revelation and a prophetic calling.

So now we come to the crucial questions: Have prophets of God been raised up in modern times? Have any revelations been recorded? Has any new light come back to the earth to solve the problems of our day?

Time would not permit mention of the many revelations that are contained in modern scripture declaring this very thing. Perhaps no headlines in any newspaper could do justice to the thrilling announcement that came during the past century to reaffirm the word of God to the children of men. Beginning in the spring of 1820, the restoration of the gospel began. And notice how it came forth:

God bypassed all the professional proponents of religion throughout the world and spoke to a humble, fourteen-year-old boy. Jewish tradition has it that this was exactly the age of Jeremiah when he received his first call. And, like Jeremiah, the young prophet was overwhelmed by his assignment. He was a youth. His education was limited, his means were very modest. And he had a most ordinary name, Joseph Smith.

But within three years, important things began to happen. Others were raised up to assist. New knowledge began to pour forth. Doctrines began to be clarified. Revelations were recorded. The original organization of the Church of Jesus Christ, which was lost sometime after the first century, was soon restored. The gospel came back into the earth in great power, just as Jesus had promised it would when his disciples asked him concerning the last days.

At first, the work progressed slowly. People said God would not speak to a mere boy. They held aloft their scriptures containing the writings of prophets from the past and said that was all the revelation they wanted. They said the new young prophet was making up his revelations — that they were not from God. But this could have been expected. These people could not recognize a living prophet any more than the people at the time of Christ. Nevertheless, Joseph Smith recorded the prophecies and revelations that were given him.

Ever since the gospel was restored, there have been living prophets of God upon the earth. They are with us today. What is their calling? To strengthen our faith, to record the will of God for our generation, to place peace in troubled hearts, and to prepare us to meet the challenge of evil among men in the world today.

The same God of Abraham, Isaac, and Jacob has a message for

the nations of the earth in this modern, jet-propelled era in which we live. It is as thrilling and vital as the message that came to Judah from Jeremiah, or to Israel from Moses.

Recently I reread of an American boy — one of the several thousand who died in the battle of Iwo Jima, a place he probably had never heard of before the war took him there — who wrote in a little ten-cent notebook his last words, his survey of the world situation, as follows:

"This is the time for new revelation. People don't think much about religion nowadays, but we need a voice from on high, brother, and I don't mean maybe.

"This thing has got out of human ability to run. I'm no religious fanatic, but we are in a situation where something better than human brains has got to give us advice."

This was the last will and testament of a twenty-year-old boy who died with the thought that mankind's predicament was one that only divine help might solve. That boy cried for new revelation, for a voice of spiritual authority from on high.

More and more thoughtful people each year conclude that mankind needs new authority and revelation from God. My friends, it has come!

I am honored to declare to you that God speaks to his children. He lives; he cares; and to those of you who have not yet had that special witness in your hearts, be in tune with me now, as I declare to you with all the fervor of my soul that there is a living prophet in the world today who reveals the mind and will of God.

19

The Meaning
of Jesus Christ
for Our Time

The experiences and messages of our Church leaders have brought to my attention, as it relates to our responsibility, an experience I had a few years ago while serving as a religion teacher on the University of Southern California campus.

Because of my particular position in directing the institute program, I was invited by that great institution to participate in what was known as a PTA convention discussing the problems concerning our youth. I suppose I was invited as a member because of the great work that this Church does for its young people.

I remember that the president of the university himself was sponsoring a little luncheon to be held before the conference. As I entered the cafeteria, there assembled around the table were those who would participate in the meeting that was to ensue. I had not met my colleagues who were to discuss the problems of youth with me, and this was a chance for us to get acquainted. I noticed when I went in to take my seat that there were appropriate name cards identifying each one of us and that I was to be seated next to a full navy commander.

As we sat down, the navy commander leaned over and said to me, "You're the Latter-day Saint, aren't you?"

And I wondered what I had done to tip him off.

I said, "Yes, sir, I am, how did you know?"

"Well," he said, pointing to the cup that I had turned over as I took my chair, "I noticed you weren't going to partake of that liquid."

I said: "Yes, sir, but I happen to know a lot of people who aren't members of my faith that don't use that liquid. How would you know?"

"Well, it is the way you turned your cup over." He said, "You have that Mormon twist in your wrist."

I immediately started to exercise my own faith as a missionary and attempted to teach him a little about the Word of Wisdom. He interrupted me and said: "Young man, I didn't invite this conversation to get a dissertation from you at this time. But I would like to take this opportunity, if I may, to salute you. May I do that?"

Well, now, to a former PFC, that is great tribute. I said, "Please, sir, go right ahead."

"Well," he said, "I don't mean you personally." I must confess that hurt my ego a little.

He went on: "I would like to take this opportunity to salute your church and that great body you represent here today. As you know, I am directing one of the navy testing programs educationally throughout the United States, and wherever I go I watch you people with great interest, and I suppose I have seen many of you without your knowing it, and I would like you to know, Mr. Dunn, that I feel secure in the presence of the Latter-day Saint people."

He said: "You have something, I don't know what it is [you and I do — the priesthood, the Spirit of the Lord which beckons all to come], but," he added, "I feel that one day this country — in fact the world — will look to you for direction. Thank you, sir, for being what you are and for the great influence of your church."

Can you appreciate in some small measure the thrill that was mine as a representative of God's true church? You have had like experiences, and I thought about that experience again as we have been reminded of our great responsibilities, as parents, as teachers, and as leaders.

I would like to pay tribute to you wonderful parents who have trained your children in the way that they should go, that you might send into the mission field the choice spirits that you have. My, what a leaven in the worldly loaf they are. And I testify to you that they are great men and women, testifying to the divinity of our Lord and Savior, Jesus Christ.

As members of The Church of Jesus Christ of Latter-day Saints, we with many others of the Christian world anticipate the coming of Easter and its celebration in commemoration of the resurrection of Jesus Christ.

Anticipating Easter in an era that has been described as "post-Christian"; in an age when modern science and technology have given rise to the "secular city," as they prefer to call it; when an analytical philosophy has described as meaningless all propositions that go beyond certain defined limits of sense experience; when biblical scholarship has mythologized the New Testament, and a new radical theology has proclaimed the death of God, I think we need to raise anew the question of the meaning of Jesus Christ for our time. Of course, for many of our contemporaries, caught up in the crosscurrents of a predominantly secular culture, the life, death, and resurrection of Jesus Christ can have little or no meaning.

I raise the question — What is the meaning of Jesus Christ for our times? — not as preliminary to the presentation of a legal brief in defense of the fact of the resurrection, nor to afford an opportunity to argue in support of our belief in the resurrection. This is not the occasion for religious argument. This is an occasion to bear witness to the hope, the joy, and the faith that we have in the divine message that Christ lives.

Jesus Christ has meant many things to many people, but there can be no mistake about what he meant to the early Christians. New Testament faith was based upon the belief that in the life, death, and resurrection of Jesus Christ, God, our Father, in a decisive manner, had prepared the way for man to enter the world, live the complete life, and again regain his presence. Motivated by this belief, early Christians went forth to proclaim the gospel, or the "good news." It was the overwhelming impact of the "good news," centering in the resurrection, that caused Christians to face the threat of the dungeon, the sword, and the cross. Early Christianity moved forward under the compelling faith that the resurrected Jesus was Christ, the Lord.

That the resurrection was central to the early Christian message cannot be doubted. Writing to the Corinthians, Paul said, "If Christ be not raised, your faith is vain. . . ." (1 Corinthians 15:17.) Read in context, it is clear that Paul is not trying to prove the resurrection of Christ in this statement. He is here appealing to the one thing that all Christians accepted in order to prove another point, namely, that because of his resurrection Jesus was the Messiah, the Savior; and through the redemptive mission of Jesus, as the Christ, as the Savior, man's own immortality and eternal life were assured. This was the gospel. This was the "good news." This was the faith of early Christianity.

Now, after almost two thousand years, in the passing time of a century characterized by a decline in religious faith, the restored gospel joyfully proclaims anew, with as much enthusiasm and vigor as did the first-century Christians, that Christ is risen. Our confidence in man's salvation through the atonement of Christ is a matter of faith, not completely understood, yet the central meaning of Jesus Christ for our time, as for all time, is to be found in that faith — faith in man's salvation through the resurrection.

Salvation in this sense is a gift to a man through the grace of God. But those who are familiar with The Church of Jesus Christ of Latter-day Saints know that it is also a religion of merit. Our concern is not only with the future but also with the past, and especially with the present. Mormonism touches every phase of life; it is a gospel of work, of play, of service, of prayer, of hope. And belief in immortality looms large in this picture.

Eternal life, however, does not merely embrace the future; it also embraces the past and the present. This means that the present is determinative of what the future holds for man, both as an individual and as society. This world, therefore, is not regarded as some condemned region in space where man awaits transportation to heaven or hell.

Man and the world share a common destiny — man and the world are to be saved together. Man's purpose in the world is to progressively know and live the revelations of God reflected in his own soul and the creations about him. Man will never be worthy of or capable of appreciating a more glorious state of existence until he has in some measure learned to appreciate the meaning, beauty, and problems of the one in which he now finds himself. This means that while the past and future are important, the present is the greatest of all time, because it holds the promise of all that is to come.

With this view in mind, I raise again the question of the meaning of Jesus Christ for today. Within this dimension of the gospel we find the meaning of Christ in the very urgent and serious problems that we face as individuals and as a nation. Some of these problems come from the past and continue to haunt us; other problems are of modern making and are peculiar to our age — peculiar at least in the sense that they are in a new setting. It is in the imaginative and creative solution of old problems and in the struggle with novel problems against the gospel of Jesus Christ that he takes on new meaning for us today.

Jesus taught in terms of universal, divine principles, and men were left with the responsibility, and their free agency, to implement those principles. When he was asked how often another should be forgiven, he answered with a statement that urged a limitless spending of forgiveness. When asked what acts were legal on the Sabbath, he answered with a statement that made it plain that people should be considered over institutions. When asked, "Who is my neighbor?" he answered with a parable in which a neighbor was described as "a certain man" who was in need of help.

If Jesus had merely given moral rules in terms of the culture of his times, his teaching would have long since been out of date. But his teachings are bound to no single culture, nor to any age. Each succeeding age is left to discover a way of making the gospel principles of Jesus Christ live in terms of its own conception of society. When this is done, we are compelled to recognize that his ideal goes far beyond not only what man has put into practice but also what most men have thought possible.

To speak of our age, therefore, as the "post-Christian" age is a mistake for the simple reason that the Christian age, in any real sense, has not yet been fully achieved. If the fault is said to be in Jesus because he was too idealistic for this hardheaded, practical world, our witness is that Jesus was as much of a realist as an idealist — the real and ideal merge in his life and teachings. It is the world that has not been realistic and has not been able to take him at his word. He said that mankind *is* a brotherhood. The world has said that mankind *ought to be* a brotherhood. We have failed to take his realism seriously, and our problems multiply and grow in complexity.

In regard to the frustration, futility, and meaninglessness in which an increasing number of individual lives are submerged, our witness is that the passing years continue to establish the validity of Jesus Christ's estimate of human personality as the supreme value in the universe. To the disturbed, wandering youth of our time, we testify that personality, that people, that human beings are precious, and that life is worth living.

As to the solution of many of the personal problems with which contemporary man is plagued, our witness is that modernity as well as antiquity give support to Jesus' view that personality is fulfilled not in the self-centeredness of either the occidental or oriental variety, but rather in service to humanity. Human experience today, as always, confirms that whosoever would save his life will lose it, and whosoever shall lose his life in the interest and service of others shall save it.

I have said that the meaning of Jesus Christ for our time is to be found in his death and resurrection, which assures man's immortality. We have also said that the application of his ideal to the central and crucial problems of our day gives us further insight into his meaning for us. He stands as an eternal symbol of our Heavenly Father's interest in and suffering for the needs of humanity. As we see God's will revealed through him for the solution of our personal and social problems, so our faith is made sure that he will be forever meaningful in the lives of men.

We believe that the best and most effective efforts being made today toward the elimination of ignorance and human suffering are in accordance with the Savior's inspiration and revelation. In him and his gospel are to be found the faith and hope of the future. So it is with a deep sense of its permanent and universal meaning that we read his statement as he departed from his disciples: " . . . lo, I am with you always, even unto the end of the world." (Matthew 28:20.)

Mastering
Self

20

Know Thyself, Control Thyself, Give Thyself

I am so honored to address this priesthood session, to sit at the feet of a prophet of the Lord, to hear his counsel and direction, and to feel his spirit. I was particularly impressed with a number of the younger priesthood bearers in the audience who were taking notes, listening to a prophet. I would hope that you young priesthood bearers have the sensitivity to go home and record what has happened in your life on this wonderful occasion. Think how many people in the world would be so honored, to sit in a special meeting with prophets, seers, and revelators.

I salute you fathers who have brought your sons to this meeting, and to others in buildings throughout the country. You young priesthood bearers might as well learn early that your dads and moms will never let you go. This was brought very vividly to my attention several conferences ago when one of the sessions in which I was a speaker was televised to California. My mother resides there.

When I got back to the office after the session was over, there was a note to "call your mother." And so I did, and I thought, "Well, she is calling to congratulate her son." When I reached her on the phone I asked, "Mom, how are you?"

She said: "Paul, I just saw you on TV. Young man, you are not getting enough sleep. You look terrible." Thank God for parents who care and who never let go!

I am grateful for you priesthood leaders, you wonderful

bishops and counselors, stake presidencies, others who have precious priesthood assignments. I think of many bishops and other
leaders in my life as I look out over this great audience.

Not long ago I had an opportunity to speak in Portland,
Oregon. Lo and behold, in the audience was my former bishop,
Raymond Kirkham. He was my bishop when I was an Aaronic
Priesthood boy. I had the courage to call on him — and you
know that can be risky, to call on a bishop who remembers you
when you were a boy. I reminded him as he took the pulpit,
"Remember, I am the last speaker."

He got bold and told those young people of some interesting
experiences involving my youth. He said: "I knew this young man
was destined for a position of leadership. He is the only deacon I
ever had who, after passing the sacrament, could crawl under a
bench and get out the back door before I recognized he was gone."
He said, "I knew he was going all the way, because he took the
whole quorum with him."

Now you young priesthood bearers, I have repented; and I am
grateful for bishops who stood at the back door and redirected my
paths.

I have reflected upon the wonderful sermons, good counsel
and advice given us by a living prophet and other General Authorities of the Church. I would like to summarize my feelings,
directed to you, the Aaronic Priesthood, for what value they
might have in your lives.

I think if I could give a whole sermon in just six words it would
be these: Socrates said many years ago, *"Know thyself,"* Cicero
said, *"Control thyself,"* and the Savior said, *"Give thyself."* Now
will you write that down, young brethren; contemplate the meaning while I just share a thought concerning each one.

To know thyself is to come to know that you and I as priesthood bearers are literally the offspring of Deity; and that means,
young men, that you and I were born to succeed; that in the
preexistence you and I earned a right by our faithfulness and by
our commitment to worthy principles to come into mortality in

order that we might learn through the priesthood how to become like our Father.

That means, if I understand the gospel correctly, that there isn't one single failure among us. The word *can't* is false doctrine in the Mormon Church. When a young man says to me, "I can't do it," I become concerned because in a sense he is saying, "I don't understand the gospel." He may not be motivated; he may have discouragements; there may be barriers in his life; but he *can* succeed.

I promise you young priesthood bearers that if you really come to know who you are through the scriptures and through the revealed doctrine of this Church, you can accomplish anything you want in this life.

I don't mean to suggest by this that you won't stumble a time or two. That is a part of the growing process. The lives of many great men will testify to you that ofttimes they have many failures, and there is no disgrace in falling down; the disgrace is in lying there. To get up one more time than you fall is to be a winner. To stay down is to be a loser.

I think of that great immortal athlete Babe Ruth when I talk about the principle of success and particularly failure. Let me just share a little experience from his life.

It was a beautiful Saturday afternoon in the summer of 1927, and thirty-five thousand wildly excited baseball fans packed Shibe Park. They were giving Babe Ruth the "razzberry" — and good! Lefty (Bob) Grove, one of the greatest left-handed pitchers of all time, had just struck out Babe Ruth on three consecutive pitched balls for the second successive time. Two runners were stranded on the bases.

As the great slugger returned to the bench, amidst wild and abusive jeering, he looked up into the stands with an unruffled smile, just as he did the first time, gave his cap a polite little tip from his perspiring brow, stepped down into the dugout, and calmly took a drink of water.

In the eighth inning, when he came up for his third time at

bat, the situation was critical. The Athletics were leading the Yankees, 3-1. The bases were full and two were out. As Babe selected his favorite bat and started toward the plate, the crowd rose in a body, as if by signal. The excitement was tremendous!

"Strike 'im out again!" pleaded the fans to Grove. Strutting around the pitcher's box, it was easy to see that the big southpaw believed he was going to do just that.

As the mighty batter took his position, the crowd became hysterical. There was a pause. Mickey Cochrane, the A's great catcher, crouched to give the signal. Grove threw one with lightning speed. Ruth swung; it was a foul tip. "Str—ike one!" roared the umpire. Again the signal, and the pitch was too fast to follow. Again, Babe took that magnificent swing — and missed. "Stri—i-i-ke two!" was the call.

Ruth staggered and went down. He had literally swung himself off his feet. There was a cloud of dust as the big fellow sprawled on the ground. The crowd was going mad. Finally, regaining his feet, the "Bambino" brushed the dust off his trousers, dried his hands, and got set for the next pitch. Grove delivered the ball so fast not a single fan could see it. Babe swung — but this time he connected! It was only a split second before everybody seemed to realize what had happened. That ball was never coming back.

It disappeared over the scoreboard and cleared the houses across the street — one of the longest hits ever recorded.

As Babe Ruth trotted around the bases and across the plate behind the other runners — with what proved to be the winning run — he received a wild ovation from the crowd. Ruth doffed his cap with that little smile, and the expression on his face was exactly like the one he wore on his first two trips, when he had gone down swinging.

Later in the season, after the Yanks clinched the American League pennant, Grantland Rice, interviewing the Babe, asked, "What do you do when you get in a batting slump?"

Babe replied: "I just keep goin' up there and keep swingin'. I know the old law of averages will hold good for me the same as it does for anybody else, if I keep havin' my healthy swings. If I strike out two or three times in a game, or fail to get a hit for a week, why should I worry? Let the pitchers worry; they're the guys who're gonna have to pay for it later on."

This unshakable faith in making the law of averages work for him enabled Babe Ruth to accept his bad breaks and failures with a smile. This simple philosophy had much to do with making him baseball's greatest slugger. His attitude of taking both good and bad in stride made him one of the game's greatest heroes.

Why is it, when we read about great athletes or men in other professions, we are seldom told about their failures? For example, we now read of the amazing record of the immortal Babe Ruth, with his total of 741 home runs; but another unapproached world's record of his is carefully buried, and that is that he struck out more times than any other player in history — 1,330 times!

One thousand three hundred and thirty times he suffered the humiliation of walking back to the bench amidst jeers and ridicule. But he never allowed fear or discouragement or failure to keep him down.

Someone has said that success consists not in never falling, but in rising every time you fall. Get up one more time than you go down, young people, and you will win. Stay down, and you lose.

My father used to say, "Paul, there are dozens of rules for success, but none of them work unless you do."

Cicero said, "Control thyself." I had the opportunity in World War II to bat against the immortal Bob Feller in a servicemen's game. If you ever want a lesson in humility, bat against Feller. Bob Feller had a unique distinction as a sixteen-year-old boy. He could take a 9½-inch, five-ounce baseball and throw it sixty feet six inches at 105 miles an hour.

Now that may not impress you, but you go to bat and you're very impressed. To those of you who may not understand that velocity, a nine-inch baseball is the size of an aspirin tablet at sixty feet six inches, at one hundred miles per hour. I submit to you, it makes a difference which side of the plate he throws it.

Bob Feller at age sixteen had a problem. *He lacked contol.* He was a great athlete. He had tremendous capacity. He was born to succeed. He knew himself, but he hadn't disciplined his great talent of speed, so that it was questionable as to whether he would stick in the majors.

But Bob Feller became the great athlete he was because he listened to wise counsel. He had great coaches, and one of them took him aside one day and said: "Bob, it really doesn't matter whether you throw 105 miles an hour or 95. If you will take a little speed off your pitch and put the ball where it belongs, you will succeed!"

We call that *control* in baseball, and you little leaguers know how important control is to a pitcher. Bob listened and became the strike-out artist of his era.

You don't know Jim Rusick, I think, unless you are related to him. I played ball with Jim. Jim Rusick was a sixteen-year-old boy on the Hollywood High School baseball team. He could throw a 9½-inch baseball 105 miles an hour, but he wouldn't listen to counsel. He didn't learn to control the talent that he had, and Jim has never been heard of since.

It's one thing to be born with ability to succeed; it's another thing to harness it and to control it.

This is the purpose of the gospel of Jesus Christ, to control that which we have been born with. That is the purpose of the Church and its programs. We need to learn how to control that which God has given us.

Finally, the Savior said, Take all that I have given you, harness it, discipline it, and then give it to the world. Give thyself.

Let me just conclude with a little experience I had in New England.

I think one of the greatest thrills that a mission president experiences is to receive a new missionary. I received notice from the First Presidency that eight young men were to be assigned to New England. Shortly they arrived. This was a great treat for

Jeanne and me, as we greeted these new missionaries in the mission home. One by one, as they came in, we tried to set them at ease.

The first one was a brilliant-looking boy. I won't describe him, but I thought, "Thank heaven he is here." The second was just like him, and the third and the fourth. Now this, I thought, will put our mission on top.

Then I got down to number seven, and I don't mind telling you some of the concerns of my heart. I thought, This will be a challenge. I couldn't believe it; and unlike the counsel that Christ gave us not to judge our neighbors, here I was judging him. I thought, This kid just doesn't have the image.

My wife gave me a glance, and her look said, "Good luck for the next two years."

Let me just describe him to you. He was wearing a shirt that was size seventeen; his neck was an eleven. I could have pulled out his collar and put another elder in it. He had on a coat that he inherited from his dad, and you couldn't see his hands. He had a trench coat that he got from an uncle from World War I, and he had a haircut that was an Idaho original.

The New England Mission contains six of the United States and four provinces of Canada, including Labrador. As my wife and I lay in bed that night, she said, "What are you going to do with him?"

I said, "It's time to open up Labrador." I thought I had to protect the Church's image from this interesting-looking elder.

Well, that morning before I made my assignments, I knelt in prayer — thank the Lord for prayer — and I asked the Lord what I should do now; and the Spirit whispered, "Keep him in Cambridge."

And I said, "Spirit, I won't." I said, "I am the president of this mission."

And the Spirit seemed to respond with counsel, "Yes, but you will keep him in Cambridge."

Cambridge is a very sophisticated area, with all of those

universities and art centers. Well, I kept him. When I went down to breakfast, my two assistants were sitting there; and they said, "What are you going to do with him?"

I said, "We are going to keep him in Cambridge."

And they said, "President, you are kidding."

I said, "I have been seeking guidance all night, and we will keep him in Cambridge."

Two days later I got a call from a distinguished professor. I haven't time to give you the details. He said, "Paul, Friday night may I be baptized?"

I questioned him a bit. He had been through several score of missionaries the past nine years. I said, "What happened?"

He said, "This little fellow you sent me." (He was referring to my new elder.) And then he described the experience.

He said, "No sooner had he and his companion entered the office and shook my hand when he asked, 'Would you mind if we had a word of prayer?' " (This was a meeting over in his school office.) The professor said, "Not if it will do you any good." Then he remarked, "Before I could get back to my desk, this little fellow fell on his knees and started to talk to the Lord." And he said, "Paul, I looked up three times to see if the Lord was standing there." He said: "I don't know what happened to me; you describe it, but I had the most wonderful feeling come over me, and I now know what the Spirit is. I want to be baptized."

We baptized him, and he is doing a fine work for the Church and is a great asset on campus. It was all accomplished because this young elder from Idaho, whom I had misjudged, guided by the Spirit, gave himself to the Lord.

And I learned a great lesson: Don't judge! "Within the oyster shell uncouth, the purest pearl may hide, but oft you'll find a heart of truth within a rough outside."

The Lord bless us to remember who we are, to control ourselves, and to give ourselves to the Lord.

21

Your Own

Temple

I'm sensitive to the subject of physical and mental health, alertness and activity, having just recently undergone open-heart surgery myself. It reminds me of an experience I had at my very first outing shortly after my recuperation. I went to a nonmember open house, where, of course, the members were trying to convert the nonmembers to the Church. They used as a theme "Open Up Your Hearts." When it came my turn to speak, I said, "Next time you ask me to speak, select a little different topic, will you?"

It further reminds me of an experience I had not long ago in the temple. One of the privileges that is mine in this office and calling is to perform temple marriages. They are sacred and wonderful. I think they are the most exciting things we do in the Church, and I'm sure some of you would agree. On this occasion I was performing a marriage for one of my former missionaries, and he was one who needed a little help and counsel. You know what I'm talking about — there are some that just don't quite get the whole vision. He was a good boy, but he just needed a little extra counsel, so I really honed in on him. You should have been there. I gave some of the greatest counsel you've ever heard. It was terrific. My wife was a witness. Out in the hall after the marriage was over she nudged me with her elbow and said, "Say, why don't you do some of those things?" Now, I guess, you might well ask me that question now.

I'm going to talk on physical fitness and some of the aspects that surround it. While I believe it and teach it, sometimes I don't do it. But I've repented. I did it for the first thirty-five years of my life as a so-called athlete. Then I got called to be a General Authority and went behind a desk, and on a plane, and in a car— I learned some other laws and rules, and I am now trying to set that in order.

Let me use as a text a statement of the apostle Paul from 1 Corinthians. This great leader, giving counsel to the people of the times, makes this statement: "Know ye not that ye are the temple of God, and that the Spirit of God dwelleth in you? If any man defile the temple of God, him shall God destroy; for the temple of God is holy, which temple ye are." (1 Corinthians 3:16-17.)

That is pretty profound, isn't it? It was the Prophet Joseph Smith who later said, "The spirit and the body constitute the soul of man." We talk about saving souls in the kingdom. To be accurate, we have to include the spirit and the body. Too often I find that Mormons just think of the spirit. The spirit is very important. But the purpose for which we have come is to gain a physical body, and the two go back in a resurrected form to be like unto him. That is just basic Mormon theology, isn't it?

I would like to treat each of those two, although there are many variables and other counterparts I would like to discuss if time permitted. The spirit is most important. Sometimes we have a tendency to judge people's spirit by just outer surfaces, and that is dangerous if we are not careful.

I learned something several years ago as a mission president. There was a time in my life, a most glorious time, when I was given the opportunity from the First Presidency of the Church to serve as a mission president in New England. It's exciting. It's wonderful. It's one of the most thrilling things that could happen to you in the kingdom; but by the same token, it's one of the most frustrating, challenging assignments. Can you imagine having two hundred young people, ages nineteen to twenty-one, given to you to care for all day, every day? They come in all sorts of sizes and shapes and with various designs and motivations. You all of a sudden get a little guy that Mom and Dad couldn't handle for nineteen years so they sent him to you, and they pray that you'll do what they didn't do. Somebody once asked me, "Paul, what is it like to be a mission president?" I have a pretty good definition. It's like taking two hundred priests on an overnight hike for three years.

You think about it. A little kid calls you from one hundred miles away and he says, "President, I want to go home." He's all yours, nobody else's. So you check the handbook; it says, "Motivate him." And then you get on the phone and you try to motivate him and take away his homesickness and his lack of spirit, and you try to put something in its place. It's a real challenge, but with it comes the greatest blessings of all because you are dealing in the realm of the spirit. And it's the spirit, of course, in the gospel that makes you and me unique in all of the world. It's the spirit that enables you and me to work to disseminate the great message of the Church throughout the whole of the earth. What a privilege! What a blessing! I hope it's a blessing for you, not just the mechanics of a job — and there's another sermon in that to be sure.

I have found out in the Church as I have toured its stakes and worked with the Latter-day Saints all over the world, that basically there are three kinds of people in the world and in the Church. There are self-starters, there are those you have to kind of crank up, and there are those you have to tow in. Even in Church headquarters you get those three once in a while, don't you? Stated another way, there are three kinds of Mormon missionaries: those who make it happen, those who watch it happen, and those who wonder what happened. Well, as a mission president you know what we are hoping for, don't you? Those who will come out and bolster the spirit and really create an attitude of interest and desire to motivate others. My wife and I were blessed to have many such elders in our mission. But we also had some who needed a little "cranking up."

I got a letter one time from a district leader in the upper part of my mission. The missionaries had labored, they thought, very diligently with no success. Their request read: "Dear President Dunn, We are in outer darkness. These people here do not want the gospel. Let's kick the dust from our shoes, close the area, and get us out of here. Sincerely, Your Elders." Now, if you were a mission president, would you take that request seriously? I would in one sense, but do you think that's a true assessment of people in the world? See, they were judging. But there was probably a reason for which they were judging. Being close to the scene, I thought I might look into it a little more carefully. I was going to start a mission tour, and though I hadn't planned to go through that city, I included it now on my tour.

I used to have a standing policy with all of my missionaries that whenever I was out in the field, chances were pretty good that I would come and visit with them. I would tell them: "I don't want to trap you. I'm not out trying to spy on you. I'm just interested in your welfare. So don't be surprised some morning at six o'clock if I knock on your door and say, 'I'm here to study with you.'" Yet some of them were still surprised. "It's you!" That was kind of fun as I'd go through the mission.

My wife and I and two assistants arrived at the city in question. It was about noon. Our missionaries used to come home for lunch because it was a better arrangement. This was an old town built in about 1730. The missionaries' apartment was located right downtown. It was upstairs overlooking a little main street. It was a quaint little town, choice and beautiful in it's own appointment.

I knocked; nobody responded. I knocked again, and pretty soon, thump, thump, thump down the stairs came this elder. He opened the door, and I'll never forget his "It's you!" He looked like he was having a revelation.

"Yes, it's me," I answered. "We got your letter of distress. I hadn't planned on coming this time, but I thought I had better. Aren't you going to invite us in?" I could see that he wanted to somehow warn his companion, but he didn't know how. In that air of frustration, trapped, in a sense, he invited us up the stairs.

The elders were in the process of preparing their noon nourishment, and I use the term very loosely. That has a lot to do with what I want to say here in a moment — proper care of the body so that the spirit can be what the Lord intended it to be. I think there is no problem in how we feel about the spirit. The question today is perhaps how it fits with the body to constitute the soul of man. And sometimes we forget the body and the physical aspect. We let it kind of go. I did for a time and have paid an interesting price here of late. Well, I've known that there is a high correlation between the physical fitness, the mental alertness, and the spirituality of missionaries and of Latter-day Saints in general.

Kind of suspecting what I would find, I invited myself into their kitchen, and I was shocked. I don't think they had done the dishes in thirty days, and I could describe the scene, but women are present. What they had for lunch that day I couldn't believe. I remember I had one pair of elders that went thirty days, thirty straight days, on cabbage. Both of them had heads that looked like it. I had an elder that went over forty days on popcorn, and they were questioning: "President, how do you get the spirit of the thing? How do you get out there and really get motivated?" Study and prepare, sure that's great, that's wonderful, but that doesn't guarantee that the Lord is going to guide and direct you if you go contrary to other basic laws of health.

Knowing what I might find elsewhere in the apartment, with the condition of the kitchen what it was, I said very boldly, "Elders, would you show Sister Dunn and me your bedroom?" They were a little reluctant, and rightly so, but they finally escorted us in. It was highly embarrassing for all parties. Beds hadn't been made since they had been in that area. The sheets were black. There was about a quarter inch of dust on the floor. Then the real clincher. Thrown carelessly in the corner on the floor were six or seven pairs of holy garments.

Now let me ask you a question. If you were the Holy Ghost, would you bless that apartment? If you were the Lord, would you give those missionaries success? I don't know what their intent was, but they hadn't earned the right of the Spirit. They had defiled the very thing that they were out to represent. We walked into the living room. I was silent for a minute and then I said to the senior companion, "I really stopped here to kind of help you rededicate the area, and I wanted to kneel in prayer with you." In an effort to teach a principle, I continued, "I can't find a place to kneel down without my wife's dress getting dirty, can you?" This little elder dropped down on his knees and took his shirt sleeve and cleaned off a place for my wife to kneel. Question, Where do you think the Spirit was in that city? It wasn't in that apartment. It wasn't with those missionaries. Would you believe a transfer would be in order, and maybe some other teaching principles? So we made some changes. We brought in some "make it happen" elders. It wouldn't surprise you if I testified that we baptized twenty-nine people in the next two weeks. Same church, same mission, same city, but a different spirit. And two little guys couldn't understand the principle behind it. It had to do with physical and mental as well as spiritual readiness, and until you can put those together it isn't going to happen. It is just a basic law of life.

Well, unfortunately, we often leave out the mental and the physical. You and I have a great challenge if we are to live the whole gospel — to live it in its fullness, which includes not only the spirit, which is vital, but the physical. Let me just share a thought or two from a prophet. This is what Brigham Young said many years ago because it was important then. I quote, "Then let us seek to extend the present life to the uttermost by observing every law of health, and by properly balancing labor, study, rest, and recreation and thus prepare for a better life." Did you get all the ingredients? They're all important. Let us teach these to our children, that in the morning of their days they may be taught to lay the foundation of health and strength and condition, and the constitution and power of life in their bodies. He continues: "Keep the Word of Wisdom, and if you want to run and not be weary, walk and not faint, then call upon me. I will tell you how. Just stop before you are tired." I defied that one time. I used to think as a young General Authority that I could go twenty-four hours a day. Look out world. And I broke the law of health. And the law of health broke me. I stand as somewhat of an example to you that you can't, no matter who you are, break a commandment or the law of God without paying a price. Now, thank God for repentance, and I'm trying to use that to its fullest extent.

The Word of Wisdom is a principle with a promise and was given as a rule of conduct that should enable the people so to economize their time and manage and control themselves as to not eat and drink in excess or to use that which is harmful to them. We should be temperate in all things. I wish I had a week to elaborate on that one. It would be quite revealing, wouldn't it? Each of us should look into his life in this area and seek to be temperate in all things, in the exercise of labor as well as in eating and drinking. Clothe yourselves properly as you can. Exercise properly, if you can, and do right in everything. I take that as much as a law and a commandment as anything that's found in the scriptures because it came through a prophet. Listen to what another prophet says, "The condition of the body limits largely the expression of the spirit." This is what I was trying to suggest through that little story. The spirit speaks through the body, and only as the body permits. That's quite a profound statement, isn't it? The body and the spirit constitute the soul of man. Hence, if the body is in poor condition from birth, man must strengthen it as the days increase. If it is strong from the beginning, we must make it stronger. That's the challenge you and I have as we progress down life's interesting path.

When I was an athlete a hundred and fifty years ago, I had no problem keeping in physical condition. For the first thirty-five years of my life I didn't vary a pound or an inch because I went, went, and went. I pushed it. I could challenge a teenager at any point. Then I got called to be a General Authority and somehow — well, you know how we justify things in our lives, we're the greatest rationalizers the world has ever known — I could think of a thousand reasons why I shouldn't exercise, but the challenge is to think of one more reason why I should. I came to Salt Lake as a new General Authority and sat at a desk and sat and sat, and got in a car and sat, and got on a plane and sat, and for years now I have been sitting. All of my former prowess as an athlete went zoom. And just because I was in great physical condition for thirty-five years gives no verification that I can win in the next thirty-five. And that's something I knew but didn't do, and I paid a price. Knowing this, the First Presidency and the missionary committee gave me the assignment not long ago to study all of the physical fitness programs in the world, hoping maybe I would grab one. I did grab one and I just want to testify that since my surgery I'll challenge any of you in any department, within reason, in terms of physical fitness, because I've repented.

The Church has come up with what we think is an excellent physical fitness program. There are many in the world that are obviously good. We've tried to be sensible in selecting one that you could do within the leisure of your own home without embarrassment. I find it is a little hard for me to get out and jog, for instance. I like to jog. I used to do it as a kid, but now as a General Authority I jog around three blocks and I get twenty-five people to counsel. You know, they all stop you and want to ask you this or want you to tell them that, so it isn't always convenient or easy to do so.

We have now published Churchwide a program which our prophet thought ought to go to all members of the Church. This program has been sent to all our missionaries because we know that there is a high correlation between physical readiness and spirituality. There are three phases to this program, and we don't have time to get into the detail of it. Some of it wouldn't matter anyway. It's just a matter of taking someone else's word for it. I don't know everything that happened to my heart. I just believed that my doctor knew what he was doing, and I put faith and counsel and trust in that.

The first aspect of the fitness program is proper dietary and health care. I know this is a sensitive area, but regardless of who we are and where we are, our diet matters, and it has a great deal to do with our spirituality. I find that at fifty I cannot eat like I did at thirty, as much as I would like to. Now don't misunderstand me. My appetite is just as great. I have favorite foods that I cannot now eat that ten or twenty years ago I could eat. Common sense and wisdom and spirit says "Don't." Fortunately I am following that counsel. There are just certain things ten years later that you don't do like you did ten years earlier, and you and I have got to be smart enough to apply that principle. So eat properly.

I found that a heart attack, whether you are a man or a woman, has about five aspects attached to it. One is heredity. If it's in your family, chances are you are a good candidate. This doesn't mean it will necessarily occur, however. Two is proper diet. There are certain foods that will kill you. We find now that cholesterol is not the villian it was thought to be. It is your triglycerides that present a problem, and there are some foods that are high in triglycerides. Potato chips are murder, and they were my favorite food. A dip and cheese is murder, and what did I love? Potato chips and dip. Some bodies can't handle it. If the heredity factor is there, those two are just crossed out for you. They create what they call a plaque in arteries and veins which becomes a real blockage in terms of blood circulation, so you have to be sensible if you are going to prevent it. You have to know that there are certain foods that are high in one area and low in another, and you have to just use your common sense. I feel good now because I am following this counsel.

The second phase of the physical fitness program is proper body composition. There needs to be an evaluation to reduce excess fat. I grew up as an athlete, thinking that if you kept the same weight all the time you were in great shape. That is a false notion. I weighed 175 pounds and was six feet two inches at age twenty when I went to play professional baseball. At age thirty-five, I was still six feet two inches and weighed 175 pounds, but I was overweight in excess body fat. Weight does not tell the whole story. There are ways of measuring excess body fat, and I don't want to get into the medical mechanics of it, but with your doctor and proper care you can find out as you grow older whether you are reducing enough excess body fat.

Finally, you have to develop a program of exercise that will maintain muscle tone and increase cardiovascular endurance. Now that's the key. You can go through a thousand exercises that will do zero good unless you are putting proper stress and strain upon the cardiovascular system. This program does just that. The key is not how many times you go through a side-straddle hop or a deep-knee bend or a lift-of-the-leg exercise. The key is how you put pressure on the heart system so that it builds an endurance level. Swimming and jogging are terrific in doing that. A lot of people go out and bicycle all afternoon. Well, you can bicycle all day and all it will do is build your legs. It won't do a thing for your chest muscles or your cardiovascular system. The only way you can properly bicycle is to cruise a little bit, say for two or three blocks, then take a two-block area and pedal until you think you are going to die. Quit and coast, then pedal, then coast. You have to build the endurance. The same is true in jogging. I see people jog five miles a day. They are running around my house like a bunch of sheep. Well, jogging is of little or no value unless you build the stress level, and that's the key in good heart conditioning. The correct way to jog is not to run five miles at the same pace. Jog for two blocks at a leisurely pace, then run like the enemy is chasing you. Quit, then walk, then run, and quit again. Well, the exercises in this program are designed to cause that to occur. There is a moderation level, then you run in place, then exercise, then you stop. The exercises are designed to cover every known muscle in your body, and it is worth the effort to do them.

I have been on this program for ten months since my operation, and during the first five months it was terrific. I could hardle wait to get out of bed. Then the interest left me and it became a drudgery. Now I have to get up and fight myself. I find a thousand reasons why I'm not going to exercise this morning, and then I have to stop and say, "Now, who's in control here, Paul?" I have to decide that I am, and I'm going to do it. And I do it. I invite you to do the same, regardless of who you are, your age, or your condition. You can't afford not to develop the whole man, or, of course, the whole woman.

The house we live in represents a wonderful structure. Physically, it has all the most modern mechanics, all the hydraulics, all the machinery known to man. There are more than 310 mechanical movements known today, and all of these can be found in the body of each one of us. There are bars, beams, girders, levers, buffers, joints, pumps, pipes, wheels and axles, balls and sockets, trestles, axles, columns, cables, and supports. Did you know you had all that in you? I have learned a lot about my body lately. When they went in to get into my heart they took a saw and went right through the sternum and just opened it up. When they put the sternum back together, they stapled it. At the airport I set those metal-detector devices off every time I go through one!

I've learned a lot about our physical make-up. The body is an inn where we eat, a countinghouse where we work, a school where we learn to study, and a sanctuary where we worship. It can be a sty where we wallow in filth, an attic where we store rubbish, a cave where we can live away from the light. But it should not be. The human body and its manifold complexities has been compared to all the various machinery and all the factories of the world packed beneath a single roof, working together for one common end — the glory of God.

God bless us to understand the whole man and to properly care for each aspect — spiritual, mental, and physical, for it is a basic part of the gospel of Jesus Christ. Not long ago I walked into the valley of death; I know what it's like, and I just want you to know that I know this Church to be true. It really is. And like you, I've committed my life to teaching it to others who will listen. God bless us to do it in a most effective way and a healthy way, that we might bring all people to an understanding that God lives and that Jesus is the Christ.

22

What Is Courage?

While fighting in the Pacific during World War II, I witnessed pain and death many times. Each time, just before going to battle, the soldiers were terribly frightened; and many expressed the feeling that they were afraid they were going to die. These experiences frequently brought to my mind one of Shakespeare's oft-quoted lines of poetry: "Cowards die many times before their deaths; the valiant never taste of death but once." (William Shakespeare, *Julius Caesar.*)

Courage has different forms. Sometimes it is a man facing a very difficult situation, such as a battle line in time of war; sometimes it is an everyday thing — a man doing his job as a policeman or a business executive. The work is hard, and it is there every day; there is no glamour, but there is always a challenge. The brave men in these cases are the ones who get the job done — every day.

There are courageous men in all walks of life, as also in each profession there are the quitters. There aren't too many of *them*, because they don't last — they give in to the problems they face. Things look too big or too tough or as though they will take too long a period of time. The quitters do not work hard enough. The man who is good is the man who works hard at it; who sticks with the difficult thing, works at it, and finally wins out.

Someone has said, "Bravery is a complicated thing to describe." It cannot be measured nor identified by color; nor does it have an odor. It is a quality, not a thing. One of the most widely quoted definitions of courage is the famous one of Ernest Hemingway. "Guts," he said, "is grace under pressure." In other words, courage is doing what you have to do in a tough spot, and doing it calmly.

A true story will help to illustrate: During the battle of Leyte (Philippine Islands) in World War II, an associate of mine led a squad of twelve infantry soldiers through some very dense jungle toward an enemy pillbox. The Americans came out of the woods and made their way toward the fortress. It was quiet, and they did not expect any trouble; but suddenly there was a burst of enemy machine gun fire from the dugout. It was what American soldiers call an ambu gun. It fired seven hundred rounds (bullets) per minute. I mention this only to show that the American soldiers knew at once that it was enemy fire.

At the instant my friend heard the ambu gun fire, he dove flat on the ground, half in and half out of a muddy pond; but with his eyes constantly on the target. For a moment all of the men in the patrol observing the action thought their leader had been hit. Knowing that their sergeant was trapped directly in front of the pillbox, the other soldiers quickly took cover. Before these men could realize just what had happened, their leader was up on his knees, firing his rifle into the narrow slits of the pillbox. Within a moment he had achieved his objective.

What had happened was this: The sergeant had heard the ambu gun and dropped immediately on his face, which was instinctive; at the same time he reacted as the leader of the patrol and did what he had to do. He was not wounded, and he did not go all the way down on his face to hide, as all the men behind him did instinctively. He knew at once that he could not stay face down on the ground because the enemy would pick off his entire patrol one by one. So he dropped only momentarily, rolled over, got to his knees, swung his rifle into firing position, and fought back. The action was soon over, and the Americans had won. What the sergeant did took *courage* — "grace under pressure."

It does not have to happen only in war. Being brave does not mean you have to be big and noisy. It means doing what you have to do even when you do not want to do it, or when it is hard to do; or when you could let the job slide and watch somebody else do it. Being courageous covers a lot of ground. Shakespeare called it being "valiant." There are a lot of other words that could be substituted for valiant: bravery, courage, spirit, backbone, fortitude, heart. If you read about a soldier climbing out of a foxhole and braving enemy fire to reach a wounded companion and carry him back to safety, it sounds right to call this "courage" or "bravery." But take an ordinary situation in an ordinary life — have you ever had the experience of standing before a large congregation? How did you feel? Were you scared? Of course you were. Who isn't?

Several years ago, in my youth, I came to know personally the great baseball player, Lou Gehrig. Because of my admiration and respect for this man, I asked him one day how I might overcome my fear and anxiety as a competitor on the ball field. Without hesitation he said: "Paul, don't ever lose your fear; just learn to control it. Fear is a wonderful asset because it keeps a person humble and reminds him that he can't accomplish his objective alone.

"There is a higher source than man," he added; "and each time I go to perform I call upon that Divine Power for assistance."

He said, "Fear also reminds me that there are eight other players on the team, and their strength is my strength." It takes the "team effort" to succeed. He pointed out further that we could learn to control our fears by discovering our individual strengths, and then apply these strengths in the areas of our limitations.

Perhaps you have had the experience of being the only person in a crowd who believed in the principles of the gospel. There is no pressure quite like the pressure that can be brought to bear when the "peer group" would have us do that which is contrary to our basic beliefs. For example: Your group of friends have the habit of taking the name of the Lord in vain. Because you don't, you are made to feel by your associates that you are the one who is peculiar. It takes as much strength and courage to stand up against this kind of pressure, and ofttimes ridicule, as it does for the athlete or soldier to perform his feats of heroism.

It took the same kind of courage and strength for men like Joshua and Gideon to accomplish the things the Lord asked them to do. Each day of our lives we find it necessary to remember Joshua's admonition: "Choose you this day whom ye will serve." To stand up and be counted, whether it is in the time of Joshua on a battlefield, or in a social situation at school, faith and courage are required.

As a young lad Gideon lacked self-confidence. In humility he had said that he was one of the least important of his father's family. It took a lot of persuading and a great deal of inspiration to make him brave enough to attack his job. But when he was convinced that the Lord really wanted him to lead His people and drive out the enemy, he measured up in a fine way. He had no fear of his townsmen when he tore down their altar to the pagan god, Baal. He was filled with daring when, with a small band of only three hundred men, he defeated the hosts of the Midianites and liberated his people from bondage.

Almost without exception great leaders in all ages have been humble men who, through faith and courage, became instruments in the hands of God. Often success comes easily to those with great abilities and talents; and when it does, bad habits of laziness and indifference come as easily. Too often, before the goal is attained, such people become defeated and destroyed by their own talents. Hard work, faith, and courage make us strong and help us overcome our obstacles. It does not matter how many talents we have; what matters is how we use them.

23

"Follow It!"

One of the physicians who attended my open-heart surgery asked a few months ago if I would participate with him on a Sunday School program. I followed him at the pulpit. He gave a tremendous address. As he took his seat, I felt prompted to say, because I felt it, "Brothers and sisters, I want you to know that this man has touched my heart very deeply."

The great messages of our presidency, those of the Twelve and others always touch me deeply. They cause me to reminisce and to remember. My mind goes back to the time when I was privileged to attend a stake conference in Oregon. Lo and behold, in the audience was my very first bishop, a man of great faith and capacity. (I had never known a bishop until I was fifteen years old and had moved to Hollywood, California.) He stood over six feet tall, weighing well over two hundred pounds, with a heart to match — and he has never let go since. I remember under his tutelage memorizing this little verse:

"There is an odd little voice always speaking within, and it prompts you to duty and warns you from sin. And what is most strange, it makes itself heard, though it gives not a sound and says never a word." "You follow it," he told me. And the last time I saw him he said, "Are you still following it?"

I remember a great, wise teacher who said, "Paul, always keep in mind that a strong man and a waterfall always channel their own paths." And I remember a dad who said, "I gave you a great name; remember, a good name is better than a girdle of gold."

I think every boy and girl ought to have in his or her life a great dad, a marvelous bishop, and wonderful teachers. Many do; some don't. Thank God for a prophet, for leaders of the Church who add that dimension.

I thought of another great man in my life — a coach who has affected my life for eternity. I am pleased to announce that he and I are engaged together in learning more fully the gospel of Jesus Christ in a missionary effort.

I will never forget the day I walked into his office, scared to death as fifteen-year-olds are, trying to sign up for a varsity team. I stood outside his door for the better part of five minutes; and then, when I got the courage, I knocked timidly. The voice said, "Come in!" I opened the door and walked in.

He said, "What can I do for you, son?"

"Where do you sign up for varsity baseball?" I asked.

He said, "Let me ask you a question — do you want to play ball or be a champion?"

"I came to play ball."

"I'm sorry," he said, "we're all filled up."

With a broken heart I turned and walked out. That wasn't the answer I wanted to hear! I stood in the hall for a minute (thank goodness my dad had taught me courage to keep trying), then plucked up my courage and again knocked on the door. The answer came as before, "Come in!" I walked in.

"Oh, it's you again."

I said: "Yes, sir, maybe you didn't understand my earlier question. I asked you where to sign up for varsity baseball."

He straightened up in his chair: "And I asked *you* a question. Do you want to play ball or be a champion?"

Well, I knew the other answer hadn't worked, so I said, "I want to be a champion."

"Oh," he said, "sign here." And I did. He said, "We build

champions." Then he turned and asked, "Have you ever signed a contract before?"

"No, sir, I'm only fifteen."

He said, "At this institution, we commit ourselves to principles."

He took from the bottom drawer of his file a contract already typed, and on it were the standards that we listen to in our great conferences. He said: "You take that home and read it over with your parents. If you can agree to the conditions, you sign it and bring it back tomorrow." I did. Somehow, I made the team.

In the contractual agreement were promises to be the kind of a Latter-day Saint I knew I ought to be. We went through a great, great season. It ended in a tie with our arch-rival high school. The play-off game was to determine the state championship. As we assembled on the field in the last-minute preparation for the great event, the coach had us around the batting cage. As he was making his little pep talk, he stopped in front of me and said, "Oh, by the way, you will pitch the deciding game." My heart dropped! He continued his counsel. And then he stopped in front of our excellent second baseman. Most of you would know him because he went on to play for the Chicago White Sox for a number of years. He said, as he looked, "Jimmy, is that a nicotine stain on your finger?" Jimmy, like the rest of us, had made a commitment to keep his body clean.

Jimmy, looking at his finger, quickly hid his hand and said, embarrassed, "Yes, sir."

The coach said in front of the whole team, "Did you sign a contract with me?"

"Yes, sir."

"And you broke the contract?"

"Yes, sir."

"Do you know the penalty?"

"Yes, sir."

"Would you turn in your uniform? You're through."

I wanted to say, "Coach, tomorrow's the big game." (Jimmy was batting .385 and hadn't made an error at second base all year.) But the coach was thinking of a boy, not a game. Jimmy turned in his uniform, but the coach kept close to him.

I drew the assignment the next day to pitch against Al Yalian, who later signed with the New York Yankees for a fabulous bonus. Thirteen innings we went, and he beat me in the thirteenth — 1-0. The run came when a ground ball was hit to second where Jimmy normally played. The ball got through a nervous substitute's legs onto the outfield grass and eventually scored an unearned run, which defeated us. And now, years later, I thank God for a great coach who taught me that principles are more important than games.

As I reflect upon these kinds of experiences and the influence that great men have had on my life, I think of the question that young people quite often ask those of us in these positions, "Why do we hold so many meetings in the Church?" The Lord understood and answered, speaking to you and me, young people, through a prophet: "And now, behold, I give unto you a commandment, that when ye are assembled together ye shall instruct and edify each other." Why? "That ye may know how to act and direct my church." (D&C 43:8.) And I thank God that in our conferences we are taught how to act. "We thank thee, O God, for a prophet to guide us in these latter days."

Like many of you, I am frequently before those who are not of our faith, and the challenge is great and wonderful. Not long ago I was given a little honor before a great group of non-Latter-day Saint athletes. In the proceedings of the convention, one of my great idols, a Hall of Famer, was to take the rostrum and speak to us. Being the great athlete that he was, respected by many, I was shocked to hear his language as he repeatedly took the name of the Lord in vain. As I sat there, I wondered, "What do you do as a Latter-day Saint in these kinds of social situations?" And then I remembered — again, a great influence in my life — the counsel from a prophet and an experience that he had had one time coming out of surgery. An orderly who was wheeling the prophet back to his hospital room on a little metal cart caught his hand between the door and the cart in the elevator and, not thinking, let go with a few adjectives, taking the name of the Lord in vain in the process. And a prophet, sick as he was physically but very well spiritually, lifted his head and said, "Please don't talk that way — that's my best friend."

Those thoughts went through my mind as I listened to my idol. As he concluded and sat down, I put my hand on his knee and said to him: "You're terrific! Did you know that when I was growing up I had you on a high pedestal? But, if I might level with you, tonight you fell off that pedestal."

He was startled, "Didn't you like my workshop?"

I said: "I loved it. But every time you opened your mouth, you offended me and a lot of other people out there. I'm going to challenge you tonight, as your friend, to clean up your language."

I thought of the apostle Paul and Joseph Smith and particularly of our prophet today, and I learned on that occasion, as I have on many others, that people really want what you and I have, if we have the courage to give it.

God grant us to have that courage and determination as we go forth, edified and fortified by the influences of great men in our lives, to be an example unto the world.

24

Be Your
Own Boss

I was deeply impressed with a comment made by President David O. McKay, concerning the need for self-conquest. He indicated that in the life of our Savior self-control was divine. I have reflected upon that. My mind was brought quickly to the hymn that we often sing which suggests that we school our feelings. Let me just refer to the first verse as perhaps a text that I would like to develop:

School thy feelings, O my brother;
Train thy warm impulsive soul;
Do not its emotions smother,
But let wisdom's voice control.
School thy feelings; there is power
In the cool, collected mind;
Passion shatters reason's tower,
Makes the clearest vision blind.

Charles W. Penrose,
"School Thy Feelings,"
Hymns, Number 340

I think about that hymn as I listen to the comments of others concerning the condition of our nation, the riots, pestilence in the land, some of the concerns that we all have today. It is interesting to note that these conditions start in such small ways, with the individual, in the home. Our nation and our communities are no stronger than the individual or the home and its basic make-up.

I hope my wonderful partner will forgive me if I share a little experience that occurred during our adjustment period shortly after we were married. I recall that one day as I was at my work I felt ill, a little blue, and sensing the need for added physical comfort and attention, I left my office a little early to go home. The heavy traffic of the Los Angeles freeway did nothing but add to my anxieties. When I arrived home, I found that my wife was not there. Here I was, expecting tender love, care, and understanding, and of all days she could have picked, this was the one she decided not to be at home. I couldn't imagine why she couldn't read my mind.

When I arrived home, I settled myself on the couch, actually growing a little more angry with each moment that she was absent. And then finally, after about an hour of anxious waiting, she appeared on the scene. Can you imagine what she had been doing? Shopping! I looked at her somewhat wonderingly and asked where she had been. "Couldn't you be more thoughtful of your husband?" I said.

She responded, "I couldn't know that you were coming home early."

I was still a bit upset.

She wanted to show me the treasures she had just purchased, and I wasn't particularly interested. One by one she unwrapped the various purchases, and finally getting to the last she had saved for the big surprise, she said, "Just wait until you see the material that I finally found to cover the couch." And she showed it to me. She said, "What do you think?"

"It is terrible," I said.

She was hurt, and with her emotions showing she left the room. I was still upset, so I let her go. An hour passed. And you know women sometimes have an interesting way of striking back. It was one of my first lessons on this subject. Without saying a word, she just did not fix my supper.

Well, one act begets another, and I thought, "Two can play this game." So in my moment of real concern, I started to play the mature adult game that sometimes goes on in the homes of people — it is known as the silent treatment. I didn't talk to her for the rest of the evening, and she responded by not answering.

I am sorry to confess to you that we retired to our bed that night without saying a word, and I was still unfed. That night as I tried to find comfort and solace in the night, I failed to go to sleep. It was a month later before I discovered that the two of us were having a like experience. All night I lay clinging to my side of the mattress, being fearful that I might roll over and touch her.

The next day added more to our anxieties, and it was not until the following night that I gained control of my compassion and feeling and took her by the hand into the living room, where we knelt down together and sought our Heavenly Father. I made a great discovery that day — that I was able in part to school my feelings. I had remembered an oath and a covenant that I had taken in the temple before my Heavenly Father as a husband and as a father-to-be. To school our feelings is a great challenge in our lives, brethren and sisters, and I see in this a direct relationship to the condition of our nation and the world.

Another very interesting experience unfolded before me that brought to my mind again this great verse from our hymn and the comment of President McKay concerning self-control. One of my very close associates made a promise at a New Year's Eve party concerning his New Year's resolution that I thought was very interesting. He swore on that occasion that he would not commit another sin as long as he lived. He said he had made a lot of mistakes in the past, but from that time on he was going to exercise perfect self-control. And then when another ac- quaintance who was standing nearby commenced to make fun of him and his resolution, the first man became so angry that he wanted to fight.

Someone has said that "the measure of a man is the things that make him angry." And I believe that we have plenty of confirmation of this statement in the life and teachings of Jesus, as well as in the experiences of other noble souls who have lived since his time.

We note that, although Jesus warned his disciples against the evil results of uncontrolled temper, he became angry himself, and on at least one occasion he prepared to use force, if necessary, in driving evil practices from the halls of the temple. (See John 2:15.) But think, if you will, of the size of the things that aroused his anger. Men called him the prince of devils, and he paid little attention to their criticism. They had said that he was ignorant, but this had not caused him to lose his temper. They had spit in his face, mocked him, hit him, and later even hanged him to the cross, but he did not lose control of his feelings.

It was quite different, however, when they criticized him for doing good on the Sabbath. Realizing that the Sabbath was made for man, and not man for the Sabbath, he started to heal a poor fellow on the sacred day. And when he found the crowd in a critical mood, he "looked round about on them with anger . . . ." (Mark 3:5.)

So long as men held him up personally to ridicule, he paid little attention. But in the presence of injustice, when men would be unfair and unkind toward each other, he threw the influence of his great, tempered personality against their evil practices. No one could hurt him by attempting to punish him as an individual, but they touched his heart when they were cruel to each other.

Let us not confuse the well-controlled use of unselfish enthusiasm with the harsh roaring of a weak, tempestuous spirit. In the teachings of Jesus there is a definite place for the former; there is neither time nor place for the latter. "Ye have heard that it was said to them of old time, Thou shalt not kill; and whosoever shall kill shall be in danger of the judgment: .

"But I say unto you, That whosoever is angry with his brother . . . shall be in danger of the judgment. . . ." (Matthew 5:21-22.)

Coming back to my friend who became angry, after making the New Year's resolution that he was going to exercise perfect self-control, I guess the poor fellow did not realize that such a goal required determination and a plan of accomplishment. Sometimes one has to work all kinds of tricks on himself to hold his emotions in check. He had set for himself a desirable goal that would be meaningful in the lives of all of us.

An energetic person works hard and studies several hours a day sometimes to develop other types of abilities. Is it not worth some practice to gain control over one's emotions? I believe that it is, but from my own experience I am quite sure that it is no easy job. It is a happy and successful person who can gain control of his emotions and use them to improve his relationships with others and bring into his own life greater peace, joy, and serenity that are so desperately needed in our world today. Suppose we look for a moment at some of the plans that others have found helpful in controlling temper as well as developing other desirable habits and characteristics.

When Colonel Charles Lindbergh was asked what method he used, he said that he came to the conclusion that if he knew the difference between the right way to do a thing and the wrong way to do it, it was up to him to train himself to do the right thing at all times. So he drew up a list of characteristics that he wished to develop and wrote them, one under the other, on the left side of a sheet of paper. Then each evening he would read off this entire list of characteristics. After those that he felt he had developed to some extent during the day he would place a red check, and after those character factors that he felt he had violated he would draw a black check. Those that he had not been called upon to demonstrate that day would receive no mark.

After checking himself in this way over a definite period of time, he would compare the number of red and black checks to see whether or not he was getting any better. He said that he was generally glad to note improvement as he grew older. He had altogether developed fifty-eight character factors, among which were altruism, calmness in temper, clean speech, justice, modesty, no sarcasm, and punctuality.

Others have noticed considerable development in character by picking one person who has achieved an extraordinary degree of moral strength and then by judging all his own actions by the life of this ideal. Have I been as good and kind in all of my own dealings this day as he would have been? If not, then I need to be more careful tomorrow. Do I have as perfect control of my temper, am I as sympathetic, do I go out of my way as much as he does to help someone in trouble? Only when we can say yes to such questions dealing with the whole field of moral endeavor may we be satisfied with our accomplishment of self-control. And if we pick some personality that is sufficiently perfect, we shall no doubt be struggling upward to the end of our lives.

Sheldon's book *In His Steps* laid emphasis on the value of picking Jesus Christ as an ideal for every activity of the day, to do as he would do if he were here today. Reaching back over a period of nearly two thousand years, to a time when conditions were quite different from those of the present day, one senses the difficulty of knowing in every case what Jesus would do. Yet in the face of this obstacle, I have a feeling that our very attempt to catch his spirit and follow his example, the example of the greatest personality of all time, will prove a constant stimulus to higher living in the present day.

It was Jean Paul Richter who said: "He is the mightiest among the holy and the holiest among the mighty. He has, with his pierced hands, lifted empires off their hinges, turned the stream of centuries out of its channels, and still rules the ages."

In the words of a great modern religious leader, David O. McKay, "Christ's life was a life of unselfish service — always helping those who were living incompletely to live completely — his mission was to give them life. In his life and death, Christ not only fulfilled the law of sacrifice but he fulfilled every conceivable condition necessary for man to know in order to rise or progress from earthly life to eternal life."

I am convinced that regardless of the technique that we may employ, and there are many techniques, that if we will apply a method using Jesus Christ as our ideal, we will come to know that he is the Christ; and that there is waiting for us, not only in this life but in the life to come, peace, joy, and eternal happiness.

Index

-A-

Aaronic priesthood, thoughts directed to, 160-166
Adams, James Truslow, on education, 51, 97
Adults, continued building of, 25
Advertising, influence on children, 72
Alma, prayer for his son, 80
America, choice land, 17, 29
  for restoration of the gospel, 29-30
  peopled by immigrants, 29
  price of independence, 27
Anger, control of, 190-192
Arlington National Cemetery, 30
Authority, way of knowing, 122
  Jesus taught with (quotation), 145

-B-

Baptism, requirement of (quotation), 101
Baseball, contract to play (story), 184-186
Baseball glove, earned (story), 72-74
Baseball player, preparation of (story), 128-131
Bennion, Lowell, on knowing, 122
Bible, teachings about prophets, 145-146
  use of (poem), 114-155
Body, condition of, limits spirit (quotation), 173
  God expects care of, 177
  wonders of, 177
Body fat, control of, 176
Boston Globe, on demise of Mormonism, 18
Brotherhood, a higher value, 98
  of man (story), 45-46
  mankind is, 154

-C-

Call, from the prophet (story), 3-11
Chaplain Protestant, conducts service on ship, 132-133
  theological school, Protestant, 136

Character, plan for development of, 193
  an eternal possession, 114
Church of Jesus Christ, the original, 147
Church of Jesus Christ of Latter-day Saints, The, men built by, 90
  continuous revelation in, 76
  goal of, 51
  influence of, 150
Church service, shipboard (story), 132
Child, friendly example of (story), 103
  and kingdom of God (quotation), 101
Children, expressions of love to, 79-80
  gospel teaching to, 77
  influence of advertising on, 72
  need for spiritual emphasis, 52
  needs of, 41-44
  of Eternal Father, all are, 45-46
  parental teaching required, 48
  potential of, limited by home (quotation), 60
  quality time spent with, 72, 75
Christmas, 105
  song delays battle (story), 107, 115
Cicero, 160, 163
Concentration camp, evacuation of (story), 61
Constitution of the U.S., inspired document, 28
  treatment of, in textbooks, 57
  tribute to, by Joseph Smith, 17
Control, achievement of, 192-193
  gaining of, purpose of gospel, 164
Courage, definitions of, 179-180
  different forms of, 179
  in ordinary situations, 181
  of Gideon, 182
  sergeant acts with, 180-181
  to give, 187
  to keep trying, 184

-D-

Daughter, day with teenage (quotation), 79
  at new school (story), 102-103

(Daughter, day with teenage, Cont'd.)
wedding of, 111-112
Davis, Guy M., baptized, 101, 104
Delinquency, prediction of, 41
Determination, in achieving goal, 192
value of (quotation), 20-21
Dickey, John, on education, 58-59
Doctoral degree (story), 127-128
Dog, stranded on ice (story), 52-53

-E-

Easter, anticipation of, 151
lilies, on Okinawa, 122
meaning of, 121
"Easter is Coming" (poem) by Grace Daniels,
119-120
Education, great purpose of, 110
in school, limited by home, 60
of spirit and body, 58-59
Emerson, Ralph Waldo, on example
(quotation), 78
Enthusiasm, lesson in, 62
Example, of Christ, 193-194
power of, in rearing children, 81
power of, in teaching, 77
quotation by Emerson, 78
Ex-convict, gospel accepted by, 92-93
Exercise, 176
Experience, way of knowing, 123

-F-

Failures, none among priesthood bearers, 161
of great men, 161
taken in stride, 163
Faith, in resurrection, 152
teacher reminded not to undermine, 56
Families, higher value of, 98
eternal, 46, 49
greatest possession, 50
sealings in temples, 48
Family home evening, 42
parents to hold, 78
Father, as influence in home, 41
blessing to family, 71
discipline from, 42, 43
leadership by love, 70
prayer of (quotation), 70-71

(Father, as influence in home, Cont'd.)
presider in home, 69
principles taught by, 74, 75
responsibility to teach, 48
ten commandments for (quotation), 42-44
Father's blessing, before school year, 74
importance of giving regularly, 74-75
to son entering army (story), 68
"Father's Ten Commandments, A"
(quotation), 42-44
Fear, an asset, 181
Feller, Bob, pitcher, gains control (story),
163
Fellowshipping, 103-104
Football player, principle of service learned
(story), 32-36
Forgiveness, 153
Frame, Ivan, tribute to, 95
Free agency, 153
Fundamentals, return to, 89
Future, hope in, 121, 125
Jesus our hope of, 155

-G-

Gehrig, Lou, on fear, 181
Girl, rescue attempt for (story), 53-55
Glueck, Dr. Sheldon and Eleanor, on
delinquency, 41
Goal, determination required for, 192
God, character of, 17
communications to prophets, 76
death of, proclaimed, 151
enemies of, killed Joseph Smith, 18
first place in life, 90
message for today, 47-48
preparation to meet, 113
seen by Joseph Smith, 17
speaks today, 92
Goethe, on reason, 123
Good name, worth of, 184
Gospel, basic law of, 113
care of body a part of, 177
good news of, 152
happiness taught by, 99-100
lives transformed by, 108
meaning of, in homes, 44
restoration of, 147

(Gospel, basic law of, Cont'd.)
taught to children, 77
true joy in sharing, 94
Great Prologue, The by Mark E. Petersen,
30
Green Bay Packers, 90

-H-

Happiness, eternal nature of, 194
Heart attack, five aspects of, 175
Heavenly Father, grand objective of, 49
Jesus as symbol of, 155
king in parable, 113
man in image of, 123
oath taken before, 190
Hemingway, Ernest, on courage, 180
Home, cohesiveness in, 42
five ingredients of happiness in, 41
role of, in inspiring children, 59
sustained by priesthood, 47-48

-I-

In His Steps (book) by Sheldon, on Christ,
193
Individual, importance of, 86
problems of world start with, 89
Inspiration, source of knowledge, 124
Institute, building project (story), 87
Interview, with President McKay (story),
8-10
Involvement, community and church, 57

-J-

Japanese soldier, wounded (story), 45-46
Jehnke, Doris, "Saturday with a Teenage
Daughter" (quotation), 79
Jeremiah, called in youth, 147
Jesus Christ, alive after death, 125
as an ideal, 193
early Christians' faith in, 152
gospel of, power to affect world, 108
hope of future, 155
meaning for our times, 151
teachings of, timeless, 154
Judge, lesson not to, 166, 170-172

-K-

Kimball, Spencer W., counsel of, to married
couples, 47-48
home country of, 105
on heeding conference messages, 76
rebukes profanity, 58
Kingdom of God, parable of, 111-113
Kirkham, Raymond, former bishop, tribute
to, 160
Knowledge, great accumulation of, 122

-L-

Law of health, missionary breaking of (story),
170-172
Letter, on appreciating parents, 67
Leyte, island, battle of, 107, 115
Little red schoolhouse (story), 85
Living, 97
Lives, Christ in, 193-194
completed structures, 19-20
well-balanced, 24
Lombardi, Vince, 89-90
Love, need for nourishment, 47
power of, in rearing children, 81
used to recover people, 99

-M-

Mann, Horace, on value of a child, 56
Man's purpose, 153
Marriage, adjustments in (story), 189-190
advice on, to former missionary, 167
basic unit of Church, 68
courtship in, 41
preparation for, 57
Meetings, many, 186
Merit, religion of, 152
Mission, purpose of, 92
Mission president, challenge of, 168
definition of, 169
Missionaries, living contrary to health law
(story), 170-172
three kinds of, 169
Missionary, former, advice to, 167
new, in Cambridge (story), 164-166
return home of (story), 63-66
value of service as, 91

Missionary work, history of, 93
 in scriptures, 91
Mormonism, demise of, predicted, 18
 impact on life, 152-153
Mother, influence of, 41

-N-

New school, first day in (story), 102-103

-O-

"Odd little voice" (quotation), 183
"Oh Beautiful for Spacious Skies" (song), by
 Katherine Bates, 31
Okinawa, death of soldier on, 121
 lilies of, 122
 monument to soldiers on, 142
Optimism (story), 143
Osmond family, book about, as missionary
 tool, 109-110

-P-

Paper route (story), 78
Parables, on kingdom of God, 111
 teach to help people, 100
 used by Savior to teach, 98-99
PTA convention (story), 149-150
Parents, appreciation to, 67
 money spent by, on missionaries, 91
 persistence of, 159
 power of example of, 78
 preparation of, 51
 "sin be upon the heads of" (quotation), 77
 tribute to, 151
Patriarchal blessing, promises of, 136
 reviewed in battle, 140
Patriarchal order (quotation), 69
Patriotism, 29-30, 60-61
Peace, possibility of, 108
Peer group, pressure of, 181
People, concern by, 97
 greatest concern of the Lord, 87
 leaders' first concern, 88
 more important than institutions, 154
Petersen, Mark E., The Great Prologue, 30
Physical attraction, emphasis on, 52
 in marriage, 47

Physical fitness, Church program, 174
"Post-Christian," era of, 151
Power, definition of, 18
 in ministry of Jesus, 145
Pratt, Parley P., as missionary, 93
 on Joseph Smith, 17
 taught by Joseph Smith, 46-47
Prayer, before battle, 135
 by husband and wife, 190
 parental, power of, 80-81
Preexistence, rights earned in, 160
Preparation, for role in life, 128
 moral obligation of, 142
 need for, 1
 precedes power (quotation), 1
Priesthood, aid to father, 69
 marriage an order of, 48
 presiding function of (quotation), 69-70
Principles, greater than games, 186
Problems, solved by religion, 110
"Prodigal Father, The," a parable, 71
Profanity, in peer group, 182
 of a great athlete, 186-187
 rebuked by President Kimball, 58
Prophet, ability of, to search soul, 8
 Bible teaches of, 145
 failure of people to recognize, 144
 in modern times, 146
 living, 148

-R-

Reason, a way of knowing, 123
Relationships, personal, continuation of,
 114
Religion, caught, 60
 problems solved by, 110
 validity of, 124
Repentance, 92-93
Resurrection, reality of, 125
Revelation, a way of knowing, 124
 mankind's need for (quotation), 148
Revere, Paul, tribute to, 26
Richter, Jean Paul, on Christ, 193
Righteousness, reward of, 24
 search for, 20-23
Roosevelt, Theodore, on education, 58
Ruth, Babe, on law of averages (story),
 161-163

-S-

Sabbath, made for man (quotation), 87
Sacrifice, necessary for achievement (story), 22-23
   of soldiers, 142
   of young friend to build house, 24-25
Salvation, gift of, 152
Santa Claus, a great tradition, 108
   letters to, 105-106
"Saturday with a Teenage Daughter" (quotation), 79
Savior, the, as teacher, 98-99
   commemorated on Christmas, 109
   teaching of "give thyself," 160
"School Thy Feelings" (hymn), by Charles W. Penrose, 188
Scriptures, for each child, 48
   reading of, 48
   search of, 100
   spiritual preparation through, 114
   use of (poem), 114-115
Self-image, collective, 60
   taught in home, 60
Sergeant, courageous action of (story), 180
Service, a higher value, 98
   Christ's life of, 193-194
   fulfills personality, 154-155
   value of (story), 32-36
Shakespeare, on courage, 179
Smile, value of (story), 99
Smith, Joseph, a prophet, 14-17
   birthplace of, 13, 14
   called in youth, 147
   character of, 15
   defines a soul, 52
   every gift possessed by, 15
   God revealed to, 13, 17
   on eternal families, 46-47
   on missionary work, 94
   physical appearance of, 14
   suffering of, 16, 17
   testimony of, 15, 17
   unspoiled, 29
Smith, Joseph Fielding, on patriarchal order, 69
   on temple ordinances, 48
Socrates, 160
Soldier, death of, on Okinawa, 121-122

(*Soldier, death of, on Okinawa, Cont'd.*)
   unknown, tomb of, 30
Soldiers, trapped by enemy (story), 140-141
Soul, definition of, 52
   infinite worth of, 51
   worth of (quotation), 86-87
   worth of (stories), 52-55
Spiritual preparation, for parenthood, 52, 56
   to meet God, 113
Spirituality, health and, 174
Standard works, 100
Stewart, Charles B., priests adviser, 95
Story, adjustments in marriage, 189-190
   Babe Ruth and the law of averages, 161-163
   Bob Feller, pitcher, develops control, 164
   call, from the prophet, 3-11
   Christmas song delays battle, 107
   church services on ship, 132
   contract to play varsity baseball, 184-186
   crippled boy buys dog, 59
   daughter's wedding, 111-112
   doctoral degree, 127-128
   dog stranded on ice, 52-53
   eleven soldiers trapped 140-141
   evacuation of concentration camp, 61
   father's blessing to son entering army, 68
   first day in new school, 102-103
   first talk in church, 126
   football player learns to serve, 32-36
   girl in well, rescue attempt, 53-55
   institute building project, 87
   Japanese soldier wounded, 45-46
   little red schoolhouse, 85
   missionaries living contrary to law of health, 170-172
   missionary homecoming, 63-66
   mother and five daughters sealed, 45-46
   new baseball glove earned, 72-74
   new missionary in Cambridge, 164
   New Year's Eve promise, 190-191
   optimism, 143
   PTA convention, 149
   paper route, 78
   piano sonata, 22-23
   prayer before battle, 135
   preparation to be baseball player, 128-131
   President Kimball rebukes profanity, 58
   profanity of a great athlete, 186-187

(Story, adjustments in marriage, Cont'd.)
   sacrifice to build a house, 24-25
   sergeant's courage, 180-181
   soldier's death, 121
   Sunday School visit, 105
   tanks on Guam, 137-139
   teacher's new thoughts, 96-97
   textbooks rejected, 57
   unfinished house, 19-25
   value of a smile, 99
   young widow, 121
"Strengthen thy brethren," 101-104
Strobeck, Louise, influence of teacher
   (poem), 62
Success, born to, 160-161
   easily attained, 182
   law of, 21
Supervision, in home, 42

-T-

Talents, use of, 182
Talk, first Church (story), 126-127
Tanks, on Guam (story), 137-139
Teacher, definition of, 97
   Savior as a, 98-99
   tribute to, 95
Temple, body is (quotation), 168
   family sealed in (story), 49
   marriage in, 48
Testimony, borne to a prophet, 11
   borne to Harvard professor, 91
   gained before battle, 135
   of Joseph Smith, 15
   of others, way of knowing, 122-123
   of young missionary on plane, 64
   verified by a living prophet, 9
Textbooks, rejected (story), 57
Theological School, Protestant, 136
Thoughts, giving of (poem), 100
   new, required of class, 95-97
Truth, ways to know, 122

-U-

Understanding, attribute of parent, 59
   of boy for dog (story), 59

-V-

Values, eternal, 130
   misplaced, 98

-W-

Washington, George, set apart by God, 27,
   28
Water, scriptural references to, 21
Weddings, ancient, 111-113
   practical side of, 112
Wentworth, John, letter to, 93
Widow, young (story), 121
Widtsoe, John A., on priesthood, 69-70
Wife, commitment of, 10
   converted, 136
   early adjustments with (story), 189-190
   honor for, 43
   respect for, taught by husband, 71
   varied duties of, 40
Womanhood, respect for, 71
Woodruff, Wilford, as missionary, 93
   on Joseph Smith, 16
Word of Wisdom, 173, 175

-Y-

Young, Brigham, on Joseph Smith, 14, 16
   on law of health, 172
   on the Constitution, 28
Young, Levi Edgar, 5
Young people, ability of, 127
   brethren aware of, 127
   Church works for, 149
   obligation of, 142
   problems of, 149
Youth, Jeremiah called in, 147
   Joseph Smith a, 147